THE DOUBLE LIFE OF THE FAMILY

Studies in Society

THE DOUBLE LIFE
OF THE FAMILY

Michael Bittman and Jocelyn Pixley

ALLEN & UNWIN

First published in 1997 by
Allen & Unwin
9 Atchison Street, St Leonards NSW 2065 Australia
Phone: (61 2) 9901 4088
Fax: (61 2) 9906 2218
E-mail: frontdesk@allen-unwin.com.au
URL: http://www.allen-unwin.com.au

National Library of Australia
Cataloguing-in-Publication entry:

Bittman, Michael.
    The double life of the family.

    Includes index.
    ISBN 1 86373 629 8.

    1. Family—Australia. I. Pixley, Jocelyn F. (Jocelyn
    Florence), 1947– . II. Title. (Series: Studies in society
    (Sydney, N.S.W.);).

306.850994

Set in 10.5/12pt Garamond by DOCUPRO, Sydney
Printed and bound by South Wind Production, Singapore

10 9 8 7 6 5 4 3 2 1

Contents

List of tables and figures

Tables

Figures

List of abbreviations

ABS	Australian Bureau of Statistics
ACTU	Australian Council of Trade Unions
AGPS	Australian Government Publishing Service
AIFS	Australian Institute of Family Studies
AIH&W	Australian Institute of Health and Welfare
ESV	Electricity Services Victoria
FVPET	Family Violence Professional Education Taskforce
GDP	Gross Domestic Product
GFCV	Gas and Fuel Corporation of Victoria
GHP	Gross Household Product
GMP	Gross Market Product
GNP	Gross National Product
HECS	Higher Education Contribution Scheme
ILO	International Labour Organization
INSTRAW	Institute on the Research and Training for the Advancement of Women
OECD	Organization for Economic Cooperation and Development
QDVTF	Queensland Domestic Violence Taskforce
TAFE	Technical and Further Education

Acknowledgments

We all live in families. The ideas contained in this book were developed over many years. During this time, we received much stimulation and countless suggestions from friends and colleagues. We would like to point out the special role played by institutions in supporting this research: Michael Bittman thanks the Australian Bureau of Statistics for its support in 1993–94, the University of Essex, the University of Melbourne and his employer, the University of New South Wales, for the opportunity to take up research fellowships at the above institutions. Jocelyn Pixley thanks the University of New South Wales for the research grant for this project from the Faculty of Arts and Social Sciences and for the opportunity to undertake research leave in 1994, and McGill University and the University of Sheffield for the support and stimulation provided during that leave.

A note of thanks is due to our publishers, Allen & Unwin—in particular our editor Elizabeth Weiss. She had the patience and belief in the project to see it through to its completion in the face of two authors juggling numerous other commitments.

We would like to acknowledge the material help received from friends and colleagues. Sue Donnellan, Amanda Elliot, Marina Paxman and Cathy Thomson provided research vital to the book. The authors gratefully acknowledge the generosity of Frances Lovejoy in allowing us to base much of our analysis in Chapter 6 on an article by Michael Bittman and Frances Lovejoy. Terry Leahy, Denise Thompson and Kate Worth provided detailed advice and suggestions on the manuscript. Bruce Bradbury, Steve D'Alton, Duncan Ironmonger, Clive Kessler, Paula Kelly and Paul Jones all read drafts of parts of the manuscript and offered the authors practical ideas, although the responsibility for the whole rests with us alone. Sociologists at the University of Newcastle, the University of New South Wales and the University of Wollongong also gave important critical commentary during seminars on sections of the book.

For permission to reproduce tables and figures, the authors would like to thank Peter Routh (of the ABS) who supplied data points for the age pyramid in Chapter 1, and in general the authors are indebted to the ABS whose high quality data underpin many of the tables in this book. The Liberal Party agreed to the reproduction of the 1993 election pamphlet for North Sydney. Fontana/Collins kindly gave permission to reproduce the table on the sexual division of labour in times past from Edward Shorter's *The Making of the Modern Family*, reproduced in Chapter 3; the Office of the Status of Women are also to be thanked for giving permission to use the cartoon in Chapter 4. Bruce Bradbury and Jenny Doyle, of the Social Policy Research Centre, University of New South Wales, kindly agreed to our use of their table on caring and dependency-related payments in the Australian social security and tax systems of 1995, reproduced in Chapter 9.

To all our relations and friends who showed remarkable forbearance during the trial of our preoccupations with the book, we express our gratitude; in particular, we owe thanks to Louisa Dawson, Sam Dawson, Lorna Pixley, Carol Morris, Stefan Keller and Cassie Rickarby.

Preface

Most of us usually think about our family lives with some combination of hope and experience. Family life arouses feelings of elation and disappointment. We suggest that a phrase such as the 'double life' of the family is a way to show how this mixture of love and bitterness is a part of most people's expectations and experiences of 'the family'. We do not argue that the idea that families are 'special' is some silly delusion. Rather, there are endless inconsistencies between 'the family' that most people hope for and the family as they experience it. Inconsistencies occur in all the arenas in which households try to manage both themselves and their relations with other institutions, often as individuals and not 'family members'. These yearnings, that are rarely diminished by experience, change as we move from infancy to adulthood, from one household to another over the span of our lives.

Modern families in Western industrialised nations exist in highly individualistic societies. Modernity emphasises how the rational actions of isolated individuals are paramount despite the fact that modern society entails a greater level of interdependence than any other known social organisation. That is, there is a major inconsistency between the ideals of collective family life, the predominant, individualistic relations between people, and the extraordinary dependency on distant and impersonal organisations and activities, to which we are all subject. A petrol shortage creates chaos and food supplies can run out rapidly, a failure of garbage collection brings the threat of an epidemic and a decision in a boardroom in the United States puts thousands out of work in Geelong. How do all these different logics become played out in family life? We point to the inconsistencies and the uneven development of these relationships, and suggest that the ambiguities reside in 'the family' as much as in the sociology of the family.

There is a social efficacy about the 'romance' of family life—from boy meets girl, to 'having babies', right through to life as an elderly couple—which involves tenacious hopes that in some way the family can live out this optimism. This sometimes results in equally tenacious opposition to such a trajectory. The myth of the family has its own reality despite the deep tensions that most people feel for their own families at different stages in their lives. We are not proposing that there is a Dark Side and a Light Side of the family, rather we explore how the 'modern family' cannot fulfil the dream of intimacy even with the best intentions. We look at how the normative expectations of the modern family have developed over the past three or four hundred years and more. The notions that families are a haven of intimacy, that women are not meant to be the subordinates of men and that children should not be useful additions to household economies but priceless young humans who cannot be sold or sent out as child labour, are part of our modern consciousness.

Yet these ideals of the modern family are also about a 'fusion' of needs and interests in this era of individualism. How does this work out for individual members of families: the women, men, children, the elderly, the sick and the healthy? In modern societies, children are economic liabilities to their parents; the people most responsible for their upbringing are no longer the whole community but isolated mothers. Inside the family, although there remains the hope of intimacy, it is continually dashed by unequal relations between spouses. Children have been sentimentalised over the past hundred years, and yet children can also be liabilities, or at least mixed blessings, while parents are hardly perfect either.

Similarly, although family life seems to offer a leisurely respite from 'outside' obligations, inside households there is a largely hidden world of hard labour. Modern technology has not reduced the amount of domestic work; instead modern societies have increased the demands on household labour. The extent of domestic production has only recently been considered by male economists (probably when their wives started to undertake paid employment), but the question of who is largely responsible for the unpaid workload which rivals Gross Domestic Product in volume, is highly political. On the one hand, if families are the site of intimacy, why have so many employed women been unable to negotiate ways of sharing domestic responsibilities more fairly with their spouses? There is a disjunction between the belief that men and women are equal and the manifest behaviour to the contrary. This gives rise within families to various forms of simulation of romance and mutuality between couples. On the other hand, if some kind of specialisation between spouses seems the only option, and given that men have higher incomes, what does a breadwinner–home-maker division do to intimate relations of presumed equality? We explore how sensible calculations of sheer survival for a household after children are born, which revolve around men's higher wages, do not provide women with a reasonable bargaining advantage in a market society.

No family survives too well without some attachment to the labour market, yet responsibility for the young and old results in market disadvantage and discrimination. For the modern women who have such family obligations, this often results in poverty in old age. In contrast, a largely unrecognised major consideration is the extent to which the market needs the family. In the long term, the market needs new workers to replace old, and superannuation relies on adult workers supporting retired workers. An economy (let alone a society) does not continue without the replacement of producers and consumers. Children are celebrated by the market, but only in their role of easily persuaded consumers.

In a market society, the market externalises as many goods as possible. Governments are always aware of the enormous difficulties of imposing regulations on markets to foster family life. Modern governments are meant to treat business organisations and family life as private spheres, that is, beyond the intrusion of governments. In the development of the modern family, the lack of state intervention was in fact combined with legal support for male domination within the household. Women and children were thus liable to the whims of the male household head, even though marriages had become free contracts between formal equals. In the twentieth century, although many legal injustices have gone, the problem remains that market societies foster an individualism where there are no individual benefits from bearing and raising children. Children are a 'utility' to employers and are sometimes a utility to the nation-state (as cannon fodder): they may be loved by their parents but they are a personal disutility. As the birthrate rapidly declined due to the expense of rearing children, governments have stepped in with family policies. These have taken the form of nationalistic fertility drives and efforts to enforce home-making on women, in particular through the family wage. More recently some countries have developed policies that provide for greater equality for women and far more support in caring for children.

In general, however, it is fair to say that governments have not supported individual members of families, but have directed support to the male household head at the expense of women and children. Family life is construed as a choice, a choice of whom to marry and whether or not to have children. The responsibilities that these choices entail limit further choices, but market societies consider that preferences as revealed in behaviour are evidence of free choices. Yet families do not have a 'choice' about meeting the needs of helpless dependants and children do not 'choose' to be born. The expense of providing families with due recognition and recompense for their fundamental contributions is substituted with sentimental rhetoric. Thus many politicians proclaim the family as the only basic welfare unit, while blithely ignoring the problems that modern Western societies load upon the individuals within families. The result of these inconsistencies and double standards is to put the members of families on collision courses.

This book traces the double life of the family through its various settings—the mental world of the individual, the private home, the labour market and the state. The first task of the book is to establish that the family has this double life and to describe the processes through which it arose and its internal tensions. Then we will move on to the uneven tensions, both inside the family and outside, created by the employment system and governments' family policies.

1

Is the myth of the nuclear family dead?

If we know something reassuringly well, perhaps even intimately or personally, we use an expression derived from the word family—we say we are 'familiar' with it. Of course this usage presumes that we know our family intimately. Because we 'know' our own families, by extension we relate to *all* families—or, as it is often called, *the* family. The family is an idea that has been used in fiction writing, in song, and in film and television. Some central themes of popular culture revolve around family issues. Seen in this way the genre of romance (girl meets boy), for example, deals with family formation. Soap operas manipulate kinship relations—rarely with much subtlety—to wring new twists out of ever-familiar plots. Commodities are presented as 'family packs'. The association between 'family' and 'family household'—or 'home' as it's usually known—is the foundation of many an advertiser's and politician's appeal. 'Home' implies security, cordiality and compassion. There is even a television genre called 'family sitcom', most of which is highly conventional. This in turn has given rise to a counter-product—TV programs such as *Roseanne*, *The Simpsons*, and *Married with Children*. Much of their humour is derived from the unexpected transgression of some of these familiar associations. Such events cannot be funny unless the viewer knows what *should* happen. Humour is a socially acceptable method of saying what otherwise cannot be said: that is why we laugh. The existence of this genre of anti-family sitcoms is, in its own way, a testimony to the normative power of the familiar. At the same time they point the way to a deeper understanding of the family.[1]

Not everything is what it seems

By contrast, there is something uncomfortable, even shocking, in reading reports that betray the fact that not all families are as they should be. The divorce rate causes great alarm to many. Criminologists tell us that more people are murdered by close relatives than by strangers (as we discuss later in the next chapter). Recent campaigns against child sexual abuse and domestic violence confirm that the danger lurks within our own homes more than outside. These are events that even *Roseanne* or *The Simpsons* rarely broach. At the same time, these events call forth the intervention of health profession-als—specialists in sickness and in breakdowns. Victims and perpetrators alike are offered counselling, therapy. In other words, the events are unambiguously treated as not normal, a disturbance of the regular and healthy state of affairs, beyond what can be morally tolerated by society. In short, such events have been treated as *pathological*. Sociologists since Durkheim have been aware of the social significance of the punishment of transgression as a symbolic way of representing the bound-aries of what society will accept as morally 'normal'. In this way the army of experts and professional practitioners are unleashed at the site of these 'transgressions' to do the necessary repair work for the maintenance of 'the normal'.

The central idea of this book is that the family has been a difficult institution for sociologists to study precisely because these regulating ideas about 'the family' have been so poorly understood. We will seek to introduce the idea of the double life of the family—normative and actual. We argue that family organisation occurs on, at least, two levels—a behavioural level and normative level. Through tracing the circumstances in which the normative family becomes visible—its forms of appearance—we will try to demonstrate that the normative family exists as a social fact. In so doing we hope to elucidate something of the character of these beliefs and the features of an individual's attachment to them. It is more than possible that the normative and behavioural can diverge, for if there was no divergence, societies would not need any police or criminal courts. Indeed, one could say, along with Durkheim, that historical and cross-national variation in Western societies is simply a product of the degree of divergence between the normative and the behavioural (Durkheim 1933; 1938).

In subsequent chapters we will explore the dynamics of tension between people's actual family relations and the normative family, tensions that hold implications for policy-makers and those with an interest in social change. This book is in large measure dedicated to the idea that the normative family—a set of historically and socially produced expectations, values, desires and yearnings—cannot be ignored. The normative family has played a central part in our culture and society, and may even have considerable influence on the electoral appeal of political parties.

Opposition between myth and reality

Sociologists have approached the normative family chiefly as a popular misconception to be dispelled by confrontation with the facts. It has been commonplace, for the last couple of decades, for sociologists to debunk the 'myth of the nuclear family'. Unfortunately, most of their energy has been expended on trying to prove that not all family households are nuclear family households. Little effort has been put into treating the myth of the nuclear family seriously *as myth*.

There is a characteristic response to this: the broadsheet press and sociologists combine to give the kind of lecture on the family that any undergraduate in the last twenty years is likely to have encountered. This takes the form of debunking the myth of the universal nuclear family. It starts by making some rather imprecise reference to the nuclear family, which is (implicitly) variously defined as anything from a husband and wife with dependent children to the somewhat narrower category of units composed of breadwinning father, non-employed housewife/mother and the standard two children. The lecture then goes on to describe how only a minority of households conform to this definition of the nuclear family, and the newspapers sermonise about being misled by nostalgia for times past.

The main point to be made here is not simply that this unmasking is careless with facts but that it also fails as sociology. If the idea of the 'myth of the nuclear family' were anything more than a convenient peg on which to hang a variety of otherwise disparate 'demographic facts'—if in other words it was taken seriously as myth—this would represent a substantial advance. In our view, what requires explanation is why politicians and their pollsters in the back room should imagine they can attract loyalty on the basis of an appeal to an allegedly obsolete social form. How, a sociologist might ask, is it possible to promulgate this 'myth of the nuclear family' when so few have any practical attachment to a nuclear family? Further, sociologists might inquire what the consequences of an attachment to this myth might be.

We will look first, then, at the main demographic patterns in the Australian population, before exploring the numerous forms of appearance of the normative family.

The spurious 'myth' of the disappearing nuclear family— statistics misrepresented

In the great exertion to prove the uncharacteristic nature of the nuclear family today, the standard approach fails to ask if this narrowly defined 'nuclear family' ever comprised a majority of households. It misses the important demographic changes it was devised to organise. The June 1994 Labour Force Survey[2] (ABS 1994a) estimated that there were approximately 4.7 million families in Australia, of which 85 per cent were 'couple families'[3] and 49 per cent couple families with dependants present. While there is some formal truth to the proposition that in the survey 'nuclear families'—consisting of Mum, Dad and the kids—were a minority of households (49 per cent), this does not mean that institutions of marriage and family are necessarily in decline. The statistical illusion of decline is in large part created by examining only cross-sectional data, that is, data collected at one point in time.

It can be very misleading to examine household types at one point in time because family households change. They pass through a series of transitions as children leave home, start new households, have children, divorce, age and ultimately die. This means that households which are not currently 'nuclear family households', may have been nuclear family households in the past or, in other cases, may be about to become nuclear family households in the near future. While slightly less than half the 'couple families' have officially at least one dependent child, the remaining 51 per cent of 'couple families' fall into two broad groups: (1) a larger group—those who no longer have dependent children; and (2) a smaller group of those who have never had children. Among this second 'childless' group, it is estimated, approximately 20 per cent will remain childless and the remainder are transitional families on their way to becoming nuclear families (McDonald 1995, p. 44).

Why the numerical decline of the nuclear family

In the following few pages we shall argue that the apparent decline in the proportion of 'nuclear family' households in Australia is the result of increasing longevity and changes in fertility, not because the nuclear family form has become unpopular. The demographer Peter McDonald has pointed out that between the 1981 census and 1991 (the most recent census at the time of writing), the proportion of 'households consisting of one or two persons increased from 47.2 per cent to 52.9 per cent'. This movement towards smaller households has been going on for 'over a century' and 'will continue into the future' (McDonald 1995, p. 23). There are three reasons for this. The first is to do with the historical pattern of fertility in Australia. The second and most important reason is the ageing of the population and the third is a combination of rising divorce rates and an increased proportion of people who will never marry.

Historical patterns of fertility: the baby boom

In the years following World War II, Australia experienced an unusual episode in its demographic history, commonly known as the 'baby boom'. The baby boom interrupted a long-term trend of fertility decline. Demographers use the measure 'total fertility rate' to estimate the number of children women will have borne by the time they complete their child-bearing. Between 1861 and 1865, each woman in Australia was, on average, likely to give birth to six children over the course of her reproductive life. By 1935 total fertility rate had fallen to a fraction over two children for each Australian woman. However, between 1945 and the early 1970s, the baby boom temporarily reversed this trend in Australia, and the total fertility rate hovered around three children for each woman, peaking in 1961 when the rate was 3.55.

The baby boom was associated with a unique combination of (1) an increasing rate of marriage, (2) a pattern of earlier marriage, and (3) low rates of childlessness. The baby boom, it has been widely argued, was accompanied by an extraordinary 'marriage boom' (National Population Inquiry 1975). A good indication of the universality of marriage is given by the proportion of women who never marry. The pattern prevailing for women born in the last half of the nineteenth century was that 14 to 17 per cent would never marry. The proportion of women born after 1950 who never marry is returning to these high levels characteristic of last century and is predicted to exceed them. Among women who were the mothers of the baby boomers (women born between 1920 and 1950) it is estimated that only 4 to 6 per cent never married (McDonald 1995, p. 33). While during most other periods of Australian history less than seventeen women out of every twenty would marry, in the period that gave rise to the baby boom, nineteen out of every twenty women married.

Not only was the rate of marriage exceptionally high during the baby boom but the age at marriage was extraordinarily low. In the years leading up to the baby boom about 30 per cent of women aged 20–24 years were married. Towards the end of the baby boom era (1971) this had risen to 64 per cent, while currently less than 20 per cent of women aged 20–24 are married.[4] A similar trend is evident among men (McDonald 1995, pp. 33–4).

The third characteristic associated with the baby boom was low rates of childlessness. During the baby boom the rate of childlessness was less than half that of earlier generations and this rate was 'only marginally above the expected rate of childlessness due to physiological reasons alone' (McDonald 1995, p. 43).

From the mid-1970s Australia has experienced an equally spectacular but far less publicised 'baby bust' (Hugo 1992, p. 15). By 1976 the total fertility rate had fallen below the replacement level.[5] The estimated number of births has remained below two per woman through the 1980s and early 1990s (Hugo 1992, pp. 8–9). Since 1971 a pattern of postponed birth has become evident, and 'the percentage of first births occurring to married women aged 30 and over rose from 7.6 per cent to 31.1 per cent' (McDonald 1995, p. 46). In 1971 one in four Australian women became a mother before her twentieth birthday, whereas the current figure is closer to one in ten (McDonald 1995, p. 47).

Longevity and the effects of an ageing population

A baby boom followed by a baby bust has produced a bulge in the age pyramid. The grey shaded area between the age of 34 and 49 years in Figure 1.1 shows how this 'middle-aged' bulge has appeared over the last two decades. In 1911 the age pyramid of the Australian population was very broad in the base and low in height, reflecting a high birthrate and much shorter life expectancy. Since that time the base of the pyramid has narrowed, so that at some ages the total population has actually shrunk in the last twenty years, while life expectancy has risen markedly. Since the fertility among those born in the baby boom is lower than that of their parents, and is expected to be lower still among their offspring, this bulge will become more pronounced. At the other end of the life course there have been remarkable increases in life expectancies in Australia. Male children born in the 1990s can expect to live for an average of 74 years and females can reasonably expect to live to 80 years of age. This is eight to ten years longer than their counterparts born in 1947, and a staggering nineteen to twenty years longer than those born at the beginning of the twentieth century (Hugo 1992, pp. 75, 86).[6] This historical trend towards greater life expectancy is elongating the age pyramid. It is expected that between 1991 and 2011 the population over 65 years of age will grow at twice the rate of the population overall (McDonald 1995, p. 59). The age 'pyramid' has begun to resemble a pear or molten Coca-Cola bottle. And this baby boomer bulge can be expected to move up the pyramid in the coming decades.

The oldest of the baby boomers are now at the age when their children are leaving home. A large number are without

Figure 1.1 Estimated resident population of Australia, 30 June 1975 and 1995 (preliminary)

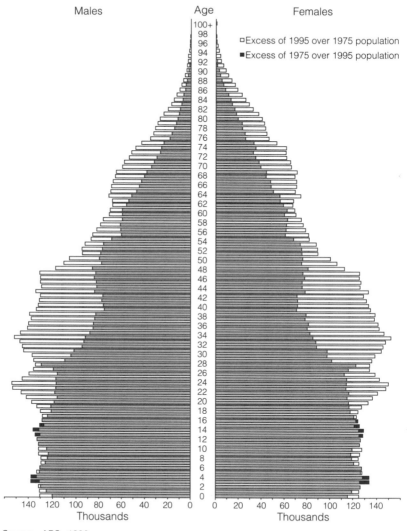

Source: ABS, 1996a.

official dependants because their children are over fifteen and not at high school or in tertiary educational institutions. These changes are producing a disproportionate increase in the number of two-person, 'empty nest' households. The post-war baby boom has led to an end-of-the-millennium 'empty nest' boom. The overwhelming number of these households were once 'nuclear family' households and cannot reasonably be produced as evidence that the nuclear family has been rejected by Australians.

Rising divorce rates and increased proportion of people who will never marry

There is no denying the growth of single-parent families, whose absolute numbers have more than doubled since 1976. By June 1994 it was estimated that there were 627 300 one-parent families, representing 13.2 per cent of all family households in Australia. Eighty-four per cent of these were lone-mother families. In the mid-1990s approximately one out of every eight children aged 0–14 lived in a single-parent family (ABS 1994a). Over one-quarter of Australian children will spend at least part of their childhood in a single-parent family (Hugo 1992, p. 30). However this should be balanced by a recognition that the bulk of Australians will spend their childhood living with both parents. Peter McDonald, using data from Western Australia in 1986, has calculated the proportion of children still living with both their natural parents. The results are shown in Table 1.1.

Concern about single-parent households arises from two sources: (1) an anxiety about the moral disintegration of contemporary society; and (2) the rising cost of government benefits paid to this group. Worry about the cost of sole parents is related to the disproportionate number of sole-parent families living below the poverty line and the consequent demand for welfare services (Saunders & Matheson 1991, p. 21). Anxiety about the family and moral disintegration is almost as old as sociology itself. Durkheim (1952), in his

Table 1.1 Per cent of children still living with both parents by age of child

Age of child	% living with both parents
1 year	91
6 years	85
12 years	80
15 years	77

Source: McDonald, 1995

1897 discussion of suicide, suggested that family membership was a bulwark against the kind of suicide that resulted from normlessness. Subsequent research has questioned whether families are equally beneficial for women (Bernard 1976, p. 43), but many thinkers continue to view divorce as a threat to social order.

Rates of divorce in Australia rose steadily from a low base at the beginning of this century until the introduction of the 1976 Family Law Act. In 1921–25, there were 2.7 divorces per 10 000 of the population. By 1960, the rate had risen to 6.9. Before the introduction of the new Act in 1974 the rate had reached 13. After the new legislation, the divorce rate rocketed to 45.5 in 1976 (when a backlog of people waiting for the new legislation was processed), and by 1991 had settled back to 26 per 10 000 (James 1979, p. 205; Joint Select Committee 1980, p. 45; ABS 1991). If current rates of divorce apply over the next 30 years, it is estimated that one in three marriages will end in divorce (McDonald 1995, p. 53).

Interpreting this apparent epidemic of divorce is less than straightforward. Firstly, before the law changed and when official divorce rates were low, there was widespread reporting of men deserting their wives (Roe 1987). However, as Pixley points out, 'desertion figures are difficult to assess partly because of enforced absences due to work or lack of work, and gold lust frequently extended for years' (1991, p. 300). The Western Australian census of 1901 found that 28 per cent of men were living away from their wives (Burns 1983, p. 51).

Secondly, few marriages at the beginning of this century would have survived 30 years without enforced separation due to the death of a partner. This implies that much of the apparent rise in divorce is a by-product of longer life expectancy. Peter McDonald has calculated that 100 years ago the percentage of couples still together after 30 years (taking into account both widowhood and separation) would therefore be about 46 per cent. The proportion of 'today's couples who can expect to be still together after 30 years is 53 per cent' (McDonald 1995, pp. 52–3).

Thirdly, high divorce rates, rather than symbolising a modern decay of marriage, may actually be the outcome of an increased value placed on marriage. Contemporary expectations of marriage are high. Mate selection on the basis of romantic love, as distinct from economically advantageous unions, places great emphasis on companionship and is far less tolerant of physical cruelty, neglect and lack of financial support (O'Brien 1988). It could be argued that the expectation of such complete companionship promotes high levels of dissatisfaction with anything less, and a search for the perfect partner (see for example, McDonald 1989, pp. 103–4). Support for this argument comes from the high rates of remarriage after divorce. As Hugo points out: 'in 1982 some 30 percent of Australia's 117,275 marriages involved at least one divorced person, and in 10 per cent of cases both participants had been divorced' (1992, p. 44). In 1992 an estimated 202 900 families contained at least one stepchild, of which 43 per cent lived in blended families (ABS 1993a, pp. 4–5, 9). The moral panic surrounding divorce cannot alter the fact that the overwhelming majority of households with dependent children (82 per cent) are currently two-parent family households (ABS 1994a, p. 1).

Growth of de facto marriages over the last decade (Brachter & Santow 1988, pp. 9–10; Khoo & McDonald 1988) has been accompanied by official moves to treat them as legal marriages for such purposes as occupational benefits and official statistics. About 8 per cent of couple families in Australia are de facto relationships. De facto couples are more likely to be young; 69 per cent are less than 35 years of age. One-quarter of the persons living in de facto relationships had been divorced. Over the last two decades the proportion of couples living in de facto relationships before beginning a marriage has risen steeply from 15 per cent in 1975 to almost 60 per cent in 1991. Only about one in three de facto couples has children present, compared with one in two married couples. De facto couples with children are fairly evenly divided between step and blended families, and children living with their natural parents (ABS 1993a, pp. 4–5, 9). Summarising the statistics on de facto relationships, Peter McDonald comments that, 'while other forms of relationship are becoming more common and are more socially acceptable, couple relationships in Australia are still dominated by marriage (1995, p. 32).

Homosexual culture in Australia in the last decade has gained a high profile, with the Gay and Lesbian Mardi Gras

through the streets of inner Sydney becoming a tourist desti-
nation and a national television event. It has been noted that
homosexual unions may also follow a path of 'normalisation',
in order that they may be officially accepted as the equivalent
of the married couple. This development is, however, by no
means certain (Gilding 1991, p. 131). There have been wildly
divergent claims made about the number of homosexual
unions in Australia. Until the 1996 census, the findings of
which were not available at the time of writing, the Australian
Bureau of Statistics treated gay and lesbian couples as cohabiting strangers. In the 1991 census only 5 per cent of all
households were households officially classified as households
containing unrelated individuals—so-called group households.
This suggests that the number of cohabiting homosexuals is
relatively low. It does not tell us anything about the number
of gay and lesbian people who do not cohabit, nor the relative
change in the number of people who prefer this lifestyle.
Group households are predominantly two-person households
and their members are likely to be young (76 per cent under
35 years of age) (McDonald 1995, p. 20).

Nor has the arrival of 'multiculturalism' altered the numer-
ical dominance of the nuclear family household. Contrary to
popular opinion, on average only 1 per cent of families where
the reference person (a gender-neutral replacement for 'household head') was born overseas are multi-family households.
The proportion is higher within some communities and lower
in others. While immigrants from Indo-China and Turkey are
ten times more likely than the Australian-born to live in
multi-family households, the proportion of people in these
communities who do so is never greater than 6 per cent. Nine
out of ten immigrants from Southern Europe, the Middle East
and Indo-China live in families (per se), compared with three
out of four amongst Australian-born households. Eighty-eight
per cent of migrant families are couple families (Bureau of
Immigration and Population Research 1994, pp. 1–8).

In June 1994, only 16 per cent of Australians (an estimated
2 159 800 people) aged fifteen years or over and living in
private dwellings did not live in a family household. Among
this group, the clear majority (62 per cent) live alone (ABS
1994a, p. 6). The proportion of one-person households has
almost doubled over the last 30 years and is even tipped by

some to continue its rapid expansion (Ironmonger & Lloyd 1990). While rising divorce rates and a lower rate of marriage have contributed to the growth of one-person households, the most important factor behind the growth of these households has been the ageing of the population. According to McDonald, 'in June 1992, 56 per cent of all people living alone were aged 55 years or older' and 'reflecting the earlier death of men compared with women, 70 per cent of these older people living alone were women' (McDonald 1995, p. 19).

The double life—the social efficacy of myth

Summarising these observations, what is often passed off as the 'decline of the nuclear family' is not what it seems. When those who believe in the disappearing nuclear family list the causes of the supposed decline, they cite declining marriage, rising divorce, the growth in numbers of single parents and the spread of gay and lesbian lifestyles. But when they require numbers to give weight to their arguments, they rely on figures relating to parents in empty nests and widows: the consequences of processes such as falling family size[7] and ageing of the population.[8] A careful examination of population statistics shows that, despite the hand-wringing of some conservative commentators, most children are born and raised in two-parent households, and that the overwhelming majority of the population has some direct experience of living in a nuclear family. To paraphrase a famous saying of Mark Twain, reports of the 'demise of the nuclear family' are greatly exaggerated.

Of course, if you have something more specific in mind, a 'traditional family' (where the father is a full-time breadwinner and the mother a full-time housewife), the case for decline is far stronger, since roughly only one-third of all families with dependent children conform to this pattern (Edgar 1992, p. 42). But even this figure can mislead. The proportion of families with infant and pre-school children where the wife is a full-time carer is much closer to one-half (ABS 1994a, p. 11), while much of the paid work undertaken by mothers of small children is part-time. As Jallinoja points out, this is consistent with a set of community values that requires a full-time mother rather than a full-time housewife

(Jallinoja 1989, pp. 107–9). Although this represents a distinct change from the 'traditional' family, it preserves many elements of this former pattern. In particular, the husband's role is merely modified to that of chief provider rather than of sole provider, and women's aspirations are still restricted to those compatible with full-time motherhood. In other words, the form taken by the increased female labour force participation is the one most compatible with the demands of the traditional family. Moreover, while there is significant and growing support for equality in domestic labour, there is little evidence of any reassignment of domestic tasks in practice. 'Non-traditional' men have not assumed responsibility for tasks which are not defined as traditionally male (Bittman 1990; Bittman 1991; Bittman & Lovejoy 1993). Sociologists and many socially progressive people may earnestly wish that the nuclear family was dead, but this not to say it is currently deceased.

More importantly, lamenting or celebrating the passing of an obsolete social form distracts attention from the more sociologically significant way in which the 'myth of the nuclear family' has enduring effects. It is an elemental tenet of sociological and anthropological analysis that the effects of myth have little to do with the truth of the matter. The ANZAC myth projects heroic achievement despite the fact that it celebrates a military defeat. The sociological tradition of the analysis of myth goes beyond the mere counterposing of myth and reality.

Luhmann and the normative family

A most important characteristic about the 'myth of the nuclear family' is that the belief in the desirability of the nuclear family does not perish when exposed to the cold light of contradictory evidence, as shown by the failure of gender equality to emerge in the realm of housework.

It is helpful to look at the work of Niklas Luhmann in this respect. Luhmann has distinguished between two types of expectations—cognitive and normative. Normative expectations are peculiar because, unlike cognitive expectations, they are not modified when they are contradicted by events (Luhmann 1979, p. xiv).

An example may help to clarify this distinction. Imagine a traveller who is waiting for a bus with the idea that the bus runs on the quarter hour. But at 4.15 p.m. the bus fails to arrive and instead it appears at 4.27 p.m. The next day the traveller needs to make the same journey and arrives at the bus stop just in time to meet the 4.27 p.m. bus. Our traveller's expectations about the bus timetable are an example of what Luhmann has called 'cognitive expectations' because they are modified when the traveller experiences clear evidence that these expectations are not factually correct.

The same traveller may believe that sexual relations between fathers and their offspring are forbidden but one day learns from his sister that their father sexually abused her as a child. Instead of modifying his expectations, perhaps taking a more benign view of incest or sexual abuse, the traveller develops a deep disgust for the father. In this case the expectations about incest are not modified in the face of factual evidence of its occurrence. This is an example of what Luhmann would call a 'normative expectation'.

Beliefs about the desirability of the nuclear family are a bit like belief in the incest taboo. Even if, at any one point in time, it can be shown that only a minority of the population live in households consisting of mother, father and their children, single individuals are still considered 'lonely', and even if they are in the company of a variety of partners and friends, their parents continue to wonder when they 'are going to settle down'. Similarly the evidence that the domestic division of labour is not an equal division, does not shake people's belief in equal partnership or in the value of nuclear families. These normative expectations are, we argue, related to the mythical dimensions of 'the family'. Chapter 2 continues this theme and discusses the significance of 'the myth of the nuclear family'.

2

The other life of the family

The importance of the normative family is clear. But how does one gain access to the realm of the normative family? In this chapter, we draw upon an eclectic array of theories dealing with the concept of myth. Our purpose is to show how, regardless of the approach adopted, there are useful things to be discovered about the mythical or normative family. Our originality, if any, consists in the application of these frameworks to the task of thinking about the myth of the family rather than proposing a new framework about myth in general.

In this chapter we use three techniques to access the mythical family:

1   analysis of narrative and ritual in the manner of Bronislaw Malinowski;
2   a semiological analysis of pictorial (and textual) representations of this myth; and
3   the analysis of humour in a television sitcom (*The Simpsons*) inspired by a Parsonian reading of Freud.

Concretely, this means (1) looking at the family foundation narrative of Desmond Morris and the ritual of Xmas family gatherings; (2) analysing popular pictorial images of filial relations and the use of the term 'family' in political campaigning; and (3) contrasting *The Simpsons* with more conventional television family sitcoms.[1]

Suppose there is a house with three windows, each showing an imperfect view of a central room and its contents. We think that the three techniques for the study of myth (outlined above) are like three windows into the central space of family myth. Since we are denied direct access to this myth, we have to be content with different, but partial, views and the possibility that the three views might be capable of being resolved into a comprehensive concept.

Characteristics and interpretation of myth— Malinowski and Morris

When social anthropology was established in the early part of this century, one of the earliest tasks of practitioners was to combat theories of myth offered by classical scholars. These classical theorists tended to see myth as either elaborate and highly camouflaged allegories about the forces of nature, or else as distorted representations of historical truth. Against this, Bronislaw Malinowski argued 'in order to explain a cultural product it is necessary to know it. And to know, in matters of thought and emotion, is to have experienced it. The first necessity in the study of mythology, then, is to grasp how the natives [sic] live their myths' (Malinowski 1962, p. 291).

> Mythology, therefore, or the sacred tradition of a society, is a body of narratives woven into their culture, dictating their belief, defining their ritual, acting as the chart of their social order and the pattern of their moral behaviour. Every myth has naturally a literary content, since it is always a narrative, but this narrative is not merely a piece of entertaining fiction or explanatory statement to the believer. It is a true account of sensational events which have shaped the constitution of the world, the essence of moral conduct, and determines the ritual contact between man and his maker, or other powers that be. (p. 249)

Malinowski believed that to study the narrative of a myth in isolation from its ritual process and moral institutions was a travesty. Only by viewing myth in this social context could its 'cultural function' become apparent. '[T]he specific social function of myth' according to Malinowski, was 'as a charter of ritual belief, ethics and social organisation' (Malinowski 1962, pp. 250, 254).

The family is often wrapped in a sacral cloak and to criticise it appears to be attacking nature or order itself, a characteristic captured in the popular expression that a self-evident idea is a 'motherhood statement' because no one is against motherhood. Conservatives often attempt to claim the high moral ground about the family. The former Prime Minister, Paul Keating, in a speech to the National Social Policy Conference at the University of New South Wales in 1995, expressed his irritation with this situation by saying 'John Howard [at that time Leader of the Opposition] keeps incanting the word "family" as his own personal mantra; he claims he is "pro-family" as if the rest of us were anti-family. Where does he think the rest of us come from—Mars? Of course, we all come from families.'[2]

The high priests in the transmission of the myth of the 'sacred' family have frequently been behavioural scientists, including sociologists. Their homage has mostly consisted in asserting that the social form of the family, or an irreducible core component of it, is given directly by nature. While this idea of a 'naturally determined' family remains constant among these theorists, the method by which nature has achieved natural determination is disputed. It can be the outcome of hard-wired biological characteristics of the human species, an evolutionary adaptation, or an imperative of the social order.

Behavioural scientists have provided what Malinowski called a 'foundation narrative'—that is, a mythical story about the beginning of a social institution. For example, 'in the beginning . . .' pregnancy and the care of young infants, say some evolutionary theorists (Morris 1968; Tiger 1969; Tiger & Fox 1972), confined women to domestic work, while men were free to roam the wide territories in hunting game. Sometimes other differences, such as average differences in the quantity of muscle fibre, difference in the use of regions of the brain, or small hormonal differences between men and women, are used as additional support for this explanation of the original division of labour.

Anthropologists have found that all societies distinguish between 'women's work' and 'men's work'. However, these above writers have assumed the sexual division of labour to be the outcome of the evolutionary origin of the human species.

Desmond Morris extends this logic into an attempted explanation of marriage. In his foundation narrative, the confinement of women to 'home base' as a result of the demands of children led to hunting parties becoming all-male groups. However, Morris argues that this really goes against the 'primate grain' because it meant that a virile male would depart on 'feeding trips' leaving his 'female unprotected from the advances of other males that might happen to come by' (Morris 1968, p. 9). The answer to this dilemma, claims Morris, was the development of 'pair bonding'. According to Morris, this solved three problems at one stroke: females remained faithful to a male while he was away on the hunt; rivalries between males were greatly reduced, with the consequence that the cooperation necessary for hunting was greatly facilitated; and finally, offspring benefited, because they received the 'maximum care and attention' (Morris 1968, p. 10).

This approach is remarkably ignorant of the variability of family arrangements in nature and blind to the perils of generalising from the behaviour of animals to that of humans. Just exactly what does follow from the sexual nature of human reproduction? Many species found in nature, including plants, have an asexual mode of reproduction, but even if we restrict ourselves to animals which do reproduce sexually, there is a wide variety of solutions to the problem of how to care for dependent young. Evidence in the animal kingdom for the division into hunters and nurturers according to the sex of the animal is relatively unconvincing. Females of many carnivorous species hunt, and the males of some species display what might be called 'maternal' behaviour. In a pattern that is almost the exact reverse of that which Morris claims to be 'natural' among humans, male emperor penguins endure months of freezing Antarctic conditions at 'home base' to keep eggs warm while their mates journey to the ocean to hunt for food.

It is remarkable that, despite his emphasis on the beast within us all (*The Naked Ape*), a theorist such as Desmond Morris should draw his characterisation of 'pair bonding' from his observation of the behaviour of birds and fish. It would surely be more relevant to give an example of the behaviour of higher primates such as gorillas (although resemblances between current human behaviour and that of primates is not sufficient to suggest that these behaviours have been inherited).[3] Presumably, this is because among the gorilla species, as among Australian eastern grey kangaroos, males compete with one another for access to fertile females: males establish a hierarchy based on ritualised combat, in which only the dominant males mate with females, and there is no evidence of 'pair bonding'.

Ann Oakley has described these speculative histories as self-serving and androcentric (male-centred), pointing out that they are a variation of the 'man the mighty hunter' myth (Oakley 1974a, p. 161). Such foundation narratives put value on the masculine activity and append the feminine activity almost as an afterthought. Anthropologists' studies of hunter–gatherer societies over the past 150 years show that while hunting is the high prestige activity, often it is women's activity as gatherers that feeds most of the members of these societies. This was certainly so with many indigenous Australians.

A similarly devastating criticism can be made of other theories which 'naturalise' the family. But the peculiar thing is the profound appeal of legends about the family. It is, indeed, extraordinarily difficult to wean oneself away from these kinds of explanations. It takes self-conscious study to absorb the idea that families are made not born.

Xmas day—a family ritual

The anthropologist Malinowski interpreted myth as an enactment of the moral order. What Luhmann has called normative expectations are expressed in both the content and the enactment of myth. Ritual, as implied by Malinowski's emphasis on the way myths are lived, is a key process for the re-creation, transmission and maintenance of these normative regulations. While foundation narratives are one element of myth which Malinowski drew to our attention, the second element is ritual. Together these two elements of Malinowski's theory of myth provide our first window into the space of the normative family. So, what is an example of a late twentieth century ritual which provides a template for living out myths about the family?

We suggest that Xmas Day is an example of such a ritual. Of course, not all families in today's multicultural Australia celebrate Xmas, although we would argue few people can avoid or ignore it altogether. Even those who follow other faiths find it difficult to avoid having their noses rubbed in Xmas festivities. Most of the families in Australia who do celebrate Xmas are not devout Christians. (Church attendance has steadily fallen since the 1960s. In the 1950s polls found that 28 per cent of women and 18 per cent of men attended church every week: Mol 1989, pp. 330–40.)

Although ostensibly Xmas Day marks an important date in the religious calendar, as a contemporary ritual celebration most of its meaning revolves around family ties. Even for people who are not Christian, some family gathering, whether large or small, often takes place. The following description of Xmas Day is typical of the kind of ritual followed in many Australian households.

Unlike a gathering of friends, the basis of Xmas celebrations is kinship. People are drawn to the celebration by a sense of obligation, which may be to some degree involuntary. Hence people look forward to the event with a mixture of anticipation and dread. In the following section, we will trace the family Xmas ritual, and try to demonstrate how these elements are connected to affirming the family myth, while simultaneously remaining aware of the tensions and difficulties engendered by this ritual.

Preparations for Xmas Day—invitations

Family Xmas celebrations frequently involve extended families, usually three generations, with lateral kin as well. Of course, people can be simultaneously involved in two distinct chains of kinship obligation such as in-laws or step-family. Membership in another kinship structure is sometimes an acceptable reason for absence, however this dilemma is frequently solved by attending both celebrations.

It is almost compulsory to be a member of a family for this day. Those without families are to be pitied as lonely, and are often invited as surrogate family members.

Presents

Getting presents for all the family invites a number of crises—who was forgotten, the problems of selecting presents, and last-minute panics. Presents are often given on the presumption that they are individual and personalised. The gifts are given with an explanation of why they were selected for each individual and should be received in the same spirit—'the very thing that I always wanted'.

The normative expectation is that gifts should be a surprise. They are meant to demonstrate how well you know just what the person wants without having asked them for suggestions—a kind of obligatory second-guessing. The function of wrapping gifts in Xmas paper relates to the element of surprise.

The requirement to show that one has thought of the most appropriate present is frequently a cause of anxiety. Attempts to temper the operation of this norm with clichés such as 'it's the thought that counts' are generally unconvincing. Presents raise the issue of generosity and reciprocity. There is a powerful financial etiquette in buying presents that conform to the family standard of generosity, a standard difficult to alter. Stinginess is interpreted as hostility or lack of interest. Over-generosity may also be a cause for embarrassment. Among adult relatives, transgressing the family cost standard is often mistaken as symbolising inferior social status because of the inability to reciprocate at the same level of generosity.

The giving of presents is usually a child-centred occasion. Children must learn the norm of reciprocity and be reconciled to less extravagant demands, giving up their ambition to possess the largest, most expensive toy. The opposite parent often buys the present with or for the child, teaching them how to consider what the other parent might like, to learn the norm that Xmas presents signal intimacy and knowledge of each person. Children also must learn that the etiquette of receiving gifts involves minimising embarrassment to the giver by pretending that the gift is just what the child wanted. Clearly the mixture of direct and deliberately deceptive messages makes receiving gifts fraught with possibilities for misunderstanding.

Activities and division of family labour

On the day, guests are greeted on arrival and offered a drink. Guests place presents under the tree, and engage in pre-dinner banter. The Xmas feast and the exchange of presents are the central ritual elements of the day's enactment. The close of the celebration is marked by a communal clean-up.

There is a definite division of labour, both in the preparation for Xmas and in the day's activities. Usually one 'nuclear family' plays host. Responsibility for the food falls chiefly to women. Often several women in the extended family provide specialty items. Typically it is the male job to supply the alcohol, greet people at the door and play Santa at the tree.

The present-giving itself is a ritual performance and has to be a public affair; even those in the kitchen are called to take part in unwrapping. There should be many third parties to witness the bilateral exchanges of gifts. The function of the tree is to provide the central prop in the drama of unwrapping.

The menu

Special food for Xmas was once more important than presents. Xmas dinner is a feast—an extension of the everyday ritual of the family meal. 'Breaking bread' together is experienced as a form of family communion.

The tradition is to eat the festive food of a northern hemisphere winter—huge roast dinners usually of turkey, stuffing and ham, heavy steamed plum puddings and brandy butter, mince pies, glacé fruit (even when fresh summer fruit is available), nuts, chocolates, and cherries. This extraordinary out-of-season menu or other special delicacies serve to set this day apart from other days. Champagne, a sparkling wine symbolically reserved for celebrations, is often served, and the best port and cognac offered around. The menu generally involves elaborate preparation, providing an occasion to symbolise nurture through 'a labour of love'. The norm of generosity guarantees an oversupply of food.

Overeating at Xmas time is common. Just why people overeat at this time is difficult to say, but one reason may be the kinship symbolism in the food. People are reluctant to ignore any food for fear of offending the various kin who contributed to the feast. The capacity to willingly overeat (which is after all a kind of self-inflicted injury to the body or physical torture) is as exaggerated a form of receiving as is the overprovision an exaggerated form of nurture. In any case, suspension of rational norms of food intake and an attitude of abandoned indulgence in overconsumption of the richest of possible foods testify that the family Xmas celebration should be an ecstatic experience. Similarly a moderate degree of drunkenness, if not outright encouraged, is amiably tolerated.

Like many other rituals, Xmas dinner prescribes the performance of processes involving both pleasure and pain to induce a profound bodily experience of the key elements of the myth. An individual who passes through these ritual elements lives the myth. This individual experiences himself/herself as an integral and equal part of a nurturing family.

Tensions

Since the family Xmas celebration is a gathering on the basis of kinship obligation and not voluntary friendship, old and new tensions lurk just below the surface. There are opportunities for conflicts: with the in-laws, between the generations, among siblings. This does not exhaust the potential sources of conflict (for example conflicts between spouses) but covers those most particular to Xmas.

In-laws, the relatives people gain through marriage, are in a sense 'chosen' by one family member only. Inviting in-laws to family Xmases has a socially obligatory character, so if people do not invite them, they generally have a well-prepared and socially acceptable justification (e.g. distance). It is hardly surprising that, in addition to being the butt of many jokes, in-laws are the occasion of considerable social anxiety and tension during Xmas events. The grounds for tension, even dislike, are mostly social. Differences in wealth, or in ethnicity, linguistic or religious background are often profound reasons why one family is largely unacceptable to another. A milder but no less common cause of tension is 'boring and boorish' behaviour. Such examples become legendary: 'Remember the time that Uncle Al slept through Xmas dinner, only waking at the mention of the distribution of the family matriarch's assets'. Often these tensions are symbolised through disagreements about politics, ethical issues, alleged 'stupidity' or dullness.

In conflicts between the generations, important sources of tension are the differences in age and authority. The formative experiences of each generation are unique. These differing experiences increase the probability that there will be strongly felt disagreements about socially acceptable behaviour, especially those connected with lifestyle choices such as child-rearing and housekeeping practices, diet, sexuality, sexual mores and feminism.

All parent–child relations are characterised by a definite structure of authority and the memories of these former roles die hard. Parents often presume that they have authority over their adult children and indeed still relate to them as children. Adult 'children' are often overcome by memories of the powerlessness of being a small and dependent child or of the struggle to assert their independence. Each party experiences disappointment and frustration.

There are also tensions between the youngest generation and their parents. Xmas is often presented as a child-centred occasion, with much of its paraphernalia being justified as important for the children. With very young children, parents suspend the norm of reciprocity in the exchange of gifts, and replace it with an exchange of gift-for-expression-of-delight. In some families or at work picnics, presents are given to children only.

So, it is hardly surprising that for children, the most significant aspect of Xmas is the gifts. Children's expectations at Xmas time are very high. In the overwrought atmosphere, presents are unwrapped in a frenzy. There is much opportunity for unhappiness caused by imagined oversights, mistaken gifts, inadequate substitutions. These felt grievances are usually experienced as the parents' 'fault'. In one instance, a four-year-old disappointed with the failure of an expected gift locked himself in the broom cupboard for the entire duration of the Xmas celebration, forlornly issuing recriminations from behind the door.

In addition to the upset of the children, parents may also experience painful disappointment because of the catastrophic collapse of the gift-for-expression-of-delight exchange. Instead of the anticipated delight, parents find themselves attempting to mollify tearful and resentful offspring.

Not all children have siblings. Freud pointed out that siblings are rivals for the affections of their parents. This is most overt at very young ages but covert tensions often persist into adult life. When the gifts are unwrapped, often the largest tantrums are between siblings who feel aggrieved that their brother/sister has been favoured over them. These conflicts are conditioned by birth order and sex.

Despite most parents' efforts to bestow equal attention and affection on every child, differences based on maturity and gender lead inevitably to disparate experiences. The youngest sibling may look up to an elder brother or sister but, from the perspective of the older sibling, the responsibility for a younger, less socially and physically capable sibling is an obstacle to their own enjoyment. The younger sibling may feel excluded.

Although it is now more widely accepted for parents to treat boys and girls impartially, nevertheless, some gender differences appear unavoidable. There remains an emphasis, whether from parents, grandparents or other influences, on the development of boys' intellectual achievements and sporting skills, whereas amongst girls there is a greater emphasis on social skills and (surprisingly still) preparation for being a housewife. Parents' choice of Xmas gifts is constrained by the availability of gender-neutral toys. In Australia most department stores rigidly divide the toy offerings by sex, and television advertisements naturally conform to store buyers' decisions. Guns, violent figures and mechanical and construction games are stacked on half the rows and toy ironing tables, dolls and miniature prams fill the other. Age and gender differences among siblings often lead to resentment at the real or imagined overemphasis on boys, guilt over being the favoured sibling, to serious feelings of inferiority and its converse.

This 'happy' Xmas occasion might be a situation where adults must be on their best diplomatic behaviour to avoid giving voice to their resentment and anger while in the background, children whine and cry. The presence of a 'stranger' (the lonely other) at these family gatherings may relieve such problems, since tensions contradict the presumption of family harmony in the season of 'peace and good will to all', and cannot be relived too nakedly in front of a stranger. Efforts to be on one's best behaviour, to overlook a repetition of old slights and irritating patronage are, however, often stressful too. The surfeit of food and alcohol does nothing to alleviate these tensions of a meal-time (or a few days) spent with people chosen on the basis of blood and not friendship.

Despite the tensions and the torments, Xmas remains primarily a family ritual. It is believed by most participants that Xmas away from the family is a deprivation, that Xmas time is an opportunity to show the warmth and solidarity inherent in the 'bosom' of families. At least once a year families re-enact this ritual, attempting to make real the morality of trusting, intimate bonds of family. From the invitations and careful selection of presents through to the final serving of plum pudding, each act in the family Xmas ritual serves to institutionalise the morality of reciprocity, generosity and mutual respect. Perhaps, family Xmas is a more taxing ritual than initiation rites. In order to maintain the normative content of the family myth, the abundant evidence suggesting covert distress and dissolution must be overlooked or rationalised and the tensions endured. The normative expectations of warm, harmonious and unbreakable bonds of family are maintained despite being contradicted by events.

Interpretations of myth from linguistics

Another approach to the study of myth has been that initiated by Roland Barthes. Barthes is perhaps the most celebrated exponent of semiotics, the study of systems of signs and the way they convey meaning. The central idea of this discipline is that pictures, gestures and events are signs which can be interpreted or 'read' in much the same way as sentences in language. This theory is heavily influenced by linguistics and it is unusual for writers to mention the work of Malinowski and Barthes in the same context. We shall try to demonstrate that the normative family conforms to the definition of myth in both the anthropological and the linguistic traditions. Semiotics has emphasised 'lived texts' in contradistinction to 'produced texts' (that is, books, films and plays). These lived texts consist of everyday images and gestures, which generate culture in much the same way that Malinowski believed ritual produced culture (Fiske et al. 1987).

Barthes

In *Mythologies* (1973), Barthes sets out to describe the production of meaning in myths. The basic unit of this analysis
is the sign. The sign is formed by the association of two
elements—the signifier and the signified. In language, the
signifier is the acoustic image, the sound of the word we utter;
whereas the signified is the concept (what is indicated by the
word) and 'the relation between concept and image is the
sign (the word, for instance), which is a concrete entity'
(Barthes 1973, p. 113). The sign is thus the third element.
Barthes uses the example of a lover who shows his passion
by presenting the beloved with a bunch of roses. To the
lovers, the roses are a single sign—'passionified roses'—roses
weighted with passion. For analytic purposes, however, there
are three terms: the signifier (roses), the signified (passion)
and the sign, passionified roses. The rose and the emotion of
passion existed before uniting to form this third object, which
is the sign. The rose is not a symbol of anything until it is
associated with passion through the gesture of the lover's gift.
The lovers 'read' the bunch of roses as indicating a definite
meaning—passion.

Myth, according to Barthes, is a system of communication—a mode of signification. It is a message whose peculiarity
is that it is a second order semiological system. The raw
materials of myth are already signs, that is signs in a first
order system (Barthes 1973, p. 109). Any sign—a gesture, an
expression, a turn of phrase, a style of dress, an image—can
become an element of myth and used for particular social
purposes. As Barthes says, 'mythical speech is made of a
material which has *already* been worked on so as to make it
suitable for communication' (Barthes 1973, p. 110).

The pre-existing (first order) sign becomes a signifier in the
second order system which generates the meaning of myth.
This is best illustrated through example. We go to visit a friend's
shared household and on the wall we notice the poster
illustrated in Figure 2.1.[4]

In the poster the shadowy figure of a young man naked
to the waist, dressed only in jeans, is shown gazing tenderly
and devotedly at an infant cradled gently in his arms. The well
lit, wide-eyed baby stares back in open-mouthed engagement.

Figure 2.1 Image of man and infant

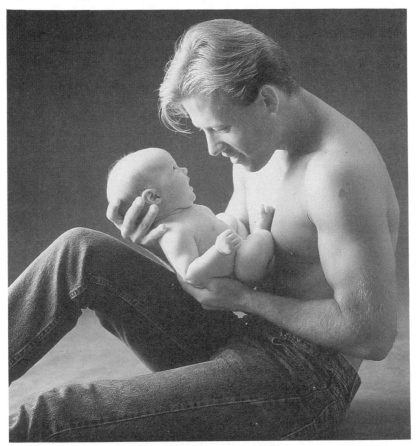

Source: International Photographic Library

All of this is the meaning of the picture. But, naively or not, we can see at a glance what it signifies: that this intent looking 'new' male is bonding with the baby. He is capable of experiencing affection and he has the desire to nurture. There is no better answer to those who allege that all men are insensitive and hostile to family responsibilities, than this image. Men care. The bonds of love and family are natural and powerful.

The first order system of representation—the photograph, which is either a good or a poor likeness of an individual man (the model) and a particular baby—becomes the vehicle of the second order system of myth and is used to represent the miracle of new human life, love between parents and children, a revolution in sex roles and progress towards a world of greater equity and freedom. The picture mimics the Renaissance images of Madonna and child in its composition. This reference is underlined by the powerful halo-like light that falls on the head of the baby. Such a figurative allusion is also part of the seizure by myth, evoking the image of the adoration of the Christ-child. This man does not just cradle the baby—he worships it. He is just as protective and enthralled as any mother.

But, of course, he is a *man*. Lest there be any doubt about this, the young man's semi-naked body, dappled in shadow, is revealed incompletely, so that the play of light and dark emphasises the perfect line of his nose, his tousled blond hair and the musculature in his chest and arm. This photograph belongs to a genre of openly titillating images—soft pornography—where the man is the object of sexual desire. The mythic image suggests: not only is this guy good in bed but nine months later he will still be around. Entranced by fatherhood, baby can safely be left in his powerful but capable arms. The mother, his unseen partner, can lead just as independent a life as any single woman.

Barthes emphasises that the myth comes to the image 'fully armed'. Myth seizes the first order representation and overlays its intended second order concept (a revolutionary new form of masculinity, etc.). The picture of the model and the baby acts as an alibi for the myth, so that if it is challenged as a myth, it can be claimed that this is only a photograph of a man and baby. There is a 'constant game of hide-and-seek' between the picture and its use as a signifier of the myth (Barthes 1973, p. 118). For the myth reader, 'everything happens as if the picture *naturally* conjured up the concept, as if the signifier *gave a foundation* to the signified' and from the precise moment when the 'new man' achieves this natural state, myth is experienced as legitimate fact (Barthes 1973, pp. 129–30, emphasis in original).

This is what allows viewers to consume myth innocently: they do not see the image as a semiological system but as an inductive one, where conclusions are drawn from the evidence of their eyes. In a sense myth hides nothing, its function is to distort—'it points out and it notifies, it makes us understand something and it imposes it on us' (Barthes 1973, p. 17). 'Myth is experienced as innocent speech', says Barthes, 'not because its intentions are hidden—if they were hidden, they would not be efficacious—but because they are naturalised' (Barthes 1973, p. 131). Myth is powerful not because we are easily duped but because its mode of expression is subtle and complicated.

In a language the choice of a sound to represent a new object is arbitrary, at the time of its invention a 'telephone', for example, might easily have been called something else (in German, for example, it is called a 'distance-speaker'). In myth, however, the signification is never arbitrary—it is always *motivated*. For the myth of the 'new father' to get hold of the image of the model and the baby, there must be an intentional analogy between the pose of the father and the standard representation of mother and child. As Barthes points out, a variety of different images may serve the myth equally well (Barthes 1973, p. 127). So in place of the man with baby, the 'new father' may be signified by other images—a man hangs nappies on a clothes line; an unshaven father coaxes a baby in a highchair by mimicking the necessary eating movements; two children play hide and seek with a delighted father who hides amateurishly behind a tree; an expectant father listens attentively at the pre-natal class.

In these respects myth resembles an ideographic language, like that used in road signs, where the presence of a steep hill is indicated by a black silhouette with wheels (the image of a generic car) shown on a wedge (the generic representation of the hill). In other words ideographic language keeps some analogies while discarding most others, so that a circle can represent a face, two dots the eyes, and an upturned semi-circle a smile (happiness). Typically, myth is conveyed by these reduced, 'poor, incomplete images', especially 'caricatures, pastiches, symbols' (Barthes 1973, p. 127).

Written text too can be seized by myth. The most obvious examples of this are provided by political campaigning. We have chosen the rear panel of a 1993 election pamphlet (shown in Figure 2.2) to illustrate this point.

Figure 2.2 Use of the sign 'family' in election pamphlet, 1993

THE NORTH SYDNEY LIBERAL

Families of North Sydney have been neglected, or worse, discriminated against, over the last ten years. Labor has treated **families** with contempt and will do worse if we let them.

Tell Canberra the past cannot be the future.

A Liberal Government in Canberra will change things for the better.

North Sydney is one of Australia's most important communities — our families need a representative in Canberra who cares — and can do something about it.

Only if we vote Liberal do we give John Hewson a chance to Fightback! for us all.

VOTE ☐1☐ McNEILLY

Send a Liberal to Canberra who cares — **and can do something for our families.**

FIGHTBACK! for North Sydney families means:

1. More jobs
2. Fairer tax
3. Better health care
4. Increases in family benefits
5. Cheaper food and petrol
6. Childcare benefits
7. Tax-free savings
8. Affordable first home ownership
9. New superannuation incentives
10. Better schools and training.

BE BETTER OFF —

VOTE ☐1☐ McNEILLY

for North Sydney

He cares — and can do something about it.

(For more information about Bruce McNeilly and **Fightback!** phone **958-5838**.)

Source: The Liberal Party of Australia, NSW Division, 1993.

In this pamphlet the word 'families' is printed only in bold type. For those scanning the document, 'families' competes with the ideograph of the ballot paper for the reader's attention. The term 'families' is repeated six times and the idea that the candidate 'cares' is proclaimed three times compared with just three mentions of 'Liberal', 'North Sydney' and 'Canberra', and only two mentions of the candidate's name and the official campaign slogan 'Fightback!'. An election pamphlet is no place for subtlety, so the candidate is seeking blatantly to associate himself with families. The skeletal information available at a glance is that voting for McNeilly and families just go together.

If one reads the text of the first paragraph, set in abnormally large type, it becomes clear that this association is pushed to extraordinary lengths. It imposes a commonality between reader and candidate. Both are addressed as defenders of their family ('Labor . . . will do worse if we let them'). Having bid the reader to recognise herself/himself as a family member, the text uses the imagery of the oppressed to address the relatively financially privileged and ethnically homogeneous residents of North Sydney.[5] They and their loved ones have been subject to 'neglect', 'discrimination' and 'treated . . . with contempt'. Having endured these insults and injuries, they are urged, on behalf of their spouses and children, to 'Fightback!' and 'tell Canberra the past cannot be the future'. These voters and the candidate want nothing for themselves, they are simply doing this for the greater good of their families. Indeed in a later paragraph, the candidate explains that he should be elected because 'our families need a representative in Canberra who cares'.

In this paragraph, there is a complex play with the associations of the words 'family' and 'families'. The intended outrage and subsequent 'Fightback!' vote are solicited on the basis of a family membership. The outrage is invoked by reminding the voter of a powerless childhood. Neglect, discrimination, indifference—the 'crimes' of the Labor government are those of a bad parent. Why hasn't the government/parent paid me attention, stood up for me in my disputes and why don't they show affection?

This is an infantile vision of authority. In this appeal to the voter, the candidate sets himself up as a caring and protective parent—'He cares—and can do something about it'. Under the protection of this good father everyone will 'Be Better Off'. The support for policies is sought on this irrational basis and not by any demonstration of the technical advantages of the policies themselves. The Fightback! platform is listed as a set of outcomes (More jobs; Fairer tax; Better health care; Increases in family benefits; Cheaper food and petrol, etc.), ignoring the kernel of the policies which will be the means of reaching these outcomes. The Fightback! document itself emphasised a consumption tax as part of tax reform, privatisation, smaller government, less regulation and the unfettered operation of the market as the means to end recession. The pamphlet, however, eschews this technical discussion in favour of a list of treats for 'North Sydney families'.

The myth of the downtrodden North Sydney family voters stands in contrast to any adult comprehension of the relation between government and citizenry. As a justification, the pamphlet absurdly asserts that 'North Sydney is one of Australia's most important communities'. Why should a government pay particular attention to such a successful and untroubled community? By what principles could North Sydney families imagine they have suffered 'discrimination'? Just how has the Federal Government (or is it Canberra?) treated them with 'contempt'? Taking the position of the signifier in the first order system, that is, the position of a concrete family in this electorate, is enough to debunk the mythical family of voter-and-candidate. The first order family has not in fact suffered these wounds and slights from 'Canberra', although the appeal of the pamphlet relies on membership in an infantilised family that is powerless. The concrete family is replaced by the caricature of the 'North Sydney family' but, as with the pictorial image, the concrete family acts as an alibi and naturalises the appeal for Liberal votes.

Popular representations of the family—subversive family sitcoms

On a daily basis, television produces a profusion of representations of family life and indeed, there is a genre of television specialising in this called family sitcoms (situation comedy). In Barthes' terms, they develop a semiological system of myth which communicates a set of values. Practically every Australian home has one or more television sets. Television is an integral part of the culture of most Australian homes. The manner in which families are represented through this medium provides our third window onto normative family arrangements.[6]

In his work *Jokes and Their Relation to the Unconscious* (1976), Sigmund Freud developed the idea that like dreams, slips of tongue and neurotic symptoms, jokes are a mode of expressing unacceptable impulses. In particular he was concerned with aggressive and sexual impulses (Freud 1976, pp. 132–62). Ridicule, humiliation and smut are the core of what he called 'tendentious' jokes. It is a short step from this theory to the idea of 'tension management' outlined by Talcott Parsons (1951), himself an enthusiastic reader of Freud. Parsons, like Freud, believed that the social order was maintained with difficulty in the face of individual impulses towards essentially antisocial forms of gratification. The tension accumulated through the frustration of unfulfilled needs could be relieved by designating arenas where its release was strictly demarcated, safe and socially sanctioned. The sublimation of aggression and sexuality in humour is an example of this process. As Gregory Bateson (1973) has pointed out, 'play' among young animals often takes the form of mock aggression. The playful nip stands for the savage bite. However, the animal must be able to distinguish between this playful simulation and a genuine attack. So must humans—which explains the phrases: 'This is going too far!' 'It is beyond a joke'.

Humour permits the sublimated expression of the unacceptable. Under the mask of ambiguity all manner of things can be said. By focusing on those elements that are so outrageous as to make us laugh, and thus sanctioning the transgression of the socially acceptable, we get an inverted image of the normative structure. It is therefore possible in our opinion to discern, in studying this humour, the normative structures that it subverts.

The genre of television comedy we have chosen—subversive family sitcoms—is complex because it is a second order form of comedy. Much of its appeal derives from its satirical commentary on the sugary conventionality of mainstream television family sitcoms. *Roseanne, The Simpsons,* and *Married with Children* are examples of the genre we have in mind. We will argue that this opposition to conventional family morality does not escape social regulation but only makes the normative family more apparent through its partial flouting of expectations. The humour relies on ambivalence, surprise, incongruity and superiority. Without a thorough knowledge of the appropriate expectations, the viewer would not find these subversive shows funny.

The Cosby Show is fairly representative of the conventional family sitcom satirised by the more subversive shows. This enormously successful show presents a father-knows-best world, where racial and economic equality are assumed to have arrived (Feuer 1987, pp. 126–30). In contrast to the 1950s television families, who 'took *the institution of the stable family for granted* . . . the Huxtables work strenuously and self-consciously at persuading viewers how well they get along' (Taylor 1989, p. 161, emphasis in original). At the heart of *The Cosby Show* is a moral etiquette of parenting and developmental psychology. Moral instruction is represented as the purpose of each episode and the ending of each show is deliberately didactic. The narrative is always resolved in a learning experience, a lesson in 'social adjustment for the children', and beneath the mildness is a casual hostility where everyone mocks and insults each other.

Ella Taylor suggests this show exemplifies television's 'aggressive reinstatement' of the nuclear family in the 1980s. The father, played by Bill Cosby, has a brand of patriarchal dominance underneath a childlike charm. This dualism may cater to viewers' unfulfilled yearning, according to Taylor, for 'a perfectly synchronised family' that easily provides for everyone's needs and that 'regulates itself through a benevolent dictatorship'. A tone of 'persistent authoritarianism' is set by Bill. His wife, Clair, works and manages the domestic arrangements, although the four children also share in chores. The independence that Clair Huxtable derives from her paid work is undercut by her husband's warnings against her becoming too assertive 'The show's endless rehearsal and efficient mopping up of mild domestic disorder stakes a claim for the perfect family that works', according to Taylor, but at the cost of the 'closure of all open endings, relative viewpoints, and ethical ambiguities and its energetic repression of the sources that afflict many families (especially black families)' (Taylor 1989, p. 164).

In contrast with *The Cosby Show* and similar family sitcoms, the programs of the early 1990s, particularly *The Simpsons*, *Roseanne* and *Married with Children*, could be seen as debunking the myth of the perfect TV family. For reasons of space, we shall only treat *The Simpsons*. In many ways *The Simpsons* is an obverse of *The Cosby Show*. Homer Simpson the father is a parody, a ridiculous reversal of the urbane, wealthy Bill Cosby the 'educator'.[7] The self-conscious reference to conventional family sitcoms in *The Simpsons* is made explicit by the inclusion of a character—a black doctor named Huxtable.

The introductory segment of *The Simpsons* is a dense and compressed overview of the whole show. It depicts a slice from the daily activities of each Simpson family member. So, Bart and Lisa, the two older children, are seen finishing their typical school day. Bart leaps out of the school window from his detention onto his skateboard, and rushes home on crowded footpaths, stealing bus stop signs and so forth along the way. Lisa's musical performance, in breaking away from an easier, scheduled piece at band rehearsal, attracts disapproving stares from the male teacher and other pupils. She departs from the classroom still playing brilliantly on the saxophone. Bart, the male child, faces no sanctions for his outrageous behaviour, whereas Lisa's behaviour, even while displaying artistic genius, is judged to be inappropriate and disruptive.

The next two shots show the daily activities of the parents, Marge and Homer, in traditional familial roles. Marge is grocery shopping with the baby Maggie (a child with a dummy, perpetually trapped in a sleeping bag), who gets mistaken for produce but ends up unharmed in Marge's grocery cart. Marge is then pictured driving home with the baby happily imitating her. Homer, in the traditional breadwinner role, is shown finishing his day's work at the local nuclear power plant. But he recklessly discards his expensive tools at the stop-work siren, thoughtlessly brushing radioactive waste from his clothing, and then hurling more glowing waste out of his car window on the way home.

As they all converge at their home, Bart skateboards over the top of Homer's car, Marge almost runs over Bart and then Homer, and Lisa nearly runs down Homer with her bike. They all race in and fight their way for a position on the couch in front of the television. The whole is a marked contrast to the structure of *The Cosby Show*'s opening sequence, which is one of 'a theme and variations', where Cosby is the theme and his wife and each child appear with him individually as variations whom the playful father treats thoughtfully and personally. The Cosby/Huxtable family exemplifies simplicity and taste, each character could be a fashion model and the family is 'well off' (Seiter 1987, pp. 36–7), whereas the Simpson family is working class, careless and messy. Homer may be self-centred like Bill Cosby, but from the opening sequence the audience can see that he is also stupid, lazy and thoughtless, and the wife and children, far from fawning around a fatherly idol, are only depicted in a scene of family 'togetherness' as collective couch potatoes. In contrast to the upright didacticism of the Huxtables, the Simpson family revels in so-called mindless, tasteless activities.

So it could be argued that audiences have turned with great relief from the saccharine-sweet, subtle authoritarianism of shows such as Cosby's. *The Simpsons, Roseanne* and *Married with Children* all subvert the myth of universal middle-classness so prevalent in the 1980s sitcoms, by their social failure, their tenuous employment in blue collar jobs and so forth. It is a moot point, however, whether these shows move very far from the ideals of the normative family, which reinforces the power of the myths.

The Simpsons scripts rely heavily on humorous transgression of normative structures. A continual breaking of the rules of family life—of husband–wife relations and customary modes of child-rearing—occurs in each episode. This technique would not be funny without the audience's preconceptions of the ideal family and the unstated norms around perfect parenting. Humorists systematically exploit an audience's capacities to understand and predict the rules of appropriate, standard behaviour, by playing on the underlying meanings and assumptions we all learn. Humour works by deviating from a conventional framework of well-known events that construct certain meanings, in altering an expected part of an event. A discontinuity of some sort between the expected and what actually occurs seems to be fundamental to the experience of humour, according to many experts on the topic (Goldstein 1972; Zijderveld 1983).

Some of the techniques of humour rely on incongruity (for example, a contrast between a significant event and an incongruously trivial one), surprise or shock, ambivalence (where feelings are incompatible, for example the mixture of mirth and nervousness prompted by Homer's carelessness with the radioactive waste) and superiority or ridicule (Homer frequently responds stupidly, and viewers compare themselves favourably with, or even triumph over, his failings). These techniques depend on members of a society sharing a number of similar patterns of behaviour, interpretations of behaviour and similar emotional responses to behaviour. Humour reflexively reveals social expectations and allows us to think what are 'normally' unacceptable thoughts.

In the case of *The Simpsons*, the major stereotypes that the scripts play with are those of the father and husband. A few examples in the father–son relationship demonstrate the technique:

While Bart prepares to go to France for three months on a student exchange program, Homer talks to him seriously, giving Bart advice before he leaves. Then Homer says, 'I guess what I'm trying to say is . . . don't mess up France the way you messed up your room'.

This is a comparison of incongruous events, a merely untidy room and a trip by a small boy to a foreign country, with the humour lying in Homer's failure to achieve conventional expectations of a father's responsible, serious role in instructing and caring for Bart. Other examples, here using ridicule of Homer or Bart, of transgressing the norms of parental love, moral uprightness and trust, and thinking the unthinkable about children, are in the following two incidents.

When Homer loses his job, he is overcome by a desire for money and alcohol. In the midst of his depression, Homer smashes Bart's piggy bank open and immediately says, 'Oh no! What have I done? I smashed open my little boy's piggy bank, and for what . . . a few measly coins. Not even enough to buy one beer. Wait a minute, let me check . . . not even close.' When Bart goes to France, Homer is not only enthusiastic about having Bart leave, but also expresses the fact that he prefers the family without Bart. Homer says, 'You know Marge, this is the way I've always wanted it to be. We've become a fully functioning family unit. We've always blamed ourselves, but I guess it's become pretty clear which cylinder wasn't firing.'

These incidents transgress the prevailing norms that children are irreplaceable, that sons are special to fathers and children are not to be blamed for a family's problems. The humour arises from this weak, not-so-special relationship, with an underlying function of easing guilt (for children and parents, since the Simpson children are as similarly cynical about their father). Such texts speak to the dilemma of parents blaming themselves for their children's behaviour, yet possibly harbouring underlying feelings that their children are the cause of their problems. The baby is 'controlled' by garments remarkably similar to swaddling clothes, a practice discarded in the late feudal era, but this restriction fails; baby Maggie is often left unattended and miraculously survives all sorts of dangers unseen by her parents. We laugh nervously at these inattentive transgressions of parenting norms.

Homer and Marge both transgress a more shaky, less entrenched norm that daughters' abilities should be encouraged as much as sons'. Lisa is highly intelligent, compared with Bart, but Homer is usually uninterested or exaggeratedly pleased with her. He is unable to communicate with his daughter. Marge, the nurturer and disciplinarian, is also an exaggerated role model for Lisa. In her stereotypical motherly functions, the character of Marge ensures that the jokes are directed more at the norms presented by other television families, where daughters are still trivialised, but far more subtly. Likewise when Marge has a romantic affair, however neglectful, embarrassing and silly Homer is, Marge conforms to the norm that marriage is lasting, even if the sexual excitement is missing, while romance is sexual, new and special but faintly ridiculous.

A number of readings from various subject positions are possible. *The Simpsons* shows that the family is not sacred or impenetrable, and holds up the lofty values of traditional families, or those of television families like Cosby's, only in order to subvert them. Audiences can identify with a 'less than perfect' family that may resemble their own, at least at the level of the contemporary family's shortcomings, and find ease for the guilty feelings of not living up to unstated normative structures and familial rules.

Nevertheless, the show revolves around the father, Homer, the most stupid and incompetent character, whose slack and wheedling behaviour to Marge could be viewed as showing men as the 'problem' in families. And yet, the humour lies precisely in Homer's exaggerated laziness and ridiculous behaviour; everyone can laugh at this uneducated, working-class bumbler, because anyone, even another man, must be superior in the humour of invidious comparisons. In our interpretation, the preferred reading offered by the script writers is of reassurance to men, and a moral lesson to children and women. It suggests not to expect too much of fathers or husbands, but to keep trying to 'get along' through accepting these stereotypical masculine traits, because most men are surely not as hopeless as the absurd Homer.

The closed window—suppression of 'pathological' family disharmony

Freud was interested in humour because it was a mechanism by which the socially forbidden found 'sublimated' expression. But some of the activities that frequently occur within family settings are too hot even for 'subversive' comedies to handle. These activities must be suppressed outright. In some religions, God is so holy that no mere mortal is permitted to say the name or make a graven image of God. Some things just cannot be spoken about. It is taboo. One understanding of taboo is that we observe taboos (for example, of silence) because the events in question (for example, domestic violence) make us anxious, being beyond our technical control. Observing the taboo is a way of reassuring ourselves. Radcliffe-Brown contests this general understanding of taboo. For him, taboos are 'the obligatory recognition in a standardised symbolic form of the significance and importance of the event' to the community at large (Radcliffe-Brown 1952, pp. 149–50).

Similarly, there are conventions for shielding us all from seeing 'polluted' incidents or 'matter out of place' (Douglas 1970). Unspoken agreements that dead bodies from road accidents should not be shown on television only become obvious when a news program upsets the convention. No one desires to see the potential fate of any of us drawn too graphically, and the car industry would also suffer.

Conspiracy of silence

Family violence is hidden by what many commentators call a 'conspiracy of silence'—a covenant against speaking out—which involves perpetrators, victims and most of those professionals and authorities who are in a position to do something about it (Hopkins & McGregor 1991, p. 8). These suppressed activities represent a limit of the normative system where acts are considered so awful as to be unspeakable.

Estimates of the extent

Since domestic violence is taboo, it is hardly surprising that it is difficult to gather information about it. Like drug use, it is a matter about which people are reluctant to speak and the extent of domestic violence is difficult to estimate. The major sources of information are police reports, the demand for refuge accommodation, phone-ins and population surveys. The highest estimates of the incidence come from population surveys (ABS 1996c; FVPET 1991, pp. 66–7, 101–2; QDVTF, 1988, pp. 43–5).[8] United States population surveys, extrapolated to the Australian population in 1984, suggest that 16 per cent of couples experience violence of some sort and 6 per cent severe violence during any one year. This implies that approximately 1 per cent of severe incidents were reported to the police (FVPET 1991, p. 70). Forty-six per cent of respondents to a survey conducted by the Office of the Status of Women reported knowing someone involved in domestic violence (Brown 1990, p. 870). A Queensland domestic violence hotline showed that only 56 per cent of women who called reported any of these incidents to the police (QDVTF 1988). Estimates based on phone-in data suggest that many more women experience domestic violence than seek shelter in a refuge (Mugford et al. 1989, p. 105).

The survey data and data derived from phone-ins are open to criticism on methodological grounds. However, the demand for places in refuges is concrete data that is more difficult to dismiss. When the women's refuge movement began in 1974, refuges were inundated by a quite unpredicted number of women and children. About 2500 people in any one day are currently using refuges around Australia (Hopkins & McGregor 1991, pp. 11–12). In New South Wales alone between 1984 and 1985, 5605 women and 6949 children were accommodated in refuges and almost twice that number (23 000) were turned away due to overcrowding (Stubbs & Wallace 1988, p. 55).

The indications are that the incidence of domestic violence is under-reported. Hospitals are inclined to report victims of domestic violence as accident patients, which leads them to estimate that one in twenty injuries result from domestic violence rather than the one in four established by follow-up interviews (QDVTF 1988, p. 43). One-quarter of all offences against the person actually reported to police and recorded in New South Wales between 1986 and 1987 occurred in private dwellings. John Avery, later a Commissioner of the New South Wales Police, argued, using police records, that '[f]amily violence and domestic disturbances consume more time than any other call on police services except for street accidents' (cited in Stubbs & Wallace 1988, p. 54). All these estimates of the extent of domestic violence agree that overwhelmingly victims are women, 85–95 per cent, and abusers men (QDVTF 1988, pp. 13–14; Hopkins & McGregor 1991; FVPET 1991, p. 74).

While domestic violence rates are difficult to estimate there can be no doubt about murder rates. Patricia Easteal in a recent study found that 24 per cent of homicides were known to be murders of sexual intimates; in another 18 per cent the relationship between victim and perpetrator was unknown. Of the 150 victims of 'intimate homicide' between 1989 and 1991, 121 were women (81 per cent). The predominant perpetrators of 'intimate homicide' were men (82 per cent) (Easteal 1993, pp. 32, 50–1). Wallace has calculated that '43 per cent of homicides between 1968–81 in New South Wales were within the family' (Mugford et al. 1989, p. 104).

According to New South Wales records, more men than women meet a violent end. Men engage in far more public assaults (rates of male pub and club violence are high), 25.8 per cent of men are murdered by 'friends' and 23 per cent by strangers, compared with respectively 9.6 and 9.1 per cent of women (Mugford et al. 1989, p. 105; FVPET 1991, pp. 71–2).

In total only 10 per cent of male victims were killed by their spouses while almost half (47 per cent) of the female victims of all murder cases were killed by their husbands.

According to Easteal, only 19 per cent of murders of intimates were committed by women. However, given women's low rate of homicide, 43 per cent of the victims of female murderers were intimates (Easteal 1993, p. 50). In almost all of the cases of women killing male intimate partners, there was evidence of previous domestic violence by the man against his female partner, often for years. Far from the popular depictions of female murderers motivated by revenge, money or another man, as in the films *Fatal Attraction* or *Basic Instinct,* female offenders are mostly responding to domestic victimisation (Easteal 1993, pp. 50–1, 92).

A high proportion of domestic homicides are 'the culmination of ongoing wife battering', many of which police and other authorities were already aware of (Easteal 1993, p. 181). Easteal argues that male domestic homicides exemplify 'the ownership-type of jealousy' acted out in the relationship, exacerbated by separation and culminating in the final act. Male perpetrators are given to say such phrases as 'If I can't have you, nobody will' and 'If you do [have an affair] I'll shoot your kid' (Easteal 1993, p. 109).

Easteal claims her findings confirm the thesis that

> control is always the primary warning sign for murder. It is also the number one warning signal for violence. Murder is the final irrevocable step, the ultimate expression of men's control over women. For some men, the need for control is not satisfied until this irrevocable step is taken. (Bean, cited in Easteal 1993, p. 91)

Comparing those homicides followed by the murderer suiciding and those where this did not happen, Easteal notes that 'the same motif is manifest: a perception of the partner as an integral part of the individual' (Easteal 1993, p. 179). It seems that if unity cannot be enforced, murder is preferable to admitting to the disunity of the family.

The need of the perpetrator to control his partner appears a dominant motive in domestic violence, not only homicide. The pretexts for domestic violence are issues about trivial domestic routines (Hopkins & McGregor 1991, pp. 93, 119). As one victim says:

> No particular thing set him off which is the hardest to cope with . . . For example, the butter may be hard instead of easy spreading consistence because you overlooked taking it out of the fridge early. This would trigger off verbal abuse, which in seconds became violent behaviour, chair overthrown backwards at the table and a mad rage—his demonstration of what I'd get if I didn't oblige every whim type of thing. (QDVTF 1988, p. 27)

The abusive partner refuses to let his wife be a separate person; these husbands try to monitor their wives' contacts with others, and isolate them from contact with their own family and friends. Social abuse usually accompanies mental and physical violence, with public humiliation ever-present as a threat to enforce a woman's isolation (FVPET 1991, pp. 62–4, 79).

Many battered wives adopt a withdrawal strategy of over-compliance and self-abnegation. 'You try to become as close to perfect as possible', said one victim (QDVTF 1988, p. 64). The woman accepts housekeeping to be her duty, and violence a punishment for non-compliance (Hopkins & McGregor 1991, pp. 93, 119). But for the abuser who has achieved his aims, there is always room to improve on perfection, for compliance seems to guarantee further abuse (QDVTF 1988, p. 66).

Under-reporting by victims is, from most accounts, closely connected to the idealised family. Difficulties in disclosing the violence are typically based on notions of privacy and community or family loyalty. Although most victims often feel ashamed of their injuries, they are also unable to overcome the idea that speaking out is a betrayal of their partner (FVPET 1991, p. 65). Fear of possible social condemnation or disrespect for the victim or offender leads to concealment. Abusers look like anyone else: as one victim says, 'He was a regular "Take home to meet Mum and Dad" type of guy'. Most victims believe that they can stop the abuse themselves: 'I thought if I gave him enough love I could change him' (QDVTF 1988, p. 22). This draws victims into the conspiracy of silence surrounding domestic violence.

Among other key conspirators are the 'authorities', professionals, neighbours and friends. Police have a large measure of discretion in recording incidents and until recently domestic violence in certain situations was not considered serious enough to be put on the public record (Edwards 1989, p. 81). Victims have tended to consult general practitioners instead (QDVTF 1988, p. 198). Yet for a long time doctors limited their treatment to prescriptions of tranquillisers, ignoring the obvious symptoms. The major response by clergy has been similar, telling victims to 'Go back home' or 'Pray'. The reluctance of friends, neighbours or family to become involved in a 'private matter' is another persistent factor. A male neighbour delivered this message to the victim of frequent and noisy bashings: 'Please stop your husband from causing such a row as he frightens our children!' (QDVTF 1988, p. 32).

Marriage guidance counsellors, like doctors, have also overlooked the ubiquity of domestic violence among their clients. According to one counsellor, the 'remarkable' long-term lack of attention to violence in the professional literature was not because 'violence and abuse was not happening; rather it was because marriage counsellors themselves . . . were caught up in the complex pattern of denial which surrounds the issue' (cited in Mugford et al. 1989, p. 111).

Combined with evidence of public perceptions, this all suggests that a deep ambivalence persists: many people overtly find domestic violence unacceptable but are still unable to call any domestic violence, even grievous bodily harm, a crime (Mugford et al. 1989, pp. 111–12). Those in positions of authority as well as the wider community still tend (incorrectly) to pathologise the victims, a misperception which also helps to explain why it remains so under-reported. Domestic violence is, indeed, a 'well-kept secret' (Longtain 1979).

A dangerous intimacy

In summary, although little is heard about domestic violence, about a hundred Australian women are killed every year and perhaps thousands are injured from criminal assaults by husbands or male partners. Studies also indicate that spouse abusers and their victims are frequently (from one-third to one-half) child abusers, and that 80 to 90 per cent of children witnessed the spousal violence (QDVTF 1988, pp. 101–4). The largest proportion of all victims of family violence are those engaged in 'home duties' with dependent children (FVPET 1991, pp. 77–8).

The incidence of 'killing the beloved', wife battering and child abuse in Australian society and elsewhere is, we hardly need add, the darkest underside of the family. Far from being a haven against a dangerous outside world, the home is for women and children, statistically, a more likely source of abuse, torture and death at the hands of males than is the public sphere of strangers. But few people want to take the 'domestic' out of the violence, and place it in the public eye and criminal courts where it belongs.

The intimate relations which draw Australians towards families also expose them to the greatest dangers. Since these relations, as Wallace says, are 'our main source of pleasure they are also equally a main source of frustration and hurt' (Wallace 1990, p. 543). How people came to seek fulfilment in their family relationships is the subject of the next chapter.

3

The rise of intimacy

The formative influences on the contemporary Australian family, like those in Canada and the USA, were imported with white settlement from the families of north-western Europe. The family form that established itself on Australian shores once the colony was secured had undergone significant development in the face of industrialisation before it arrived in Australia. The character of this 'Australian family' bears the marks of its origins. The diverse cultural influences on family life in Australia today arising from post-war migration encounter well-established norms defining 'Australian family life'. Therefore, we will now turn to a consideration of what features distinguished this recent and hegemonic north-western European family form.

Orthodox sociology contrasts the contemporary north-western European family with the pre-modern or traditional family. The modern family is modern because it is the only family form compatible with a modern society, that is, the kind of society created by the industrial revolution. According to orthodox sociology, industrialisation required a particular set of institutional underpinnings. Talcott Parsons, who was perhaps the leading figure of this line of thought, argued that societies could be understood by analogy to embryology (Parsons 1966). Society evolves by a movement from simple to complex, like the development of a foetus, initially resembling the organisation of more primitive organisms, with each stage marked by a progressive differentiation. The simplest organism is a single-cell organism. Differentiation is a process whereby cells and organs become specialised in their function. Parsons believed that in simpler societies kinship provides the framework for all other social organisation. Complex modern society is characterised by specialised, impersonal processes of market allocation and bureaucratic organisation. Following Weber (1968, pp. 86–109), Parsons argued for the incompatibility of modern enterprises with methods of organisation characteristic of patrimonial household forms[1]—modern society requires the separation of home and work.

Many sociologists thought that industrialisation left the family in crisis—an institution without significance or function. Parsons did not agree. On the contrary, he believed that the differentiated modern family performs a crucial role in social reproduction. In modern society, the family is charged with responsibility for producing socialised newer members, and with the stabilisation of adult personalities. This is achieved by strictly limiting the relevance of kinship. Stem or extended families containing many generations give way to an irreducible nuclear family. Parsons called this the conjugal family, in order to emphasise that the group is formed by marriage and contains only the marital partners and their immature offspring. Like others, Parsons believed this structure to be most compatible with the demands for geographical mobility originating in industrial organisation. More importantly, he thought a nuclear family organisation was modern because of its specialisation in the indispensable functions of socialisation and stabilisation. Only the modern form of the family can mediate between the impulse for anti-social gratification of infant needs, and the complex requirements for achievement and performance which will be demanded in later life. The modern family alone can secure and stabilise the personal identities of adults in the face of a world which judges them by abstract, universal, impersonal and affectionless standards. The realm of the family not only becomes the last refuge of intimate relations but also intensifies this intimacy.

What's modern about the modern family?

Historians have disputed Parsons' narrative of extended families shrinking to a nuclear core under the influence of industrialisation. The failure to find a widespread pattern of stem or extended families in pre-industrial records of north-western Europe led to a collapse of faith in Parsons' story (Anderson 1979; Pollock 1983; Poster 1978: Harris 1983). Consequently, the nuclear family could no longer be regarded as a creation of industrialisation. If any evidence exists for the shrinkage from extended to nuclear family, then it is among the higher ranks of society, not the geographically mobile propertyless (Stone 1979, p. 421). Hence, the newer set of theories has regarded the differences in household size as broadly disproven, and has concentrated instead on changes in the qualities of relations within the family (Shorter 1977; Stone 1979; Aries 1973), and on the relationships between family households and the new institutions of industrial society (Anderson 1979; Davidoff & Hall 1987). According to these writers, similarities in form mask significant differences in the content of relations. These differences express a transformation in the normative expectations governing family life.

Major differences between the pre-industrial family and the contemporary family consist of:

(a) altered relations between husband and wife;
(b) privatisation of the family;
(c) revaluation of infants and elaboration of the mother–child bond; and
(d) separation of home and work.

Collectively, these developments have been labelled 'affective individualism' (Stone 1979), and the 'surge of sentiment' (Shorter 1977), since they all describe an increase in patterns of intimacy. Despite slightly different emphases, the similarities between Lawrence Stone's and Edward Shorter's historical accounts are striking. Both assert that in the pre-modern family, mate selection is primarily an exchange between kin groups in which considerations of property and alliance are predominant.

Altered relations between husband and wife

As Macfarlane notes, 'the majority of people in most societies believe that marriage is too important a matter to be left to the individuals concerned', and 'hence the personal feelings of the marriage partners, their "love" attraction, is largely irrelevant to arranging a marriage' (Macfarlane 1987, p. 123).[2] Shorter, in *The Making of the Modern Family* (1977) reproduces an eighteenth-century picture of a marriage proposal drawn by the artist Cornelius Troost. It depicts three men sitting around a table with a woman shown in the background ready to provide for the men's needs. The men are the father of the bride, the father of the groom and the prospective groom. The woman is the prospective bride's mother. The bride-to-be is not in the picture at all! The marriage bargain between the two kin groups was a bargain struck between men on the basis of economic considerations. Once married, the pre-modern husband and wife were unequal partners— patriarchal authority was absolute. Marriage was a hierarchical relation between a woman and a man, and was, in turn, itself subordinated to higher authority. The custom of *droit du seigneur* (the lord's right) illustrates this chain of authority, being the right of a feudal lord to have sexual intercourse with a vassal's bride on her wedding night.

The pattern of marriage combined with romantic love is a culturally peculiar development in north-western Europe. The first European tradition of writing about romantic love is the literature on courtly love. But courtly love was typically adulterous love, demonstrating that it was considered improbable that a man could love his wife. The novelty of the modern family lies in the fact that the figures of mistress and wife are combined. The modern family brings marriage, romance and sex together for the first time. A wife becomes more than a helpmeet, more than an economic resource. A wife becomes a lover and companion as well.

Shorter and Stone contend that obedient inferiors make poor companions. Marriage must therefore become more a relationship between equals. Wives must stop standing behind their husbands at mealtimes, obediently waiting to ladle out a second portion to the man of the house. They must begin to sit at the same dinner table, to banish the servants from sight, and even be bold enough to 'hold hands in front of the fire' (Shorter 1977).

Shorter argues that the housing conditions of the majority of the population in pre-industrial times made intimate sexual play unlikely. He paints a picture of sex for reproduction in peasant households which has the emotional texture of animal breeding. Relying heavily on evidence of illegitimate births, Shorter claims that the move to the pattern of love-marriage was simultaneously the 'first sexual revolution'. It is clear that in the latter part of the twentieth century, the sexual life of married couples is assumed to be a litmus test of the health of the marriage. Indeed it could be said that this era has been characterised by an obsession with the importance of sex and with its technical performance. Manuals on 'the joys of sex' abound urging a variety of positional changes, new procedures and emphasising the importance of foreplay. Women's magazines advise readers on the most memorable and reliable ways of reaching orgasm. By contrast with the earlier part of the century when family medical encyclopedias illustrated harnesses to prevent children from engaging in 'self-abuse' (Melendy 1914), psychiatrists now earnestly endorse masturbation.

A whole therapeutic industry has grown around these topics and it may not be unreasonable to suggest that the result has been widespread anxiety about sexual under-performance and lingering dissatisfaction that sex has not cured all problems in life. Anthony Giddens has noted that contemporary manuals for psychotherapy also concentrate on developing the idea of a 'pure relationship' which is a relationship entered into for its own sake (Giddens 1992). We shall be returning to these themes later in this chapter.

Privatisation of the family

These historians of the family argue that for such dramatic changes to take place certain other developments were necessary. In addition to the increasing equality of partners, there had to be some relaxation of the control exercised by external groups (principally other kin and community), over courting, mate selection, and the details of marriage thereafter. This implies the construction of a 'wall of privacy' between the new conjugal unit and the outside world.

In past times, the community took an intimate interest in the affairs of each household. At festival times, villagers staged a commentary on marital fidelity by parading representatives of cuckolded husbands through the streets sitting backwards on raised chairs (Shorter 1977, p. 217). Villagers also signalled their disapproval of couples who infringed the moral code by gathering in the dead of night at the windows and doors of the transgressors and making 'rough music'—banging loudly with pans and lids (Shorter 1977, pp. 72, 216).

The lack of privacy was evident in the architecture of European household dwellings. The typical dwelling contained only a few rooms, most often only one. Houses were shared not only with other relatives, but also with servants and frequently with farm animals. The separation of bedrooms from more public rooms, doors and corridors with rooms leading off them, gained popularity among the newly-wealthy middle classes of the eighteenth century and diffused to more common folk slowly over the subsequent centuries. Up to that point, it was difficult to shut out other members of the household. Sexual privacy between marital couples only became possible following these inventions. Some historians have suggested that in past times many householders slept in a communal bed. Probably the norm of one person per bed only became established by the middle of this century.

A striking illustration of this is provided by Flandrin, in his discussion of a rape case brought in 1533 by 'Marguerite, widow of Jean Jacomart, against her seducer Pierre Pellart, nicknamed Mordienne'. Flandrin relates how 'a girl of eighteen testified that one night, when she was in bed with Maguerite in the latter's room, the accused came there and had carnal knowledge of Marguerite. She knows this because she was lying beside Marguerite and was touching her' (Flandrin 1979, p. 99).

The process of privatisation has continued into this century. Michael Gilding, writing about the Australian family, has noted that until recently a high proportion of Australian households contained 'outsiders' such as adult domestics, friends, relatives and lodgers. In 1911, 'Max Kelly estimated that 15 to 20 per cent of Sydney's adult population were boarders or lodgers' (Gilding 1991, p. 60). Gilding also cites a survey from the mid-1970s, which 'found that the proportion of couples starting life with relatives had fallen from over 10 per cent in the 1930s to almost zero' (Gilding 1991, p. 111). Gilding notes that in a pamphlet of advice to middle-class women written in 1944, the author advised that outsiders were 'generally an undesirable influence, whereas "good homes and family groups [were] of indispensable national value"' (Gilding 1991, p. 46).

Eli Zaretsky (1976), in a suggestive work, has proposed that privacy is one important precondition for the development of the idea of a subjective, personal life. The other is a thorough separation between home and work, which will be dealt with later in this chapter. These developments reached a new plateau in the nineteenth century.

The highly elaborated 'wall of privacy' ultimately gave rise to anxieties that the nuclear family walls may be so complete that it is hermetically sealed or entombed in the suburbs in the second half of the twentieth century. Aldous Huxley illustrates this by having one of the characters in his novel *Island* say, as though reading instructions from a cookery book:

> Take one sexually inept wage slave . . . one dissatisfied female, two or (if preferred) three small television addicts; marinate in a mixture of Freudianism and dilute Christianity; then bottle up tightly in a four-roomed flat and stew for fifteen years in their own juice. (Huxley 1976, p. 104)

This new privacy has its dark side, as we pointed out in our discussion of domestic violence in Chapter 2.

Revaluation of infants and elaboration of the mother–child bond

According to Shorter, Stone and de Mause, children benefit from the sentimentalisation of private domestic life (Shorter 1977; Stone 1979; de Mause ed. 1976). Instead of being regarded as born into original sin, children become a symbol of innocence. From being considered a burden they are now considered a blessing, a source of amusement and pleasure. The evidence for these changes can be found in the interpretation of iconography (Aries 1973), the cessation of the practice of swaddling,[3] the diminishing use of wet nurses, the reduction in the incidence of abandonment or infanticide, and the end of the practice of sending children away on apprenticeships (Pollock 1983, p. 23). Stone advances a theory of emotional capital to account for many of the changes over the eighteenth and nineteenth centuries.[4]

According to Stone, the prevalence of infant mortality is a cause of the neglect of children in pre-modern times. Parents invest in emotional bonds with an individual offspring only when there is some expectation of that individual's survival (Stone 1979, p. 407). The emotional investment in them is, in modern times, seen as a further guarantee of their survival.

In opposition to Stone and Shorter it could be argued that even though infant mortality was high in the pre-industrial era, those children that survived were considered economic assets to their households. In addition to the significant contribution children made as farm labourers, apprentice tradespeople and servants, children were also an asset because the alliances formed through marriages could consolidate family wealth. Commentators have long recognised that in peasant societies, parents hoped to rely on their children for security in their infirmity and old age. Perhaps the emotional bonding between mothers and children described by Shorter and Stone substitutes for the previous pattern of parents' economic interest in the welfare of their children.

According to Stone and Shorter, each 'advance' in the treatment of children is signalled by an alteration affecting women's activities. The narrative is, therefore, chiefly about motherhood, but, since there can be no mothers without children, it is the mother–child bond which is modern. The burden of emotional capital in children has been unequally borne.

Indeed, the discovery of 'the child' led to extensive elaborations of the concept of motherhood of various kinds during the twentieth century. Ehrenreich and English (1979) point out that, with the exception of state schooling, public interest in the child was expressed not with material help for 'mothers' but a torrent of 'advice, warnings and instructions' from child-raising experts. Mother as 'the all-powerful maternal sculptress' (Eyer 1992, p. 127), however 'professional' she may be, was 'shadowed' by another professional, 'one who would make it *his* speciality to tell the mothers what to do', as Ehrenreich and English emphasise (1979, pp. 166–7). As they say, this emerging science 'comes to see the mothers not only as the major agents of child development but also as the major *obstacles* to it' (Ehrenreich & English 1979, p. 166, emphasis in original).

Yet experts kept changing their minds, witnessed in numerous fads in child-raising. The 'industrial approach', influenced by behaviourist psychologists and popularised by Truby King, emphasised regularity, schedules and precautions against 'spoiling'. Thus the behaviourist J.B. Watson was always outraged at leniency:

> If you expect a dog to grow up and be useful as a watch dog, a bird dog, a fox hound, useful for anything except a lap dog, you wouldn't dare treat it the way you treat your child. When I hear a mother say 'Bless its little heart' when it falls down, or stubs its toe, or suffers some other ill, I usually have to walk a block or two to let off steam. (quoted in Ehrenreich and English 1979, p. 185)

By the 1920s such routines were said to strangle children's spontaneity. A new regime of permissiveness, where mothers must indulge children's wishes, reigned until the 1970s (when child-health expert Benjamin Spock was blamed for student dissent). Psychoanalysis stressed the romance of mother–infant love—mother would need to 'regress' to an infantile state (Ehrenreich & English 1979, p. 200). It is hardly surprising that psychoanalysis' main focus was on 'bad mothers'—of two sorts, the rejecting mother and the overprotective mother. As Spiegel points out, evidence for links between mothering and mental illness is 'weakest when the outcome is psychiatrically, the most disastrous', namely schizophrenia (Spiegel 1982, p. 105). Experts' attribution of blame to nearly any form of mothering did not mean that the fantasy of perfect mothering was diminished (Chodorow & Contratto 1982). Whether firm discipline or instant gratification was required, mothers must learn what was 'natural', if not instinctual, from male professionals.

Ideas about 'maternal deprivation'—popular in the decades after World War II—were derived from studies of war orphans in institutions, and theories about 'attachment' from experiments with infant monkeys. The maternal deprivation thesis suggested that antisocial and mental disorders in children were 'caused' by nearly any separation of children from their mothers. John Bowlby, most well known for stressing the need for 'continuous' mothering, in his pamphlet entitled 'Can I Leave My Baby?' answered his presumed female questioner implicitly in the negative: mother might leave her child for an hour or so, in an emergency (Riley 1983, p. 101). Concepts such as 'maternal deprivation' and the 'failure to thrive' were subsequently found to be methodologically faulty, sometimes fabricated. In the famous case of the children of female prisoners, whose 'failure to thrive' ended with high mortality rates, the researcher failed to mention that in addition to the apparent depression, many of these infants also suffered as a result of a measles epidemic (e.g. Eyer 1992, p. 60). Infants studied in institutions often had twenty to forty caretakers in their first two years, and were deprived of stimulus, sometimes kept in enclosed cubicles with only their hands and feet to play with. In the case of research on 'attachment' in infant monkeys, the experiment involved deprivation of *all* animal contact, not just the nurturance of their mother. Moreover, antisocial disorders of children are usually connected to discord within families that leads to separation, not separation itself (Eyer 1992, pp. 66–7). Lacking in this research was any focus on the situation of 'mother' or the influence of other members of families.

In the 1970s the notion of mother–infant 'bonding' appeared to provide some relief from 'continuous' mothering, by suggesting that 'bonds' after birth, through 'skin-to-skin' contact, were more important than the constant presence of 'mother' through an entire childhood. Yet the bonding thesis was directly derived from the research on animal 'attachment', suggesting an 'instinctual' link or an hormonal 'chemical glue'. Diane Eyer argues that bonding was an answer, less for women themselves than for problems with the medicalisation of childbirth. The bonding thesis helped preserve the authority of medicine: hospital childbirth was reformed, with the family brought into the process, but 'bonding' came with a requirement that mothers now should give 'active love' to their babies right after birth (Eyer 1992, pp. 10–13). The corollary was that 'failure' in bonding would distort the infant's personality development and capacity to make subsequent social 'bonds', and was thought a factor in child abuse—research that was all discredited in the 1980s (Sluckin et al. 1983, pp. 90–5).

Moreover, reformed hospitals have not reduced the rates of medical intervention: birthing rooms have as much technology as operating theatres, and new mothers, feeling 'groggy' after the birth, now face a 'ceremonial' perfunctory procedure of bonding where they are watched to see if they fall in love with their babies in less than ten minutes (Eyer 1992, pp. 193–4). Fathers' presence in the birthing process was another big change which, along with 'bonding', may have led men to be more interested in their small children.

As Denise Riley argues, the 'synthetically conceived mother' of all these kinds, the packages blandly wrapped up as 'motherhood' conceal delicate histories, wants and attributions. The validation of motherhood rigidly separates 'women' from 'mothers' (Riley 1983, p. 196), in that *mothers* are assumed to be married and always at home and *women* are assumed to be periodically at work. The promotion of 'motherhood' as a self-evident value works against understanding or doing anything about the needs of women with children, whether women are employed or not, and debate about women's needs is often obscured by rhetoric about their maternal function (Riley 1983, pp. 152–4). For women, the contradictory prescriptions of motherhood have brought numerous forms of guilt and shame—an unjust situation, desirable for neither women nor children.

The reverse side of the coin of the elaboration of modern motherhood has been the sustained pattern of father absence. In households before industrialisation, men as fathers or as masters of young apprentices were intimately connected to children's education for life; today most of the expert literature focuses on the mother–child bond mainly to the exclusion of the influence of the father, despite recent efforts to include the 'new father' and a shift in the discourse from 'mothering' to 'parenting'.

Men and women ultimately follow discrete paths, reaching a point of great divergence in the latter part of the nineteenth century, when men dominated the public world and women were confined to the private. It is necessary to devote a little space here to an explanation of the nature of these two spheres—the public and the private.

Separation of home and work

Development of the public—male wage labour

Of course, the simple explanation for father absence is that they are doing market work. At the heart of the industrial revolution lies the shift to a new form of labour—wage labour. In wage labour, the worker hires out their capacity to labour for a specific period of time. In the pre-industrial period, the market was much less developed. Most households provided for themselves through a system of subsistence production. Most of what they ate was produced by themselves for this purpose and the same applied to clothes, fuel and shelter. Some surplus goods were traded, and in towns artisans produced goods on commission and to a lesser degree for sale on the market.

Industrial capitalism is organised on the basis of a pool of propertyless labourers. The creation of a large number of such workers could not have been possible without the destruction of forms of life based on the rural family household. In England, this process occurred from the fifteenth to the eighteenth centuries, mainly through the enclosure of common lands and the expulsion of rural peasantry. Markets came to replace forms of household organisation as the chief way of coordinating economic activity.

A full market society is only truly established when all goods are bought and sold on the market and human labour itself becomes a commodity (Dobb 1963). 'Free' labour replaced bonded or indentured forms of labour such as serfs, apprentices, journeymen and even slaves. This labour was not only 'free' in the sense of having no specific master, but also 'free' in the sense that, once labour was separated from the means of subsistence, it was now free to starve. Before labour became a commodity, masters had pecuniary interests and social obligations in relation to the welfare of their workers. Maltreated or undernourished workers reduced the effectiveness of the master's local labour force, and therefore masters had a strong interest in maintaining their workers' welfare. In contrast, with the development of a market in labour, each and every worker becomes an interchangeable competitor and therefore from the employers' point of view, dispensable. In this heartless, new public world, the market for labour is no longer local and each and every worker must restlessly roam the countryside in search of employment. It is therefore a severe disadvantage to be encumbered by local kinship or other social ties. This brutal regime institutes a highly individualistic ethic which ultimately advantages the least encumbered—'every man for himself'. The process by which men come to dominate the sphere of paid work is analysed in greater detail in Chapter 8.

Basis of individualism

In this new society of free competition, individuals appear to be equal and free from the bonds of kin and community, which in pre-industrial times gave them a definite position in a finite social order. It was difficult for people to think about themselves except in relation to others, a fact which is captured in the phrase, 'to rise above your station'. By contrast, markets appear to be composed of individuals each pursuing their own interests. The forms of sociability which underpin this market order are rarely visible. This gave licence to thinkers to imagine a whole new world based on the unit of the individual. As we shall see later, this isolated individual also becomes a subject possessing a personal life.

Given the invisibility of social bonds in market societies, the historical origins of the 'individual' also become obscure. The new individual appears as 'an ideal whose existence belongs to the past; not as the result of history but its starting point' (Marx 1973, p. 83). This historical amnesia is evident in the works of classical liberal political theorists (particularly Hobbes and Locke), who tried to understand market society and to develop an appropriate normative theory. Society, according to liberal theorists, is formed by a contract between otherwise completely unconnected individuals. Individuals, they presumed, were born free and equal—possessing the same natural rights.

Individual rights become the essence of human nature. 'What makes a man [sic] human is freedom from dependence on the wills of others', as C.B. Macpherson explains in his celebrated commentary on the foundations of liberalism in the seventeenth century. In principle, the independent individual should be free from 'any relations with others except those relations which the individual enters voluntarily with a view to his own interest'. Under market conditions the individual is supposed to be 'essentially the proprietor of his own person and capacities, for which he owes nothing to society' (Macpherson 1962, p. 263). What makes people human is ownership of property, even if this property is only in their own person. For example, wage labourers are 'free' to offer their capacity to labour, indeed, this may be their only 'property'. Thus a link is forged between property, the market and individualism, leading to what C.B. Macpherson calls the theory of 'possessive individualism' (Macpherson 1962).

Markets and marriage

There is an intimate connection between the rise of the market and the new ideas about equality in marriage. We can see how, from the experience of meeting as atomised individuals exchanging property in the marketplace, men and women tend to understand themselves as individuals—equals free to make contracts, according to their own preferences The intrinsic structure of both romantic mate choice and the market are essentially similar, based on the idea of free and equal autonomous individuals spontaneously following their own interest. Henceforth women must appear the equal of men. Likewise, marriage is justified as the result of a process of coincidence of romantic interest in much the same way as market transactions are supposed to result in the optimal reciprocal satisfaction of buyer and seller. Marriage itself takes on the character of a contractual relation.

Carole Pateman compares marriage to labour contracts. She argues that liberal notions of consent and contract privilege those whose property is capital, and just as importantly, those who are male. So Pateman agrees with Macpherson that the wage contract is not a freely made contract between equals because it does not conform to the three elementary propositions about the rights of possessive individuals outlined above. (These are the rights to freedom from dependence on others, to voluntary and purely self-interested relations and to private ownership of one's person and capacities: Macpherson 1962, p. 263.) The power of capitalist property is evident in the labour contract, which is inherently unequal. The employee has the choice between on the one hand, employment and on the other, the workhouse or starvation. In this sense, the labour contract can hardly be described as a *voluntary* contract. Although the employee may in theory choose amongst employers and is no longer assigned to a master, there is little choice about employment as such. Despite the claims of liberal theorists, property in one's person—the capacity to sell one's labour—does not establish *independence*. The seller of labour is dependent upon the existence of a buyer. A peculiar characteristic of property in the person, such as the capacity to labour, is that it resides in the person of the worker. Unlike other goods, the seller cannot wait for a long time until a favourable price is offered. They may well have starved before this offer comes, suggesting that this form of property is unlike any other. The implication is that workers are not 'possessive individuals' at all and cannot claim the same rights.

Moreover, once the contract is made, the employee has placed her or his capacity to labour at the disposal of the boss for a specified period of time in exchange for a wage. Once their labour is sold, it belongs to the purchaser (during working hours), who is free to direct this labour at whim. The wage is an exchange of freedom for obedience.

Similarly, the marriage contract does not entail a 'free' choice, or a freely assumed obligation. Although marriages were no longer arranged by fathers, 'choice' and 'consent' became basically reduced to the initial acts of choosing a partner and then saying 'I do'. In the marriage contract, women had no formal or legal rights to own property until relatively recently. Women could rarely choose to survive independently, that is beyond the authority of a male household head. In the marriage contract, husbands were therefore in a position to impose duties on wives in return for the provision of bed and board for a woman's lifetime (Pateman 1979, pp. 169–70; Pateman 1988b).

Contemporary marriage, based on romantic love, has been modelled on the personal choice of alternatives available in the market. However, although this modified the previous institution of arranged marriage, it did not alter the involuntary lifetime character of this union. Liberalism idealised the family, and tried to understand it in terms of the market, but succeeded only in describing relations of superordination and subordination in inappropriate terms drawn from the market.

The reformulation of marriage as a contract reflects Locke's ideas of common interest, property and the right to pursue happiness, as Stone correctly points out (Stone 1979, p. 164). Locke's ideas were developed in opposition to those of his seventeenth-century conservative contemporaries, such as Robert Filmer, whose doctrine of passive obedience to the state derived the king's authority by analogy to the father's authority within the family. Locke made an argument against the rule of the father, while at the same time removing the family from the political domain. That is to say, he considered it a private sphere beyond government regulation in which individuals are free to pursue their happiness. However, he acknowledged that natural patriarchy reigned in the home (Eisenstein 1981, pp. 33–54). Even if one were to overlook Locke's acknowledgment of patriarchy in the private sphere, equality between men and women cannot be established on the basis that both men and women own property in the person. This is because those whose sale of property in the person is 'encumbered' by the duties of care (dependent children etc.) cannot compete on equal terms with those who are unencumbered by such responsibilities. Moreover, 'property' in the person is dependent on those social responsibilities of others during childhood. Despite Stone's and Shorter's claims of the growth of companionship and equality, the history of the division of household tasks by gender is striking because of the dissolution of the economic partnership evident in the pre-modern pattern.[5]

The development of a personal life

The obverse of the development of a public world is the creation of a private sphere, which cannot be characterised as a residual phenomenon. Privacy is not just the null category in opposition to the category of the public. Those areas of life that remain uncommodified are positively elaborated, and the idea of privacy is developed extensively.

Liberalism simultaneously celebrated individualism and promoted the idea of the family as a private sphere, 'separate' from production, in which individuals would be freely pursuing their happiness. As Eli Zaretsky has pointed out, it was a short step from these conceptions to the idea that individuals have a 'personal life'. 'Introspection intensified and deepened as people sought in themselves the only coherence, consistency, and unity capable of reconciling the fragmentation of social life', Zaretsky explains. The impersonal and affectionless cash bonds which bring people together in the marketplace 'generated new needs—for trust, intimacy and self-knowledge, for example—which intensified the weight of meaning attached to the personal relations of the family . . . [and] . . . encouraged the creation of a separate sphere of life in which personal relations were pursued as ends in themselves' (Zaretsky 1976, pp. 65–6). These ideas reached their high-water mark among the middle classes during the Victorian era, and were later adapted by the working classes when economic circumstances permitted.

To the Victorian middle classes, the family home was a 'tent pitch'd in a world not right' or even 'a sacred place, a vestal temple' (Zaretsky 1976, p. 51). The Victorian cultural critic William Ruskin declared:

> this is the true nature of home . . . it is the place of peace; the shelter not only from all injury but from all terror, doubt, and division . . . So far as the anxieties of the outer life penetrate into it . . . it ceases to be a home; it is then only part of the outer world which you have roofed over and lighted a fire in. (quoted in Zaretsky 1976, p. 51)

The experience of alienation from the new forms of market work lay behind both the emerging labour movement and the romanticism in poetry and other arts. Romanticism takes the conception of a personal inner life to its extreme. Under the threat of the industrial mass production of art tailored to market demands, artists began to place 'a new emphasis on the originality of the artist and the uniqueness of the work of art'. Beginning with romanticism, artists declared that art was the product less of a particular craft or discipline than the artist's inner life. 'Romantic individualism's final expression, in twentieth century art', says Zaretsky, 'would confine the individual to an entirely subjective and psychological realm wholly divorced from the rest of society' (Zaretsky 1976, pp. 59–60).

The rise of subjectivity results from the great transformation to a market society. The family, .as Zaretsky points out, 'became the major sphere of society in which the individual could be foremost—it was the only space that proletarians "owned"' (Zaretsky 1976, p. 61).

The development of the 'pure relationship'

The celebrated British sociologist Anthony Giddens has suggested that, ultimately, the creation of the private sphere gives rise to a whole new form of self-identity, characteristic of modernity itself. Self-identity at the end of the twentieth century, according to Giddens, is qualitatively different to what came before (1991, 1992). In traditional societies a person's identity is defined by place and position in the social order. A person's identity, their relationship to a definite locality and to others, was presumed to be largely fixed at birth. 'The fate of the individual', says Giddens, 'in personal attachments as in other spheres was tied to a broader cosmic order' (1992 p. 41). In Giddens' view modern societies are characterised by an extreme dynamism, in which practically everything changes, little is fixed and most activities are open to self-conscious revision. In English grammar when an action turns back on the subject, when the subject of a verb is identical with its object, as in the case of the verb *wash* in the sentence 'I wash myself', it is called a reflexive verb. Giddens uses the term 'reflexive' to capture just this self-conscious turning back of activity. Contemporary self-identity is reflexive because it self-consciously modifies its own activity. In Giddens' opinion this quality of reflexivity is characteristic of all 'high modern' social arrangements (Giddens 1991, pp. 1–34).

Individuals view their lives as a project of constructing and progressively developing themselves, usually understood as an autobiographical narrative. They conceive of their life course as a series of 'passages'. Modern rites of passage are private and personal, not marked out by social rituals with points of reference outside the self. Instead, the anchorage points of this trajectory of the self are established by referring to qualities of the self or events drawn from within the narrative of the self (Giddens 1991, pp. 77–80). 'I am the kind of person who makes up their mind quickly, I do not like to hang about' one might say, or 'That was before I escaped my parents' control by travelling overseas'. Or maybe 'That was before I broke up with my first partner'.

In Giddens' view, there is a constant, reflexive monitoring of subjective states. Events in the individual's life are understood as providing the stimulus for self-actualisation. Each new phase presents the individual with opportunities for growth but entails risks (such as failure, disappointment, etc.). Two key questions guide this activity—Who am I? and How shall I live? (1992, p. 198).

The moral meaning of modern self-identity is given as the duty of 'self-development', 'self-actualisation', 'fulfilment' and a radical freedom from dependency, physical and psychological. The modern moral instruction is to 'find yourself' or 'be true to yourself'. According to Giddens, 'the self is seen as a reflexive project, for which the individual is responsible . . . outside events or institutions . . . only intrude in so far as they provide supports for self-development, throw up barriers to be overcome or are a source of uncertainties to be faced' (1991, pp. 75–6).

Against the background of the modern quest for self-actualisation, Giddens develops his concept of the 'pure relationship'. According to Giddens, what we described earlier in this chapter as the tradition of 'courtly love' is an example of a type of love—passionate love—found in all cultures and all epochs. Passionate love is sexual love. Its urgent emotional impulses cause partners to ignore their everyday obligations. Since lovers behave as though they were enchanted and ignore social conventions, the pre-modern community viewed passionate love as an inappropriate basis for marriage. In contrast, romantic love, as we have seen, domesticated passionate love by associating it with marriage. In so doing, romantic love, for the first time in Western history, 'associated love with freedom, both being seen as normatively desirable states' and unified them in a mundane everyday relationship (marriage), which was presumed to last forever (Giddens 1992, p. 40). Romantic love, according to Giddens, contains the kernel of the idea of freedom (choice) in personal relationships, but assumes that marriage is a fixed, 'final state'. The pure relationship, argues Giddens, extends this revolution in personal relations by radically developing the notion of freedom or choice to the limit. Pure relationship seizes the idea of the emergent tie between freedom and self-realisation implicit in romantic love and develops it to the extreme.

Giddens describes pure relationships as 'intimate emotionally demanding relationships—between, for example, same-sex lovers or between very close friends', which in its most developed, or ideal-typical, form is a relationship maintained exclusively (or 'purely') for its own sake (1991, p. 89). Historically prior forms of intimacy are embedded in social and economic bonds, whereas the pure relationship is 'free-

floating' and self-defined. In an era where there is no longer
a link between sex and reproduction, friendship becomes the
model pure relationship. Friendship is a relationship free of
necessity, engaged in purely for the benefits and pleasure
intrinsic to the relationship and which ends as soon as the
participants no longer enjoy each other's company. All pure
relationships are undertaken on the basis of 'until further
notice' (Giddens 1992, pp. 58–63). Gay women and men, says
Giddens, are pioneers of the pure relationship between sexual
intimates because 'they have had to "get along" without the
traditionally established frameworks of marriage, in conditions
of relative equality between partners' (1992, p. 15). Whereas
romantic love placed great importance on finding that 'special
person', the more contemporary form of love places the
emphasis on the 'special relationship'. In the era of the pure
relationship, Giddens says:

> marriage becomes more and more a relationship initiated for,
> and kept going for as long as, it delivers emotional satisfaction
> to be derived from close contact from one another. Other
> traits—even such seemingly fundamental ones as having
> children—tend to become sources of 'internal drag' on pos-
> sible separation rather than anchoring features of the
> relationship. (Giddens 1991, p. 89)

Pure relationships are inherently risky, because it is difficult
to maintain the perfect coincidence of interest between partners and ensure the relationship's long-term survival.
'Commitment, within pure relationships', says Giddens, 'is
essentially what replaces the external anchors that close personal connections used to have in pre-modern situations'. In
the context of a close relationship, a committed person is one
who is aware of the tensions and inherent risks in this form
of relationship yet 'is nevertheless willing to take a chance on
it . . . a friend is ipso facto a committed person' (Giddens
1991, p. 92). Pure relationships have no supports other than
intimacy itself and such relations have the character of 'everyday social experiments' (Giddens 1992, p. 8).

Individuals in pure relationships chart a course between
self-actualisation and dependency—between addiction, including addiction to the relationship itself (co-dependency), and
what he (rather unhappily) calls 'confluent love' (Giddens

1992, pp. 87–110). Only confluent love conforms to the ideals of the pure relationship.

Giddens defines addiction as a compulsive form of behaviour, which the individual finds difficult to give up and experiences as a loss of control over the self. These compulsions offer a narcotic release from anxiety but generally are succeeded by feelings of inadequacy and shame, beginning the cycle all over again. The problem of addiction is characteristic of late modern societies where very little is determined by tradition and the individual must continually negotiate lifestyle options. The individual's lifestyle choices help define, in the individual's own eyes, who they 'are'. 'Addictions', says Giddens, 'are a negative index of the degree to which the reflexive project of self moves to centre-stage in late modernity' (1992, p. 76).

Co-dependence, according to Giddens, is a form of addiction where individuals avoid responsibility for themselves by being compulsively dedicated to the needs of another. The individual defines themself in terms of the other and gets lost in the needs of the other. In 'fixated relationships' the relation itself becomes the object of the addiction and in these relationships the consequence is also that individual identity is lost—subsumed in the identity of belonging to a 'couple' (Giddens 1992, p. 89).

In Giddens' view, confluent love (modern intimacy) is the opposite of co-dependence because it requires a strong sense of personal boundaries. These boundaries prevent a loss of self through pathological identification with the other, and become the foundation for intimate communication ('opening out to the other'). Only when people have a powerful sense of themselves as individuals are they able to build trust and intimacy through mutual disclosures about their inner, private selves. Like Shorter and Stone, Giddens believes that social hierarchy is inimical to intimacy. Intimacy in pure relationships presupposes a balance of power between the parties, which in heterosexual relationships entails the increasing liberation of women from male domination (Giddens 1992, p. 94).

According to Giddens intimacy also becomes the quality of the relationship parents strive to achieve with their children, displacing, in Giddens' view, the notion of parent authoritativeness (1992, p. 98). The modern public demands that the emotional needs of children be considered. 'Children', says Giddens, 'have rights not just to be fed, clothed and protected but rights to be cared for emotionally, to have their feelings respected and their views and feelings taken into account'. In short, the characteristics of confluent love appropriate to adult relationships are no less relevant to relations between adults and children. Equalisation of power between the parties to a relationship, Giddens argues, 'is an intrinsic element in the transformation of intimacy, as is the possibility of communication' (1992, p. 149). The peculiarity of parent–child relations is that 'people when they *are* children, especially tiny children are not yet able verbally to articulate needs' or rights (Giddens 1992, p. 109, emphasis in original). The statement of children's needs and the assertion of children's rights must be done for them by adults in the form of ethical principles.

The difficulties of forming pure relationships with young children illustrate how important the ideas of autonomy and communication are to Giddens' notion of a pure relationship. 'Intimacy', he says, 'is above all a matter of emotional communication, with others and with the self, in a context of interpersonal equality' (1992, p. 130). Giddens considers that the emergence of this new model of intimacy is one of the major social changes in the latter part of the twentieth century. The transformation of intimacy leads to a 'democratisation of personal life' (1992, p. 184). In pure relationships individuals determine the conditions of their association. In this kind of relationship open communication and negotiation are the functional equivalent of a parliament that is permanently in session. 'The imperative of free and open communication', says Giddens, 'is the *sine qua non* of the pure relationship; the relationship is its own forum' (1992, p. 194).

Giddens' concept of the pure relationship extends the many ideas put forward by Stone, Shorter and Zaretsky, drawing out the implications of the rise of affective individualism and the autonomous conduct of family relations and personal life, now separated from the control of the wider community. Giddens see this autonomy as characteristic of high modern social institutions which set their own goals and reflexively monitor their own performance. The pure relationship is simply the culmination of this process in the sphere of personal life.

There are, however, significant ambiguities in Giddens' presentation. Has the pure relationship arrived or is it still emerging? Is it an ideal or a behavioural reality? Giddens generally conveys the impression that the pure relationship has emerged in identifiable outline but cannot yet be generalised to all personal relationships. Occasionally he acknowledges that one reason why pure relationships are not yet general is because key conditions are not yet met. Pure relationships, as we have seen, can only arise between equals, and amongst heterosexuals this has been delayed by the still incomplete social emancipation of women. Women, Giddens haltingly acknowledges, are disadvantaged relative to men in the area of paid employment and domestic responsibilities. It follows that in describing the pure relationship Giddens must be describing an ideal. We agree that the pure relationship, generally, accurately describes contemporary expectations about intimacy, even intimacy between parents and children. Giddens' conception summarises what we have been calling 'normative expectations' about family relations. It is our contention that it is possible for these normative expectations and the behavioural actuality in families to diverge. In order to better understand how this divergence comes about and how it is expressed, we will now turn our attention to the issue of how inequality in domestic responsibilities came to be neglected and how this affects communication between intimates.

Sleight of hand—the invisibility of housework and responsibility for children

In this chapter so far we have attempted to show what aspects of contemporary family relationships are the focus of normative expectations and how these expectations have been transformed. In this section we want to explore how normative expectations can blind us and prevent us from recognising elements of our situation. Later chapters also amplify this theme. In dealing with this misrecognition, it is useful to use metaphors relating to conjurers and alchemists: conjurers because much of their stage act consists of making objects 'appear', 'disappear' and 'reappear' and alchemists because their activity focused on changing one object into another—turning base metals into gold. We shall try to expose these sociohistorical sleights of hand and explain how they apparently succeed. This will involve explaining the social conditions under which illusions can arise.

Uneven development

The industrial revolution transformed work and politics, and created the public world of markets and the state. However the domestic sphere was modified only indirectly. In the pre-modern era, economic and political life entailed a set of relations between households which were dissolved by the market. The isolated domestic sphere now faced the market and the liberal state. The household itself, however, was not industrialised. We shall refer to this process whereby social institutions were modified to different extents and at different rates as 'uneven development'.

In the pre-modern household before the domination of cash transactions, the contribution of both men and women to the economic welfare of the household was plain. Since household production was more or less identical with social production, this domestic division of labour was more or less identical with the sexual division of labour in society. Men and women shared the tasks of breadwinning and home-making. Following industrialisation, men came to dominate the emerging public world and this process was accompanied by the gradual exclusion of women from much of this realm (Pateman 1983, pp. 282–9). The development of the market for human labour also divided home-making and breadwinning where formerly the two had been combined in a single unit. The fact that men ultimately managed to have themselves defined and recognised as the breadwinners complicates the relation between the sexual division of labour and the domestic division of labour. In other words, the separation of tasks in the household by gender is overlaid with a gendered division between public and private. As we shall see, once the division between public and private has been established, each follows a different trajectory.

One of the major consequences of the physical removal of much formerly male activity from the household, was that

Table 3.1 Division of labour by sex in traditional rural French households

	Women's work	Men's work
Inside house	Child-rearing	Lighting oven
	Cooking	Farm accounts
	Cleaning	
	Household accounts	
	Cottage industrial work	
Outside house	Wood gleaning	Wine storage
	Water-carrying	Cattle feeding
	Vegetable gardening	Cattle marketing
	Poultry/dairy care	Care of implements
	Poultry/dairy marketing	Spading
	Larding	Ploughing
	Hay-tossing	Scything
	Weeding	Pork slaughtering

Source: Shorter 1977, p. 76

only a few insignificant domestic tasks remained men's responsibility, as can be seen by comparing the tasks listed in Table 3.1 with the typical domestic activities of the contemporary male.

Table 3.1 shows how women's indoor responsibilities have largely continued whereas practically all men's domestic responsibilities have been removed and substituted by indirect production, that is by men supplying cash to the household. Whereas production outside the home became the subject of the 'industrial revolution', as we shall see in more detail in Chapter 5 the history of attempts to mechanise and to rationalise what remained of production at home had less than dramatic effects on its output (Reiger 1985; MacKenzie & Wajcman 1985; Faulkner & Arnold 1985). As Davidoff argues, the goals of the family household, that is, 'the maintenance of hierarchical boundaries and ego-servicing of superiors' were obstacles to rational calculation (Davidoff 1976, p. 133).

The world of the market revolutionised economic production and exchange. At the same time political relationships were recast in terms of values appropriate to a market society. Market relationships give rise to the 'appearance' of individual freedom. The transactions which appear to take place in the market are those between buyers and sellers. In theory, buyers and sellers only agree to those sales that correspond to their wishes. Each is the possessor of property, even if only in their own person. Neither is compelled to form any relationship and each is guided only by self-interest. Individuals in a market society are presumed to be radically free and independent of the wills of others. As we have seen earlier, this apparent freedom actually masks a situation of unequal exchange (Macpherson 1962).

The private world of the family largely escapes this revolutionary reconstruction. Only the marriage relationship took on the character of a market contract. As we saw, for women this was in essence a pseudo-contract because it only provided the freedom to choose a particular male household head. Even under the regime of romantic love or affective individualism, the woman could not escape subordination to patriarchal authority. Although the French Revolution had banished the authority of the father-king in national politics, liberal theory retained the authority of men in the household. Thus the assignment of domestic status escapes this revolutionary reconstruction of freedom from the 'father-king' authority, and continues to be ascribed on the basis of gender. This is why somebody who does housework is a 'housewife'.

Stone and Shorter present their case for the rise of affective individualism as a story of progressive emancipation of women and children from traditional forms of indifference, maltreatment and patriarchal domination. What they actually describe, however, is a series of changes in the sexual division of labour—not the end of patriarchy but a change in its form. The theory of the growth of 'affective individualism' tends to be the victim of the very processes it describes—this theory mistakes the dominant values of market society for reality, the belief in the desirability of equality and autonomy in human relations, for the actual content of domestic relationships. Sociologists and historians are not the only victims of this social illusion. As we shall see, all family participants themselves daily struggle under the same difficulty.

Money and the priceless value of housework

Markets bring with them a new experience of social life. In a market society, certain pivotal goods become exchangeable. In particular, rights to use land, formerly the basis of people's subsistence, are removed and land becomes alienable. Land can be exchanged against any other good or the representative of all goods—money. Similarly, as we have seen, human labour itself becomes a commodity, something which can also be bought for money. These new forms of property and commodification gave rise to new ideas. Money becomes the measure of the value of all things.

One of the most enduring of Karl Marx's observations on capitalism is his description of 'the fetishisation of commodities'. Commodities are goods or services which are exchanged in the marketplace. Commodities have particular properties which make them useful to humans. The usefulness of commodities arises from human need. A coat, for example, is useful because it answers our need for warmth. In a market society, each and every good can be exchanged against all other goods. Our coat, for example, can be exchanged for a definite quantity of tea, so many text books, a certain amount of cosmetics, etc. In this process, the individual qualities of the commodities being exchanged are suppressed and the emphasis falls on determining equivalent quantities. In other words, the characteristic that the coat provides warmth is neglected while effort is expended in determining just how much tea, how many text books or what amount of cosmetics the coat is worth. Eventually, one commodity, typically a precious metal such as gold or silver, is selected to represent the value of all other commodities, so that the value of the coat, the tea, the books, the cosmetics, is rendered as a particular weight of silver (pounds sterling). A further development is the use of paper tokens (bank notes) to represent quantities of precious metal.

Marx points out that underlying the quantities in the exchange is a social process which regulates the output of the various industries through supply and demand. If too many of a nation's resources are expended in the production of one commodity, such as coats, it leads to a glut where the supply of coats exceeds the demand for them. This causes the price of coats to fall. As a consequence, tailors are laid off until the supply of coats reaches a balance with their demand. Conversely, if the supply of tea is too scarce relative to demand, this will stimulate more employment in the tea industry. In summary, what governs the proportions in which commodities exchange is a complex process by which society (the market) proportions its productive effort.

Participants in the economy only experience this process of social regulation when commodities are exchanged. To them, it appears that commodities have value, that is, they are worth a certain amount of money. In the exchange, the fact that the money value of commodities regulates the balance of effort between the various industries is not revealed to them— the price of the commodity simply fluctuates. The fetishisation of commodities, according to Marx, consists of the fact that for the participants 'a definite social relationship between men [sic] . . . assumes in their eyes, the fantastic form of a relation between things' (Marx 1954, p. 77). Just as some people develop sexual fetishes for feet or underwear, by which non-sexual objects become erotic, so participants in a market society come to see objects—or their representative, money— as the very incarnation of worth. Money appears to be the marker of the value of objects; in technical terms it valorises objects.

Most products of domestic labour, such as meals, laundry, cleaning and childcare continue to be consumed directly by their producers, with no cash changing hands. A family meal is produced because the family is hungry and the cook and the rest of the family sit down and consume it. The cook does not charge the family for her or his labour. The family meal has no money price. Even when the cook accepts money to shop for the ingredients of the meal, the money is a payment for the ingredients and not for the labour of either shopping or cooking.

In a society where commodity fetishism prevails, everything that has no money value appears to be worthless. The fact that the products of housework and childcare (with one exception discussed below) do not have a price and the fact that the labour of housework and childcare do not attract a wage means both the products and the labour of producing seem of no account, they are literally without value—worthless.

There is one important exception to the rule that the products of domestic labour are consumed by the family household, this is the 'human capital' created in the rearing of children and the support given to husbands' capacity to do paid work. A key product of the household is individuals who can offer their ability to work to employers. Infants come into the world, in the phrase of the anthropologist Ralph Linton (1936), as 'barbarian invaders' who must learn language and culture. The years of patiently naming objects, conversing, reading stories, helping with homework and instructing the young in the ways of the world represents a considerable investment. Human capital is only valuable, moreover, as long as the individual is capable of work. Even among adults, this involves daily maintenance through the provision of suste-nance and emotional support necessary to maintain the desire to work. In the case of professionals, human capital is augmented by such activities as help in further studies or in promoting careers by entertaining important guests at home.

The value of this labour that household members offer on the labour market has a money price—the wage that the employer is willing to offer. However, the value of this labour attaches to the person of the seller of labour and the process which produced the capacity to labour itself has no money value. This is another instance of the fetishism of commodities where the value apparently belongs to the commodity (human capital) rather than the work that created the human capital. In these circumstances the labour of housework continues to have no apparent value.

Under these particular historical circumstances, house-work—as work—disappears. In fact it is so thoroughly invisible that for all practical purposes it does not appear in the works of historians, sociologists and economists until 1970. We shall discuss the economic invisibility of housework in more detail in the next chapter, so for the moment we shall disregard this disappearing trick and concentrate on other aspects of social alchemy where base metal housework is 'transformed' into a golden expression of love.

If housework as menial labour is invisible, and if family ties are presumed to conform to the tenet of affective indi-vidualism and the pure relationship, then acts of domestic labour come to be seen as expressions of 'sentiment'—gestures of care and affection. Advertisers regularly play on this alchemy. Ruth Schwartz Cowan notes how after World War I advertisers no longer based their appeal on reducing the drudgery of domestic labour. Instead they presented it as 'an emotional "trip"'.

> Laundering was not just laundering, but an expression of love; the housewife who truly loved her family would protect them from the embarrassment of tattletale grey. Feeding the family was not just feeding the family, but a way to express the housewife's artistic inclinations and a way to encourage feelings of family loyalty and affection. Diapering the baby was not just diapering, but a time to build the baby's sense of security and love for the mother. Cleaning the bathroom sink was not just cleaning, but an exercise of protective maternal instincts, providing a way for the housewife to keep her family safe from disease. Tasks of this emotional magnitude could not possibly be delegated to servants, even assuming that qualified servants could be found. (Cowan 1985, p. 194)

The accompaniment to this emotionalisation of housework is guilt. Wives are made to feel guilty if there are germs lurking on the bathroom or if the family meal is not enticing, low in cholesterol and nutritionally balanced. Mothers are made to feel guilty if the contents of their children's school lunchboxes are not sufficiently healthy, if their school uniforms are dirty or unironed, their school shoes are scuffed or if they fail to notice the first signs of influenza. Honest toil is hidden, only to appear as a 'token of affection' or 'expression of love' accompanied by the gnawing guilt that any concern about oneself constitutes failing to care for others.

Communication tangles

In the 1940s and 1950s psychiatry became very interested in the distortions that could affect human development. Such distortions include 'symbiotic ties', 'double binds' and 'pseudo-mutuality'. Each of these terms was developed in the course of trying to explain the genesis of schizophrenia. By the late 1960s many argued that they were a distinguishing feature of the modern family (Morgan 1975: Boyers 1971). We argue that each of these distortions is explicable by reference to the process of uneven development.

This line of theoretical investigation into so-called 'schizo-genic' families began with adolescent patients who presented themselves at the psychiatrist's office. The psychiatrist noticed something odd about the relationship between these patients and their families, leading him or her to investigate the family circumstances of the patients. At first suspicion fell upon mothers, who were believed to be domineering, indulgent and overprotective. Such 'schizophrenogenic' mothers, it was claimed, reveal to the trained eye a pattern of possessive and conditional love that results in a 'symbiotic tie' with the child. Symbiotic mothers prolong the period of the child's complete dependence upon them in order to meet their own needs for love and identity. In the literature of the time it was occasionally acknowledged that such mothers only existed where fathers were 'weak' and absent.

Later it was proposed that the schizophrenogenic mother's dominant hold over her child was achieved by pathological forms of communication. Best known amongst these are 'double binds' and 'pseudomutuality'. Bateson and his group of researchers in Palo Alto, California, believed schizophrenics were creations of communicative deformities. Bateson argued that human communication can, and indeed always does, operate at a number of contrasting levels of abstraction. Observing the play of young monkeys at a zoo, Bateson was struck by the resemblance between play and fighting. Yet none of the young animals mistook what appeared to be outward signals of aggression and hostility as such, but somehow distinguished them as mock symbols of an attack, and responded in an apparently aggressive manner which fell short of inflicting injury (Bateson 1973, pp. 150–66). As Bateson says, 'the playful nip denotes the bite, but it does not denote what would be denoted by the bite' (1973, p. 153).

Bateson inferred that there must be signals which effectively communicated to the participants that the situation was one of play. This signal must be at a *higher level of abstraction* since it modified all other signals, transforming an aggressive signal or response to a playful one. Bateson called this level of communication—a signal which comments upon communi-cative signals at a lower level—'metacommunication'. Meta-communication is an example of the reflexive process referred to by Giddens because it involves using the self-conscious knowledge of signals as symbols to modify the meaning of symbols. The playful nip stands for the bite but does not indicate the mood sign that a genuine bite would. Thus the recognition of the nip as a symbol of the bite, while not itself being a bite, is a necessary condition for play.

As can be seen from the example of the monkeys' play, metacommunicative signals are often implicit communicative symbols. This characteristic creates a whole new field of possible paradoxes and contradictions. Take, for example, the signal 'this is play' or 'only kidding'. This message contains the elements necessary to generate a logical paradox. An example of this paradox is expressed in the ancient example of Epimenides the Cretan. 'All Cretans are liars', says Epimenides. What Epimenides says is true only if it is not true (Copi 1971, p. 13).

The message 'This is play' takes this paradoxical form. The relationship between linguistic symbols and the object they purport to represent is analogous to the relationship between a map and the territory it describes (Korzybski 1941). In play, the map and territory are both equated and discriminated. The signal 'This is play' allows actors to draw a boundary around a certain set of messages, as in the examples of the monkeys' play gestures associated with combat, and Epimenides' claim that Cretans are liars. The bite is not a bite, it is a playful nip. The ever-present danger is that the signals indicating this boundary will become included within it. Were this to happen, the messages would quickly tumble into irresolvable self-contradiction, into a paradox like that described above. The statement that this is 'just kidding' cannot be differentiated from the class of untruths. In the case of play, the whole game would change, shifting from 'play' to the more sinister game of 'Is this play?'. This kind of ambiguity can sometimes occur in sarcasm—is this message a mock insult, a sign of affection; or it is it an insult smuggled into a jocular situation; or is the most florid praise intended as the gravest insult?

Schizophrenics, Bateson and his co-workers argued, were individuals who had difficulty identifying and interpreting those signals which should tell an individual what sort of message a message is, that is, trouble with signals of the same logical types as 'This is play'. This may be manifested as a difficulty in assigning the correct communication mode to a message sent by others. Or difficulties may arise from the individual's employing inappropriate or incorrect metacommunicational markers to their own messages. Finally, schizophrenics may have difficulties in assigning the correct communicational mode to their own thoughts, sensations and percepts.

This suggestion does seem to offer an explanation for the characteristically bewildering speech of schizophrenics. False assignment of the messages of others could result in suspicions of threat in every gesture of the other, hostility in the face of kindness, inappropriate laughter and so on. The schizophrenic's idiosyncratic 'word salad' is rife with unlabelled metaphors, so that map and territory are constantly confused. The thoughts of the schizophrenics appear to them as voices commanding them or, conversely, they are frightened of the power of their cogitations, and the capacity of their wishes to influence the events around them and like some contrite sinner in religious texts, exert themselves frantically to resist temptation but cannot rid themselves of impure thoughts.

If schizophrenia is a condition identified by the sufferer's inability to discriminate between the levels of messages, the question naturally arises as to how such a state has come about. Bateson and his colleagues took the bold step of suggesting that the patient 'must live in a universe where the sequences of events are such that his [sic] unconventional communicational habits will be in some sense appropriate' (Bateson 1973, p. 177). This led Bateson's group to posit the 'double bind' theory of schizophrenia.

A double bind occurs in a social setting (two or more people) when a *'primary negative injunction'*, either prohibiting or requiring a particular action on pain of punishment is contradicted by a *'secondary injunction conflicting with the first at a more abstract level, and like the first, enforced by punishment or signals which threaten survival'* (Bateson 1973, p. 178, emphasis in original). This metacommunication may be transmitted by non-verbal as well as verbal means. Examples of the content of this secondary injunction offered by Bateson and his co-authors are: 'Do not see this as punishment'; 'Do not think of what you must not do'; 'Do not question my love . . .' (Bateson 1973, pp. 178–9). The double bind is completed by a *'tertiary negative injunction prohibiting the victim from escaping from the field'* (Bateson 1973, p. 179, emphasis in original). The authors indicate that it is often redundant to list this tertiary injunction separately because it is entailed in the first two injunctions or, as in the case of infants in care, is not possible anyway. Where it is a possibility, it may be blocked by positive inducements such as 'capricious promises of love' (Bateson 1973, p. 179). Bateson and his co-authors offer the following illustration of a double bind:

> A young man who had fairly well recovered from an acute schizophrenic episode was visited in hospital by his mother. He was glad to see her and impulsively put his arm around her shoulders, whereupon she stiffened. He withdrew his arm and she asked, 'Don't you love me anymore?' He then blushed and she said, 'Dear you must not be so easily embarrassed and afraid of your feelings'. The patient was able to stay with her only a few minutes more and following her departure he assaulted an aide and was put in the tubs. (Bateson 1973, p. 181)

At the same time as Bateson and his Palo Alto group were developing the theory of the double bind, on the east coast of the United States Lyman Wynne and his co-workers were developing their concept of pseudomutuality. Subsequently, Wynne was to speak of these two theories as a case of simultaneous discovery, indicating his belief that both concepts were developed to describe and explain the same kinds of phenomena. Wynne and his co-authors identified three possible states of complementarity in human relations; (1) mutuality, (2) non-mutuality and (3) pseudomutuality. They regarded pseudomutuality as a 'miscarried "solution" of widespread occurrence' (Wynne et al. 1967, p. 444). Pseudomutuality arises when the participants in a non-mutual situation engage in actions which conceal this fact and instead portray the situation as mutual. A mild example of pseudomutuality occurs when a customer has decided against a purchase but is embarrassed by the trouble (effort) they have caused a sales attendant and promises to 'come back' after they have completed another task. The customer creates a false sense of complementarity, giving every verbal indication of a sale when the situation is decisively non-mutual and there will be no sale.

The effect of pseudomutual communications between parents and their adolescent children is that: 'those dawning perceptions and incipient communications which might lead to an articulation of divergent expectations, interests or individuality are instead diffused, doubled, blurred or distorted' (Wynne et al. 1967, p. 449). The result is that individuation of adult personality is blocked by an attempt to reabsorb every assertion of independence within a framework of false mutuality. Wynne and his co-workers believed pseudomutuality scrambled messages, undercut the adolescent's confidence in sending and receiving messages correctly and prevented the development of a secure and independent identity.

As noted earlier these clinical theories were born in psychiatrists' professional rooms. These clinical observations lacked 'controls', that is, they did not study 'normal' families (where no one had been diagnosed as a schizophrenic). Instead they *assumed* this pattern of relationship to be extraordinary and distinctive of the families of schizophrenics. Hirsch and Leff (1975) in a careful review of the controlled and uncontrolled studies found no significant evidence of difference in the family relations of schizogenic and normal families. Since the genesis and treatment of schizophrenia is Hirsch and Leff's main concern, they do not pause to consider whether these psychiatrists had inadvertently stumbled across hitherto neglected characteristics of the modern family. It is our contention that these so-called 'schizogenic' characteristics can be found to some degree in practically all modern families.

The elaboration of motherhood in the modern period has meant that fathers have not been psychologically important in the development of their children. In this sense they have been 'weak' and they have, as we shall see in the next chapter, often been literally absent. The celebration of motherhood, together with the sexual division of labour, has isolated many mothers from the identity that can be derived from a career and urged them to turn instead to motherhood for personal fulfilment. The troubling 'symbiotic tie' found in the psychiatrists' rooms seems little more than individuals in a modern structural setting following the cultural prescriptions of their time.

The uneven development of family and society creates conditions that require tangled communication. The industrial revolution has changed the form of the patriarchal division of domestic labour but not its patriarchal character, while at the

same time it has promulgated the notion of the 'pure relationship', so that one's understanding of a relationship is viewed
through this cultural lens. This means that actors in an unequal
situation where one party has disposal over the labour of the
other must communicate what are fundamentally commands,
in the language that presupposes equality. Clearly this cannot
be regularly done at the explicit level, so it takes the form of
a metacommunicative marker. A husband may say, innocently:
'Where's my tie?'. While this message says explicitly only that
he cannot locate his tie, most of us will recognise that it can
also carry a metacommunicative marker, which turns it into a
command ('Find my tie!') or even the accusation of failure of
duty ('You've bloody well lost my tie!').

It is clear that intimate communication abounds with such
tangles, which helps explain the boom in psychotherapy and
the commercial success of Deborah Tannen's popular linguistics
books *That's Not What I Meant!* and *You Just Don't Understand.*
We shall see in Chapter 6 how the recently acquired value of
equality in housework promotes pseudomutuality as couples
strive to maintain the impression of reciprocity in the face of
objective indications of non-mutuality.

This framework explains the kinds of pseudomutuality that
pervade relations between parent and child, as well as husband and wife. The treatment of children as equals and
intimates by recasting the parent–child relationship as a pure
relationship requires systematic communicative distortions
(Habermas 1970). The power differential between parents and
their children produces a range of double binds around
parental responsibility and friendship ('I'm doing this for your
own good'), and heteronomy and autonomy ('You're old
enough to leave home when I think you can look after
yourself').

The existence and regularity of communicative tangles in
contemporary family relationships are rarely acknowledged.
The reasons for these tangles have even less been the focus
of scholarly attention. Professional observers of family relationships have been as much victims of the social alchemy of the
double life of the family as any other participant in these
relations. Under the conditions described in this chapter, many
of the activities of family households have become 'invisible'
and have reappeared in disembodied forms. Communication

has often become puzzling if not menacing. Individuals' striving for intimacy produces outcomes that bewilder them because, in a sense, they are making their lives behind their backs.

4

Working for nothing

Family life contains an invisible world of hard labour. The value of the labour that takes place inside the household has only now begun to be measured. Any recognition of the economic value of family activities requires a different mindset, one that puts aside the usual concentration on the emotional quality of family relationships. If this seems an artificial procedure, it is because we have become so accustomed to the idea that family relationships should be about intimacy and affection. At the same time, we are so inured to this normative view that we are also complicit in the process of denying the existence of mundane housework such as putting out the garbage and cleaning the toilet, not to mention the repetitive cycles of laundry, cooking and washing up. Even if the performance of these domestic tasks appears to the participants as gestures of affection, the tasks themselves are nevertheless an important and necessary component of the way that economies function.

The divisions of labour between men and women in the household are economic relationships. The inherent inequality of the exchanges between men and women is masked by the belief in pure relationships, so that we are convinced that we have moved beyond the old systems of servitude where women waited on men. Indeed, Western people often cast their family relations in a superior light. Couples are partners and the whole family just gets on with the few simple chores remaining in private life. The real world is outside in the market: the home is the place to dump the schoolbag, briefcase or toolbox at the front door and move into the warmth and fun. Only the shopping bag moves in further. Because of these beliefs, a close examination of how house-work is shared makes everyone uncomfortable. This discomfort applies just as much to the sociology of the family.

Practically everyone has some experience of housework (even academics) but, strange as it may sound, social scientists only 'discovered' unpaid domestic labour comparatively recently. This seems all the more strange because, now that there are official estimates of unpaid work, it is clear that unpaid household production is a major aspect of the economy in Australia (the labour inputs alone being valued at 50–60 per cent of the conventionally measured Gross Domestic Product). Just how did modern societies—including social scientists themselves—become blind, or choose not to see, this massive quantity of unpaid work and its significance?

In Chapter 3, we explored how the development of a public market created the private sphere as a mere by-product of the separation of home and work. Before this development, 'the economy' had few other meanings than 'householding', which was carried on within broader economic systems of households. In the absence of full public markets in labour and goods, there was a household division of labour between men and women which, although rigid and hierarchical, occurred in a framework where the contribution of each to the output of the household was obvious to all. With industrialisation, men came to specialise in paid work and women in unpaid work. The separation of home and work created a sexual division of labour which was not obviously an economic partnership. At the same time that home and work were separated, domestic life was transformed from life in a communal village to life in isolated, privatised domestic dwellings.

As a result of these changes, modern housework has acquired peculiar characteristics. The growth of the market implies that individuals engage in specialised production and acquire their other needs through purchases in the market. Thus cash becomes the standard of value and the obvious means of support. In a money economy, housework has become a realm where goods and services are exchanged without the intervention of money, and therefore the value of these goods and services is not apparent nor counted in national economic ledgers.

Moreover, unlike industry, where crafts have been fragmented into detailed, specialised tasks, in housework there is a minimal division of labour and little specialisation. Since the housewife is not employed, there is no employer with an interest in the value for money he receives for the outlay of a wage. No one has any powerful interest in the output per hour of housework. As Ruth Schwartz Cowan remarked, the land of households is inhabited by 'workers who do not have job descriptions, time clocks, or even paychecks' (Cowan 1979, p. 59).

In a world ruled by money, housework as work becomes invisible.[1] Western women's (unpaid) work is done largely in the privacy of their homes and does not attract a wage, as we saw previously. These facts endow this work with the peculiar tendency to 'disappear'. Housewives are classified as 'not in the labour force', their economic contribution is negated, absent from national accounts, and accorded little recognition or social prestige. Yet housework, however apparently trivial, is essential and the unseen half of the double life of the family.

The unpaid economy and its significance

Back in 1974, when Ann Oakley wrote *The Sociology of Housework*, every Western schoolchild knew that the person doing the job 'housework' was called a housewife, although calling it a job or work would have been odd. Housework is a gendered occupation. When asked at school 'Does your mother work?' children always knew the right answer was: 'No—she's a housewife'. Oakley's book raised many problems particular to housework, each connected with the fact that it was a woman's 'occupation'. Housework lacked recognition—it was a low status activity, with low rewards and performed in relative isolation. The daring element of Oakley's study of British housework was the simple gesture of treating housework as work.

In her autobiography, *Taking It Like a Woman* (1992), Oakley describes the difficulties she encountered in insisting that a study of women's attitudes to housework as work was not an academically absurd or laughable subject for a PhD thesis. Her supervisor initially thought she was talking about harmony in the marital bed or 'the marvellous things that could be done with the handles of vacuum cleaners', but she pressed on despite the 'patronising jocularity' (Oakley 1992, p. 74). Most of her contemporaries thought there was something irritatingly far-fetched about considering housework as an occupation let alone discussing at academic conferences the job satisfaction and worker alienation associated with housework. Yet many of the problems associated with housework seemed to be connected to its invisibility. Oakley's advocacy on behalf of housewives joined a chorus of voices campaigning to reverse the process of women being hidden from history (and virtually every other academic discipline).

The institutional support for this campaign has now reached beyond a small group of women trying to change the academic studies of industrial workplaces and modern societies that failed to see housework as work, to include major international and national agencies. Support for giving official recognition to women's unpaid work has arisen from the United Nation's Institute on the Research and Training for the Advancement of Women (INSTRAW); the International Labour Organization (ILO), and from statistical agencies in many nations around the globe (Ironmonger 1994a, pp. 55–7). Australia has been at the forefront of these developments, and public interest grew during the 1980s. More recently, the ABS (1994b) issued an occasional paper on *Unpaid Work and the Australian Economy 1992*, an official estimate of the value (in dollars and cents) of unpaid work of women and men, which superseded an earlier estimate (ABS 1990).

Duncan Ironmonger, working from the Households Economics Unit at the University of Melbourne, has argued that it is high time to make a distinction between Gross Household Product (GHP) and Gross Market Product (GMP—or as it is conventionally but ironically known, Gross Domestic Product, GDP).[2] That is, the conventional GDP does not include household production because it only counts work that is paid for, whether to repair a smashed car, make a bid on the futures exchange or to build a bridge. Ironmonger provides an estimate of the relative magnitude of household and market production. His ideas about how to apply input–output analysis to this problem have been influential in Finland, Norway, Canada and Sweden (Ironmonger 1994b). Graeme Snooks (1994), in a reappraisal of Australian economic history, argues for an incorporation of household work into our picture of the total economy, and elaborates a complete revision of Australian economic history on this basis. Given these developments, perhaps it would be fair to say that Australian women's unpaid work is less hidden from (economic) history than ever before. Accounting for the economic value of housework certainly puts a different light on the everyday world of the family, so cherished because it is 'beyond work'.

Unpaid work is considered work by modern economists because it is an activity that combines labour with raw materials to produce goods and services with enhanced economic value. Take for example home cooking—ingredients are turned into a meal which has more value than the ingredients alone, and which would cost money in a restaurant. This is what economists mean when they talk about 'value-added'. Since most unpaid work consists of households producing goods and services for their own consumption and no cash changes hands, these unpaid work activities are not captured by conventional measures of economic activity, such as the system of National Accounts, which are designed to measure market activity (Chadeau 1992; Goldschmidt-Clermont 1991).

In deciding what household activities shall count as productive activity, economists have relied on the 'third party criterion'. According to this criterion, productive activities generate goods and services that could have been provided by some other economic unit. For example, cooking, cleaning, childcare and mowing the lawn are productive activities because you could pay someone else to do these tasks for you. Describing these activities as 'tradeable' is an alternative way of expressing the same idea. The 'third party' test excludes non-productive, leisure and personal activities because it makes no sense to have someone else sleep for you or watch television for you and so on (Hill 1979).

The Multinational Time Use project, under the directorship of Alexander Szalai, standardised the classification of activities in the 1960s (Szalai 1972). This makes possible the analysis of unpaid work across nations and over time (Harvey & Niemi 1994).

Following these conventions and applying the 'third person criterion' to exclude personal and leisure activities like taking a bath or having a nap, the following household activities are regarded as unpaid work. That is, these are tasks that could be done for pay in a market society:

- Food preparation and clean up
- Laundry, ironing and clothes care
- Other housework (chiefly cleaning and tidying)
- Garden, pool and pet care
- Home maintenance and car care
- Household management (paying bills, doing paperwork, etc.)
- Transporting adult household members
- Purchasing goods and services
- Physical care of own and other children
- Care for child, sick or with disability (own and other children)
- Playing with own and other children
- Teaching own and other children
- Minding own and other children
- Travel associated with child care
- Other child care activities
- Travel associated with any of the above activities
- Travel associated with purchasing goods and services

As we will now discuss, all the activities listed above are taken to constitute the operational definition of household productive activities, and hence of 'unpaid work' as economists now conventionally understand housework.[3]

How big is the unpaid economy?

The usual method for expressing the size of the unpaid economy (that is, calculating extended national accounts), is to compare a valuation of all unpaid labour with the conventionally measured Gross Domestic Product (GDP). In 1994, the Australian Bureau of Statistics calculated that the value of all unpaid labour was equivalent to 48–64 per cent of GDP (ABS

1994b). But in calculating the magnitude of the unpaid economy, the ABS measures labour inputs only, whereas when measuring GDP, both labour *and* capital inputs are included. Ironmonger (1994c) has calculated that if the value of the capital goods used in household production (housing, vehicles and domestic appliances) is counted, then the value of 'Gross Household Product' is 94 per cent of 'Gross Market Product'. In other words, the aggregate value of the goods and services produced in the household sector of the economy is equivalent to the entire output of the market economy. Just as an iceberg is mostly out of sight, unpaid work is a huge invisible mass of value. In ignoring the unpaid work of men and women, and concentrating exclusively on the market economy, most economists are remaining blind to half of all economic activity. We hardly need to add that this blindness about family life is not exclusive to economists.

Nevertheless, the extent of the output of the household sector is indeed staggering. Ironmonger compares various household productive activities to commercial activities so that home cooking can be described as an industry, home laundry as the home laundry industry and so on.

> From these measurements we know that the industries of the household economy are collectively larger users of labour than the combined sectors of the market economy. For example in Australia in 1987, as measured by weekly hours of labour input, market industries used 252 million hours and household industries 282 million hours. Unpaid work exceeded paid work by 12 per cent . . . 76 million hours per week are used in meal preparation, 63 million in cleaning and laundry and 53 million in shopping . . . *[T]he three largest industries in the economy are the everyday activities of households (1) in preparing meals, (2) in cleaning and laundry and (3) in shopping.* These three household industries compare with the three largest market sector industries: wholesale and retail trade with 49 million hours per week, manufacturing with 43 million and community services with 41 million. (Ironmonger 1994c, p. 38, emphasis in original)

How gross household product is measured

The most widely adopted methods of valuation—imputing a cash value for unpaid work—have been based on placing a dollar value on the labour involved in unpaid work activities. Any attempt at valuation, of course, unsettles our sense that family activities are beyond price. However, these tasks can be given a price in Western societies. It is as fair to investigate their potential value as it is for anthropologists to impose Western calculations about the relative economic contributions in hunter–gatherer societies.

All these methods of valuation begin with the measurement of time spent on unpaid work activities. Generally the list of unpaid work includes indoor and outdoor housework (cooking, laundry, cleaning, gardening and pool maintenance, home repairs, car care, pet care, paperwork), childcare and shopping. There are three methods of valuing the time spent on these activities:

1 the opportunity cost method—which calculates forgone earnings of unpaid workers;
2 the replacement cost method—which calculates the cost of hiring a replacement worker(s);
3 the market substitution method—which calculates the cost of substituting for the products of unpaid labour by purchasing a similar basket of goods and services in the market.

The *opportunity cost method*, while being the easiest to operationalise, is perhaps the most variable measure. It varies according to the wage rate used as the basis for imputing the cash value of the time spent in unpaid work. For Australia the opportunity cost estimate of the cash value of all unpaid work varies from 52 per cent of GDP to 69 per cent of GDP (cf. ABS 1994b, p. 1). The key assumptions involved are whether to use gross or net wage rates and whether to include the costs of labour market entry (for example, costs of work clothes, childcare and travel). If net wages are the basis of the calculation, and if a further deduction is made for labour market entry costs, then the opportunity cost measure can provide a very low estimate of the value of household production, perhaps as little as 30 per cent of GDP. A further problem arises because male wage rates are higher than female wage rates (as explored in Chapter 7). This results in identical tasks being given different values depending on whether they are performed by a woman or a man (cf. ABS 1990, p. 121).

Once again it means that women's unpaid work is under-valued.

The cost of purchasing the services of a housekeeper is the basis for estimating the *replacement cost method* of valuing unpaid work. Two problems unique to this method are the problem of coverage and the problem of supply. The problem of coverage arises simply because the range of activities conventionally included involves activities that no housekeeper could reasonably be expected to do. Examples of these activities are yard work; car and pool maintenance; voluntary caring for sick and elderly relatives and neighbours; helping with children's homework; and perhaps even counselling and sexual services. Valuing unpaid labour time at housekeeper wage rates must necessarily exclude some activities and, therefore, produce an undervaluation.

The second problem unique to the replacement measure is the problem of supply. The occupation of a live-in servant, despite the payment of wages, retains many of the elements of pre-industrial labour—membership of the household of the employer, personal service to master and mistress, payment chiefly in kind (board or lodgings) rather than cash, and so on. Employment as a household servant declined rapidly in industrialised countries in the early decades of this century. In practice, workers in such occupations are still more plentiful in less industrialised countries, and in advanced industrial societies servants are often illegal immigrants from less industrialised countries. This illegal employment particularly occurs in the United States. Under these circumstances, esti-mating the value of unpaid work on the basis of the hiring of a housekeeper is a bit like estimating the costs of a modern car basing it on the labour of wheelwrights, blacksmiths and carriage makers.

Importantly, this method also builds in a sexual bias. Housekeepers, where they can be found, are typically female and in a sex-segregated occupational structure are typically less well paid than those in 'male' occupations. Thus, in common with the opportunity cost method, there is a tendency to understate the value of household productive activities because they are done by women. Once again, bringing the hidden labour of households into the light of day is achieved at the cost of accepting a lower value placed on the work of women.

The *market substitution* model avoids some of the difficulties mentioned above, but not all of them. The advantage of this method is that each particular service has a definite cost recognised by the market. Problems arise whenever the market and household activities appear to be non-commensurate. This includes those activities for which there is no real market equivalent, for example, socio-emotional companionship. Also the problem of coverage still remains. Exactly which basket of services available on the market could be said to substitute adequately for the diverse activities of unpaid work in the home?

This problem is compounded by the existence of simultaneous (or so-called 'secondary') activities, for example doing the ironing and watching the baby as she plays with her toys. Secondary activities are uncharacteristic of market-oriented behaviour. Estimates suggest that perhaps three-quarters of the time spent in childcare is when childcare is accompanied by another primary activity (ABS 1994c, pp. 8, 15). Ironmonger observes that when considered in this way there are 203.4 million hours per week devoted to primary and secondary childcare in Australia, compared with 272 million hours per week devoted to all forms of paid work (Ironmonger 1994b, p. 50). Ignoring secondary childcare, for example, gives a completely misleading impression, underestimating the practical time constraints of caring for children. For example, one cannot leave the house while the baby is asleep, and one probably finds another chore to do meanwhile. Nor can the market substitution method completely avoid the problem of adopting gender bias in its pricing assumptions. While this bias is less obvious than in the case of the opportunity cost method, it is nevertheless true that in a sexually segregated labour market, 'male' occupations are better rewarded than 'female' ones, drilling plant operation more valued than nursing care (ABS 1993a, pp. 38–40).

Most importantly, can one assume equivalence in time between market and household activities? Much of the appeal of paid specialist services consists in the fact that they can achieve their results quickly, whereas those engaged in household productive activities are unspecialised workers operating without the benefits of economies of scale. Cleaning of carpets may more easily be done by a specialist operator with commercial machinery. This raises the implication that market and household services may not be interchangeable. Once interchangeability is open to doubt, the method of valuation no longer has any foundation.

While none of the methods of valuing household production is without problems, the conventional national accounts which calculate GDP also involve contestable assumptions, which mean that these measures are only approximate estimates. A clear example is that conventionally an imputed value for owner-occupied housing contributes to final value of GDP.

Information that would increase the solidity of the estimates of GHP would be a measure of the outputs of household productive activities. Output, a more direct measure, would obviate the need to impute the value of housework by using labour time. An output measure would compare the products of household labour directly with market products. Unfortunately, to date, no research organisation has developed a method of collecting these output statistics. In the absence of output statistics, the current methods of calculating extended national accounts will produce varying estimates but every one of these estimates indicates that household production is a sizeable and significant form of economic activity.

Family and the social organisation of unpaid work

It cannot be stressed too much that the vast majority of unpaid work takes place in a family setting. This is not to dismiss other voluntary work in any way other than sheer volume. Social scientists have come to expect that most behaviour will be related to a number of standard factors. For example, much of people's voting behaviour is explained by their occupation, income and education. It is even possible to predict on the basis of educational attainment how long, on average, people will engage in sexual foreplay. So it comes as a surprise to find that time spent in housework, childcare and shopping is unaffected by standard factors such as occupation, income and education. The factors most strongly related to the time spent in these activities are age and gender. Age, it transpires, is a proxy for stage in life course, that is, age is related to whether

an individual lives at home with their parents, flats independently, is married,[4] has children (of a certain age), lives
in an empty-nest household, or is retired or widowed.

Gender and the household division of labour

Amongst commentators, it is widely believed that of all the
social changes in Australia since 1945, the 'revolution' in
attitudes about gender roles and family relations has had the
most profound 'impact' on modern society (Mackay 1993,
p. 24). The sociologist Ulrich Beck, after noting that the
contemporary works on the family tend to have tempestuous
titles (for example, *The War Over the Family*, *The Battle of the
Sexes*, or *The Terror of Intimacy*), believes that these titles are
indications of 'the deep insecurity and hurt with which men
and women confront each other in the everyday world of the
family (or what is left of them)' (Beck 1992, p. 103).

Time use statistics and the domestic 'revolution'

Despite the claims of a 'revolution', when we consider the
division of labour in terms of time spent on household work,
we find in fact that men do much less: in round terms, it is
a 30/70 split between men and women (ABS 1994c). This
figure is based on the broadest definition of domestic labour
and includes the time spent in 'outdoor' tasks, like house
maintenance and car cleaning, in which men specialise. The
time spent in various activities is collected by a special survey
carried out by the ABS called the Time Use Survey. The most
recent Time Use Survey was national in scope and collected
data at four separate periods (with the aim of representing
seasonal variation) over 1992. Some people may be aware of
several earlier studies, but few will have any conception of
the extent of effort put into estimating the time that Australians
spent on work. Two-day diaries were collected from all
persons over the age of 14 years in randomly selected
households (private dwellings). The final national sample
contained over 7000 people or diaries for 13 937 days. Analysis
of the best available evidence—the ABS Time Use Survey (ABS
1993c)—tells us that the division of labour in the household
plainly remains unequal.

It is important to note that these estimates imply that there are always *some* variations from this average pattern. A small number of households share work differently—for example in some households the man is responsible for the laundry. As well, there are cultural variations—Filipino families in Australia, for example, regard vacuuming the house as a 'masculine' job because it is 'heavier' work than sweeping, a job reserved for women (Soriano 1995, p. 106). Also, the kind of food that is cooked, whether a barbecue is preferred to a stove and the extent of preparation before cooking, vary according to diverse tastes and ethnic backgrounds. These surveys measure the aggregate time spent on domestic tasks and show that on average, women do far more housework than men.

Feminism as a social movement has been based on the contradiction that in a society committed to the principles of equality of opportunity and promotion by merit (what sociologists call 'status achievement'), roles are assigned by gender (what sociologists call 'ascribed status'). The fact that individuals should be assigned a role as 'home-maker', or 'principal carer' for young children or frail relatives simply on the basis of an accident of birth—their sex—rather than on the basis of their achievement (for example their educational attainment), has provoked widespread unease, even anger. Major responses have been legislation against discrimination at work,[5] programs designed to promote equal access to the labour market,[6] and campaigns to encourage a greater sharing of family responsibilities.[7]

Segregation

Given these efforts, it is surprising to find just how stereotyped the assignment of unpaid work tasks remains and how little evidence there appears to be of any 'revolution'. Most unpaid tasks around the house appear to be classified as either 'men's work' or 'women's work'. Australian women, on the whole, are responsible for 'indoor' housework such as cooking, laundry, cleaning and the physical care of children, while men are responsible for the 'outdoor' tasks like lawn, garden, pool and pet care, and for maintaining the home and the car. Shopping, gardening and playing with children are the activities most

Table 4.1 Women's and men's shares in selected unpaid work tasks, 1992

Activity	Women's share %	Men's share %
Laundry, ironing and clothes care	89	11
Physical care of (own) children	84	16
Other housework (cleaning)	82	18
Food preparation and clean up	75	25
Care of other children	75	25
Shopping	61	39
Play with (own) children	60	40
Household management	56	44
Gardening, pool and pet care	42	58
Home maintenance and car care	17	83

Source: ABS 1994c

likely to be gender neutral, although women spend more time in these activities than men.

The extent of sex segregation in domestic labour is indicated by the fact that very few activities are shared 50/50 by men and women. The strength of the segregation between 'men's jobs' and 'women's jobs' in unpaid work is very conspicuous. Women's share of laundry is nearly 90 per cent and men's participation is meagre. Women work eight and a half times longer than men on laundry, ironing and clothes care. The next most segregated activity is physical care of children, which, when compared to playing with children, is disproportionately done by women who spend more than five times longer than men in the physical care of children. Men are almost as reluctant to clean and tidy the house, leaving women an 82 per cent share of this activity: the question of who cleans the toilet is no longer a secret. Food and drink preparation, Australia's largest household industry, is a heavily female industry. For every hour that men spend in cooking, women will spend, on average, three. Only a small amount of time is devoted to care of other people's children, for example, asking playmates over for the day, but three-quarters of this is done by women.

Shopping, playing with children, household management and gardening are the activities where time use most closely approaches equality between the sexes. In the first three of these activities, men's share is approximately 40 per cent. Gardening, pool care and pet care on the other hand, are

Table 4.2 Women's and men's daily participation rate in selected unpaid work
activities, 1992

Activity	Women's participation rate %	Men's participation rate %
Laundry, ironing and clothes care	57	12
Physical care of (own) children	25	11
Other housework (cleaning)	71	26
Food preparation and clean up	86	56
Care of other children	5	1
Shopping	58	45
Play with (own) children	15	8
Household management	27	22
Gardening, pool and pet care	40	36
Home maintenance and car care	9	22

Source: ABS 1994c

activities where men's share is greater than women's. The single heavily masculine-dominant activity is home maintenance and car care. Men provide 80 per cent of the time devoted to home maintenance and car care.

Not every activity is performed with equal frequency. Some activities such as food and drink preparation are daily activities, while other activities such as mowing the lawn are more likely to be weekly activities and even then, only in summer. Winter may well be a nice quiet time for men. The participation rate in Table 4.2 expresses the proportion of people engaging in each domestic activity on a nominated day. As such, it gives a reasonable indication of the frequency with which activities are performed.

The activity most often performed by women—laundry—occurred in 57 per cent of all the days recorded in women's diaries and only in 12 per cent of men's diaries. So, for 88 per cent of the days on which men recorded their activities, they neither laundered, ironed, folded or put away any clothes. As we suggest in Chapter 6 however, men's aversion to doing the washing does not appear to be linked to any preference for wearing filthy or crumpled clothes.

Few people complete a day without eating a meal or drinking a cup of coffee or tea, although 44 per cent of men compared to 14 per cent of women apparently had someone else do the food and drink preparation for them and clean up the meal afterwards on the day of the diary. Cleaning activities continue the tale of sex-segregated participation, with three times as many women as men involved in dusting, wiping down, scrubbing and picking up toys and stray clothes. Cleaning and tidying is also clearly a daily chore, with 71 per cent of women recording some cleaning activity. Since only 26 per cent of men recorded an episode of cleaning, either they are less sensitive to dirt or somebody else (most likely female) cleaned for them.

Shopping is an activity in which there is strong participation by both men and women. Although shopping occurs at least weekly, household management such as paying bills, organising insurance and registering the car is also a frequent activity shared fairly evenly between men and women. Despite the folklore which suggests that control of the household purse strings is a corollary of the male provider role, paying the bills is in fact a job which falls by a narrow margin to women.

Gardening, pool and pet care, similarly to playing with children, seem to present an oddity, in that men's episodes of gardening are longer than those of women but less frequent. Men seem to have the luxury of devoting longer periods of time to an activity while women's unpaid work has a more interrupted character. Participation rates in home maintenance and car care are consistent with the heavily 'masculine' nature of this task. On almost one-quarter of all the diary days collected, men engaged in this group of activities. Perhaps these figures capture a tendency among men to retreat to the male domain of the garden shed. In contrast, women engage in home maintenance and car care activities on average about one day out of ten.

Since not all people have children, naturally only a small proportion of respondents to the Time Use Survey would record any time spent on the physical care of children. The participation rate of women in this activity is more than double that of men, despite the fact that there are almost as many fathers as mothers in the sample. A small proportion of people care for other people's children on a daily basis, but the same sex imbalance applies.

Mothers who were involved in caring for pre-school age children spent nearly 25 hours per week in this direct childcare activity alone, ignoring the time spent in preparing food for the child, washing the child's clothes, or tidying after the child. The mothers of pre-schoolers spent over 56 hours per week on primary unpaid work—all housework, childcare and shopping activity. Fathers who participate in the care of pre-school age children spend less than 10 hours per week in direct and nearly 22 hours per week in all unpaid work.

It is worth noting that this time spent in childcare refers only to childcare as the 'main' activity. One must also take into account the fact that caring for children frequently occurs as an activity accompanying another 'main' activity ('primary' activity). For example, while a woman is cooking for her partner's party for work friends, helping a twelve-year-old with homework and trying to make the house presentable, she may also be darting in and out of the bathroom where a two-year-old is playing in the bath. Similarly, even a spell in front of the television may be also spent standing in front of an ironing board while the baby is upstairs having an afternoon nap. In these two cases all activities other than the cooking and ironing are 'secondary' activities. When primary and secondary childcare activities are considered, the average time spent in childcare by both men and women increases threefold.

What determines the amount of unpaid work?

As suggested earlier, contrary to expectations, neither income, education nor occupation has a consistently powerful influence on the amount of unpaid work an individual does. This means that within nearly every family, the household division of labour has virtually nothing to do with whether the adult couple are highly educated or unskilled, relatively well-off or close to the poverty line. Gender, age, and to a lesser extent employment status are the most influential factors.

Employment has an important effect on the time spent in unpaid work but this effect is stronger for women. Heavy unpaid work commitments (such as childcare or care for an elderly person) drastically reduce the opportunity for women to participate in the labour force. Alternatively, a shorter working week in employment means substantially longer hours of unpaid work for women. The trade-off between paid and unpaid work among men is so weak that men's unpaid work only decreases slightly as the length of the (paid) working day increases. Alternatively a drastic reduction in time devoted to the labour market (such as with retirement) only leads to a very slight rise in the time men spend in unpaid work (Bittman 1991, pp. 20–2).

A major variation in the amount of unpaid work an individual does is associated with transitions in the life course. As everyone knows, an individual passes through a variety of stages in the course of a lifetime. In sociological terms, this movement is called the life course. These transitions involve changes to a number of distinct social statuses, that is, an individual ceases to be regarded chiefly as a son or daughter and becomes regarded as a husband or a wife, a father or a mother, a retiree, a widower or a widow, and so on. The sequence of these stages may not always be rigid but neither can the stages be arranged in an arbitrary order.[8]

While changes in time use accompanying the transition from one life course stage to another provide important information, there is only space here to deal with some of the most striking findings—the changes in the extent of unpaid work at independence, at marriage, and when retired men and women become widowed. Another important aspect of domestic work revolves around how much is shared when married women are also in the paid workforce.

The transition to independence

For those people with vivid memories of their teenage to adult years, the effect of independence on time spent in selected household tasks may not be too surprising. We will touch on the average time devoted to these tasks in three 'premarital' life course stages—living in the parental home (son or daughter), living alone and living with others (non-relatives) in a 'shared' household.

The Time Use Survey demonstrates both early sex segregation and an apparent reluctance by sons and daughters to do much housework at all. First, within this category young men spend less than half the time spent by young women in the unpaid tasks of cooking, cleaning and laundry. There is a very distinct pattern of sex stereotyping of activities even at this point in the life course, with young women specialising in cooking, cleaning and laundry and young men specialising in outdoor tasks. Second, it is clear that there are substantial differences among the premarital stages, most obvious in the remarkably few hours spent in domestic work by *all* young adults (over fifteen years of age) living with their parents. These findings are consistent with the idea that parents bear a disproportionate amount of the housework burden, that is, parents are in a sense slaves to their children.

Where parents start refusing to treat their teenagers as helpless infants, teenagers' own rooms often simply remain untidy. Many people may be familiar with this practice: in one spectacular case, a teenage girl living at home mislaid her bicycle for three months. Although the outcome is nearly inconceivable, her father swears that she eventually found the bike in her own bedroom. For parents, however, at least if children have their own room there is a door to it, and neither party need be disturbed. It is less easy, it seems, to entice teenagers to do their own laundry or cooking.

Where there are no parents to assume this burden, things are very different. There are three major forms of households formed by offspring after they leave home. The first one is a married couple household, which will be dealt with later. The other two are living alone, and sharing with non-kin. For women, time spent in both indoor and outdoor housework in these other two household categories is roughly double that spent by daughters living at home.

In the transition from daughter at home to woman in a shared household, the increase in housework is of the order of one and a half times. Daughters at home spend 7 hours 10 minutes a week on a combination of indoor and outdoor household work, whereas a woman living alone spends twice that time on these tasks, and a woman in a shared household spends 10 and a half hours. The same order applies to time spent in shopping—daughters at home spend the least, women living alone spend the most. Independent women, it is important to note, have an extraordinarily small workload compared with later phases of their life course.

Among men, the most dramatic increases occur in the indoor housework tasks—cooking, laundry and cleaning. The transition from son at home to man living on his own brings a fourfold increase in cooking time, close to a sixfold increase in laundry time and a doubling of time spent in cleaning.

Moving from one's parents' house to a shared household also requires dramatic adjustments although not as large as those of living alone. Sons at home spend a total of 2 hours 12 minutes a week on all indoor housework tasks, but once they have left home, 5 to 8 hours per week in these same tasks depending on whether they are in a shared household or living alone. These figures might explain the appeal of comedy sketches which revolve around an 'expert' in a demonstration kitchen giving advice to young men who have just left home:

Lesson 1: Wiping the Bench

Expert: For this task, you'll need some hot water, a detergent and a sponge-cloth. First, clear the bench. Then mix detergent with water (not too much detergent). Wet cloth in mixture and squeeze. Using a side to side motion . . .

The Time Use Survey shows that when sons are at home, 36 per cent of the already small amount of time devoted to housework is spent on outdoor chores. Upon achieving independence, men significantly increase time needed for shopping.

The rise in men's unpaid work on leaving home is, however, made more dramatic only because it is an increase from a very low base. Whereas at home sons devote 12 minutes in a whole week to laundry, ironing and clothes care (perhaps about the time it takes to dump one's dirty washing in the laundry basket), this increases to 1 hour 9 minutes per week among men living alone. It is almost half the time spent by women living alone. The same is true of the increase in cleaning and tidying. In relation to cooking, however, men living alone spend a comparable time to their female counterparts, despite the fact that those still at home barely do any cooking.

In the case of shared households, women's hours spent in indoor work are marginally lower than those spent by women living alone and considerably higher than those of daughters at home. Men in shared households, in contrast, spend substantially less time than men living alone on these indoor tasks and in some cases this represents only a fractional change from their pattern as sons at home. Since these figures

Figure 4.1 Effect of marriage on time spent in cooking, cleaning and laundry

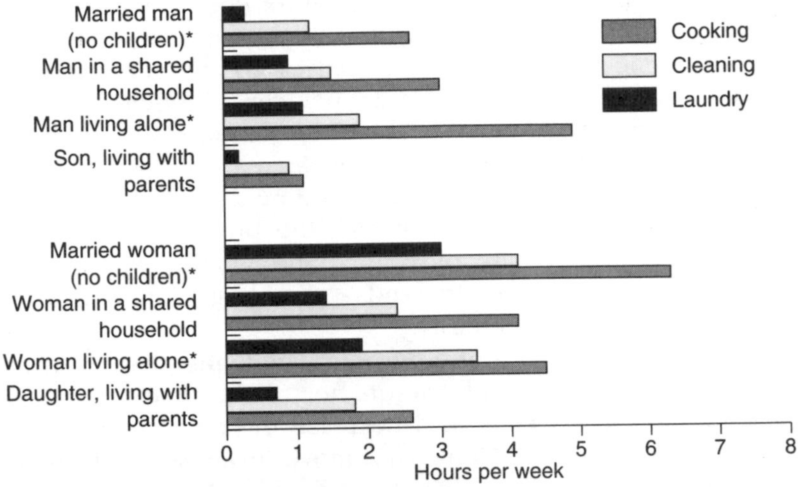

Note: * Men aged less than 65 years, women less than 60 years.
Source: ABS 1992, Time Use Survey, author's own analysis

about shared households are an average of all shared households regardless of sex composition, it appears that if women share with women, the standards of housework are higher than if men share with men. If women share with men, it would seem that women do a disproportionate share. It is possible to conclude that shared households are not, as was sometimes believed (Barrett & McIntosh 1982, pp. 140–2) in the vanguard of the movement to gender equity.

The transition to marriage

In Figure 4.1, the effect of marriage on time spent in selected household tasks is shown separately for each sex. The average time devoted to these tasks in three 'premarital' life course stages are shown in comparison to average time among married couples who haven't yet had children.

Despite many newly-weds' hopes that marital life will involve a partnership of sharing and mutual caring, the Time Use Survey shows that, when it comes to housework, these hopes are not fulfilled. The effect of marriage is diametrically opposite for men and women. Among married men, cooking, cleaning and laundry time are all reduced whereas for women, the time devoted to these tasks is dramatically increased by marriage. Compared to a single woman of equivalent age living alone, a married woman spends 40 per cent more time in cooking, time spent cleaning increases by 17 per cent, and the time taken for laundry by 37 per cent. Women who live in shared households would face after marriage a doubling of time spent on laundry, a 73 per cent increase in cleaning time and a 49 per cent increase in cooking time. The steepest increases in indoor housework face the bride who has come directly from her family of origin. She would experience a fourfold increase in laundry and a doubling of her previous cleaning and cooking times.

Compared with men of equivalent age living alone, married men can expect to spend one-quarter of the time in laundry, half the time in cooking, and decrease their cleaning time by roughly 40 per cent. Men who move from solo to shared households could also anticipate reductions in the time spent in indoor housework, although these reductions would not be as large. The family sociologist, Jessie Bernard (1976), argued that because the effects of marriage were so different for each of the sexes, one should talk not about marriage but about 'his marriage' and 'her marriage'. Although Bernard was not talking about housework, it is clear that her comments apply here equally well. The pattern for independent adults is one where, upon marriage, men transfer most of their domestic burdens to their new-found partners. Hartmann has suggested that 'husbands are a net drain on family resources' (in Berk 1985, pp. 10, 161).

The only category of men to devote more time to indoor housework upon marriage are those who move straight from living in their parents' household to establish a family household of their own. It seems that for men, the only deal which minimises indoor housework more than marriage is having Mum do it for you.

The development of a traditional division of labour cementing the sex segregation incipient among those living at home is also demonstrated in the survey. Men, however, give up most indoor housework and leave it to women while increasing their outdoor housework activities (ABS 1994d, p. 122). Marriage seems to ensure that the indoor/outdoor division is set in place.

Figure 4.2 His marriage and her marriage

Source: Office of the Status of Women 1991

There is some indication that the outdoor specialisation of men can be elaborated into a whole subculture of 'sheddies'. In a book on this phenomenon, called *Blokes and Sheds*, one 'Sheddy', having spent much time in what the author describes as a 'classic shed' supplied with a beer fridge, a 'fine collection of blues CDs and tapes', a workbench and a potbelly stove for winter, advises 'young blokes, when they get married, to "buy a shed"' (Thomson 1995, p. 52).

The effect of children

Everyone knows that children create work for their parents. Whatever the arrangement before the children, however, their arrival heralds a radical separation of men's and women's future pathways. The effects of children on these pathways and on substantially increasing women's domestic work cannot be emphasised too much. Men's commitment to paid work peaks, when the youngest child is between two and four years of age, at over 44 hours per week including travel. Women, in contrast, are in paid employment on average less than 10 hours per week but at this juncture of their lives, their unpaid work hours are even greater than the hours their spouses devote to paid work. The modern division of labour between the sexes is almost as profound as that praised by Lord Tennyson (1847):

> Man for the field and woman for the hearth;
> Man for the sword and for the needle she;
> Man with the head and woman with the heart;
> Man to command and woman to obey;
> All else confusion.

Figure 4.3 illustrates the differential impact of children on the unpaid work time of women and men. The amount of unpaid work time of mothers of pre-school age children is more than double that of married women who have no children. Mothers of infant (0–1 year) children spend over 59 hours per week in unpaid work, and there are strong reasons to believe that this understates the constraints of responsibilities for children, as we discuss below, and that a better representation is about 90 hours per week. While unpaid work time diminishes as the youngest child ages, even when the youngest is fifteen or more years of age or all the children have left home (empty nest), the time spent in unpaid work never returns to the levels before the birth of a child.

There are some peculiarities with figures expressing average time spent on childcare. The first is the problem of secondary activities and the second concerns the definition of childcare. For some reason respondents have a tendency to list childcare as the secondary activity in these circumstances. As noted earlier, for every hour recorded as a primary childcare activity there are three more hours recorded on childcare as

Figure 4.3 Men's and women's unpaid work time (hours per week) by age of youngest child, 1992

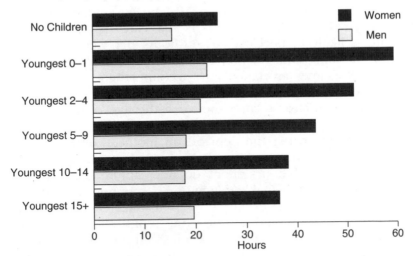

Source: ABS 1992, Time Use Survey, author's own analysis

a secondary activity (that is, accompanying another primary activity). Roughly half of this 'secondary' childcare accompanies a leisure activity or some activity associated with personal care. Frequently this means that respondents are watching *Playschool* on television, or are at the municipal swimming pool with their youngest child, which would both be coded as leisure activities, or are in the bath with a toddler (coded as personal care). These coding procedures produce the illusion of voluntary leisure and time for oneself. It means that there are still some considerable underestimations of the constraints imposed by caring for small children.

The other peculiarity arises because of the danger of double counting. Is tidying up after children time spent in childcare or time spent in cleaning? To avoid double counting, the convention is that cleaning is always coded as cleaning, and only those activities involving the direct care of children—physical care and minding of children, care of sick children, teaching, helping or reprimanding children, playing, reading to or talking with children—is coded as childcare. This convention also applies to time spent shopping for children and preparing children's meals.

If only the time spent in primary childcare in this restricted sense is considered, mothers of infant children spend over 30 hours per week in childcare. If the secondary childcare accompanying 'leisure' and 'personal care' is included, this figure is likely to be closer to 60 hours per week. When the extra shopping and the preparation of special children's food at separate times are taken into account, then the amount of time women spend caring for small children is even larger.

There is a clear relation between the age of the youngest child and the time women spend in childcare. The younger the child the greater the demand on mothers' time. Although it is a cliché to mention that babies are demanding, even the sheer quantity of hours spent do not capture the immensity of the task. As Ann Oakley suggests, it was not until after her own experience of exclusive responsibility for two young children that she could see how the typical Western arrangements for child-rearing are so 'peculiar'. At the time, she simply felt 'exhausted and incapable' but with hindsight, she rightly claims that she had 'every reason to feel exhausted'. Like most babies, her children had 'limitless energy', 'one of them woke up several times a night for five years' and even though her partner 'took to coming home early and doing more' she was very lonely. Yet she embarked on motherhood with great enthusiasm: as she says, 'I took the plunge into family life earlier, more deeply and with my eyes more completely closed than anyone else' (Oakley 1992, pp. 69–70).

For fathers the experience is rather different. To return to the Time Use data, in contrast to women, the new father's unpaid work time increases from a low of 15 hours 42 minutes per week before children arrive, to peak at 22 hours 22 minutes per week among the fathers of infants, before settling at a level of around 19 hours a week. Fathers of infants spend about 8 hours a week in direct childcare as a primary activity (nearly 33 hours per week including childcare as a secondary activity, accompanying leisure and personal care). Mothers of infants spent 264 per cent more time in unpaid work than fathers. Like their spouses', men's childcare time falls as maturing children take more care of themselves. Fathers' domestic work and shopping time is effectively invariable until their youngest child reaches fifteen years of age, but increases by about 3 and a half hours a week after that point. By then,

Table 4.3 Retired men's time spent in housework (hours per week), 1992

	Laundry	Cleaning	Cooking
Husband retired couple	0.4	1.7	4.5
Retired, living alone	1.5	3.8	9.4
Per cent increase	354	226	208

Source: ABS 1994c

men's total unpaid work per week is 19 hours 36 minutes compared with their spouses' hours at this same stage of 36 hours 24 minutes per week.

Effect of widowhood

For older men and women whose partners have died, there are notable changes in the extent of unpaid work. Women living alone above 60 years of age reduce their overall unpaid work by 24 per cent compared to women of the same age living with a male partner. Most of this reduction occurs in housework activities—cooking, laundry and cleaning. With this significantly reduced time comes an increase in time to spend on extra social life and entertainment.

For men over 65 years, on the other hand, the loss of a partner signals tremendous increases in unpaid work. Table 4.3 sets out these changes. The scale of these increases is truly breathtaking, with laundry time quadrupling and cleaning and cooking trebling. Retired men living alone are the only category of men who spend more time in food and drink preparation than their female counterparts.

Husbands' and children's contributions

The increasing participation of married women in the paid labour force has provoked many commentators, as noted earlier, to talk of a 'revolution' in the relations between men and women. So the question arises as to how couples combine paid and unpaid work when married women are in paid employment. If there has been a revolution, then men and women now sharing the role of provider would reorganise the domestic division of labour so that unpaid duties were shared. But if women simply add the demands of paid work

Figure 4.4 Contribution of family members aged fifteen years and over to unpaid household work, 1992

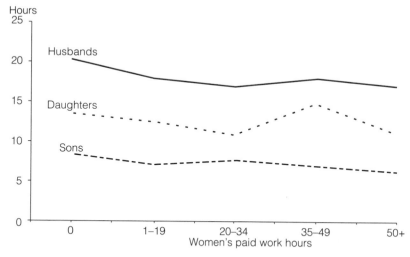

Source: ABS 1994d, Time Use Survey, p. 124

to the same level of responsibilities for unpaid work, then we would have to say that they are carrying a double burden.

It might be expected that other family members, such as husbands and teenage children, would increase their hours of unpaid work in support of married women's labour force activity. By considering whether the average amount of unpaid work of husbands and children over fifteen (living at home) increases as mothers' hours of paid work increase, we can construct a simple test of this alleged revolution. While some fluctuations are evident, in general there is a slight trend downwards suggesting that, on average, the amount of unpaid work of other family members tends to decrease rather than increase as women's paid work increases. Apparently the 'revolution' has not yet reached husbands and children (except perhaps in fantasy) and women are indeed exposed to the possibility of a double burden.

Most women cope with the potential for a double burden by reducing the time that they devote to unpaid work. The hours of paid employment, therefore, are not simply added to the domestic load of women who are not in the labour force. Rather, some of the work is either not being done or

Table 4.4 Comparison of women's 'share' of selected unpaid work activities

Activity	All women's share %	Full-time employed women's share %
Laundry	89	90
Physical care of children	84	76
Cleaning	82	84
Cooking	75	75
Shopping	61	62
Play with children	60	59
Gardening, pool and pet care	42	32
Home maintenance and car care	17	16

Source: ABS 1994c

market substitutes have been made, for example with childcare, cleaning, ironing, meals out, and so forth. Nevertheless, the total paid and unpaid work of these women is higher than that of a full-time housewife. And the trade-off between hours of paid work and hours of unpaid work is not one for one. When all other factors such as age, income, number of children and age of youngest child are held constant, there is some reduction in the time devoted to unpaid work. The rate of this reduction for cooking, laundry and cleaning, all other things being equal, is estimated at about 5 and a half hours a week for a woman employed for 40 hours a week.

There is also a question of whether the sex-segregated allocation of tasks changes with women's paid employment. That is, do men take on more indoor tasks and women possibly turn to some of the 'masculine' outdoor tasks and reverse the traditional pattern?

Take, for example, full-time employed married couples with children under fifteen years. A similar pattern of sex segregation is observed as in the population as a whole. Table 4.4 shows that, if anything, segregation is slightly more pronounced when both partners are employed full time. Apparently, full-time employed women in these couples are almost exclusively responsible for laundry, cleaning and most of the cooking and leave the gardening, car and home maintenance to the men. The one exception to the pattern of inflexible segregation is that the men in couples where both adults are employed full time spent more time in the physical care of their own children. Married women's employment has, then, had little impact on role stereotypes in the allocation of unpaid work tasks.

Conclusion

The family, we have shown in this chapter, is a hidden economic sector where the volume of productive work which takes place is equal to the market sector. Yet somehow the household economy, despite its size and significance, has been neglected. The household sector is the double of the market sector or its 'repressed underside' (Beasley 1994). If one were to believe conventional economists, the social arrangements that cater for people's personal lives in households have no value. Inside the hard labour of the family, the next generation is born and raised and the current generation of workers are able to revive themselves for another day of work.

It is clear that the workers with greatest responsibility in the household economy are chosen according to gender. Women's, not men's family responsibilities vary according to their relation to others. The fact that a woman is someone's wife or partner, or mother and/or daughter has an enormous impact on the extent of the domestic work she will do in these different relationships. Men, in contrast, show little variation in the time devoted to domestic responsibilities throughout their life course and various relationships. Upon marriage, men transfer to women practically all the responsibility for cooking, cleaning and laundry. Women's careers, not men's, are interrupted to provide care for young children and the effects of this responsibility last a lifetime. While it might be possible to juggle the extra housework that women gain as their 'bonus' upon marriage and still maintain a career, when children arrive it is extremely difficult to manage a similar juggling act, because the hours devoted to caring for children are so extensive. Men, it seems, benefit from the work of mothers and spouses and only when they are widowers do they seem to assume comparable responsibilities.

Given these facts, the double burden is a very real danger, especially because it seems that husbands and children do not compensate for mothers' new provider role by accepting more responsibility in the home. Thus, we are still waiting for the great leap forward.

This chapter has presented the current facts about the household economy and the division of labour within it. Of course the way the world is now is not as it was in the past or may be in the future. People may feel that, compared to the experience of their grandparents, housework and the raising of children is neither so onerous nor so unequally shared. Ellie Vasta reports that in many Italian-Australian families, second-generation women whose mothers also worked the double shift insist that 'men do help a lot now' (Vasta 1995, p. 159). Similar comments have been made by Australians of all backgrounds.

It is possible that, although families currently exhibit a marked inequality in responsibilities for domestic work, they are in the process of becoming more equal. In the following chapter, we will investigate the idea that families, and especially the sexual division of labour, are changing.

5

At home: the more things change, the more they stay the same[1]

A revolution in family life?

Most observers assume that Australian families are in the midst of some significant change. Some even talk about a 'revolution'—Australians' intimate world turned upside down. Among social scientists, a number of theories have been formulated to explain this revolution. Perhaps the most influential of these theories argue that sources of change are (a) changes in the nature of marriage (the symmetrical family thesis), (b) changes in technology and (c) changes in sex-role attitudes ('lagged adaptation'). In this chapter, we will examine each of these theories. For the first time in the discussion of these changes, extensive use will be made of hard data about changes in time spent in housework, childcare and shopping.

The symmetrical family

This description of the emerging family form was first developed by Young and Wilmott (1973) in their book of the same name, and has been enthusiastically promoted in recent times. They claim that the symmetrical family is a culmination of processes which began with the dissolution of the pre-industrial family. The pre-industrial family was the basic unit of production. Most individuals depended for their existence upon membership in a household which was broadly self-sustaining. Most of what they ate was produced by themselves for this purpose and the same applied to clothes, shelter and fuel.

There was a strict segregation of tasks by sex and anything less than conformity with the gender appropriate behaviour brought a swift response from other villagers. Although there was an obvious connection between all tasks performed and the economic security and wellbeing of the household, men were considered more important than women. The patriarch expected and received the submission of wife and children and, where they could be afforded, servants. The brutal exercise of this power was tempered by a common recognition of the economic value of wives and children (Shorter 1977, pp. 66, 74).

Gradually the factory replaced the cottage as the centre of industry and the family lost its productive function, or so the story goes. Men became breadwinners. This converted wives and children from economic assets (helpmeets) to economic dependants, and indeed from the husbands' point of view, into liabilities. As Young & Wilmott say: 'The husband could exercise his power more despotically even than in the past because, if they had children, the wife needed him more than he needed her. The marriage was asymmetrical' (Young and Wilmott 1973, pp. 75–6).

Husbands enforced obedience through beatings and by control of the purse. Evidence of this asymmetrical relationship is provided by husbands' choosing to spend the greater portion of their meagre wages on themselves, rather than upon their dependants, and having the pick of the paltry supply of protein at mealtimes. Home was a place where husbands slept and ate: they sought company and entertainment away from home in the ale house and the betting shop.

The origins of the contemporary symmetrical family are said to lie in the middle classes of the late nineteenth century. They were affluent enough for wives to be an ornament to a man's property as well as part of it. The comfortable private haven they established weakened what remained of dependence upon extended kin. 'The man's physical comfort, the general good order of the house and the sense of spiritual contentment gained from a consciousness of his own goodness depended upon the circumspection and the affection with which he treated his wife'

(Young & Wilmott 1973, p. 84). This provided fertile soil for the first feminist movement which began altering the legal status of women, making them persons in their own right and not purely the property of their husbands.

According to this view, once a man's wife had become his companion, and he began to centre leisure upon his home, then it became a natural extension that he should 'help' his wife with her tasks. Thus from the middle of the nineteenth century the rigid segregation of domestic roles began to be undermined. When wives are also employed, they shed their former dependence on their husbands. The organising principle of this new form of domestic organisation is equality:

> All major decisions should be made together, and even in minor household matters they should help one another as much as possible. This norm is carried out in practice. In their division of labour, many tasks were shared or interchangeable. The husband often did the cooking and sometimes the washing and ironing. The wife did the gardening and often the household repairs as well. Much of their leisure time was spent together, and they shared similar interests in politics, music, literature, and in entertainment. (Bott in Young & Wilmott 1973, p. 30)

There is some initial plausibility and appeal to this theory. Certainly women are steadily increasing their labour force participation. As we have seen, the Time Use Survey data also show that men are indeed doing a proportion of tasks around the house that might formerly have been considered unmasculine. According to the 1983 Australian Values Study, 87 per cent of Australians agree with the statement: 'men and women should share household jobs' (Holmstrom 1985, p. 4).

There are three kinds of evidence which would be necessary to make this theory a convincing description of the direction of change for future households. First, evidence is required that men and women are increasingly competing on equal terms in the labour market. If the symmetrical family theory is correct, then one would expect that women's labour force participation rates, the distribution of female employees across industry and occupation, and women's earnings, would increasingly resemble the pattern for men. We will consider these issues in detail in Chapter 7.

Second, the theory requires that women's increasing responsibilities for breadwinning translate into greater independence and equality within the household. On the basis of this vision of the future, one would expect, too, that the distribution of assets and income within the home would be divided equitably.

Third, there would need to be evidence that there is a trend for men to begin to share the burdens of home-making and child-rearing. We will be considering these claims in detail in this chapter.

There has been spectacular growth in the rates of women's participation in paid employment over the last few decades, most dramatically in the participation rates of married women. Nevertheless, in 1990, female employees still earned about two-thirds of average male weekly earnings (National Women's Consultative Council 1990). Women are heavily concentrated in particular industries and occupations. This labour market segregation has proved to be remarkably durable.

Moreover, there is considerable evidence to suggest that women's lower rewards for paid work have their roots in the gender-specific burdens of the household division of labour. Women's work histories are more likely to be discontinuous (McDonald 1986, pp. 76–7; Young 1990, pp. 17–18). As we saw in Chapter 4, time use studies have found significantly less time is devoted to paid employment by women with young children, while at this same point in the life course men's time in paid work usually increases.

While any observer is forced to acknowledge the profound changes in women's labour force participation, it does not necessarily follow that the cash income translates into a greater power for wives vis-a-vis their husbands. Too often this is simply assumed by proponents of the symmetrical family view. An English study of dual-earner households found that although women's earnings contributed very substantially towards the primary needs of the household and underpinned the household's achieved standards of living, a gendered division of responsibility also developed in expenditure patterns. This mimicked the traditional domestic division of labour, 'with men responsible for the roof over the family's head and women for the day-to-day shopping and childcare' (Brannen & Moss 1987, p. 84).

Meredith Edwards' study of the financial arrangements of 50 Australian families found that nine of the 30 wives contributing more than 30 per cent of family income had no control over family finances. Edwards found that wives tended to manage the family finances when it was a case of stretching to make ends met. Three wives as opposed to fourteen husbands received a set amount of personal spending money, and the husbands' expenditure on themselves was almost always greater than that of their wives (Edwards 1984, pp. 133–51). Details of internal distribution of household income are discussed in more detail in Chapter 8.

The major stumbling block of the symmetrical family thesis has been to demonstrate that where wives do paid work, husbands do correspondingly more domestic work. In the light of the material presented in Chapter 4, there can be little doubt that comparisons between husbands whose partners are employed and husbands whose partners are non-employed reveal little by way of compensating domestic labour.

The fall-back position has been to argue that the symmetrical division of labour is the result of a slow evolutionary change and hence changes over time are more appropriate than straight comparison of subpopulations. Before we begin a detailed examination of this issue (aided by data from Australian surveys covering the period 1974 to 1992), we will continue our overview of theories of domestic change.

The technological conception of the future

As soon as the issue of change in the time devoted to housework is raised, there is a tendency for people to slip into discussions about domestic appliances. Before we realise it we have moved from the issue of change in social arrangements to the properties of microwave ovens, dishwashers, and a possible future of computer-controlled 'smart houses' (Berg 1994). In this view, the domestic division of labour will ultimately disappear because machines will first make domestic tasks significantly less burdensome, before abolishing them altogether through automation or robotisation. It has even been proposed that women's increased labour force participation is the direct result of their being left with nothing to do (Cowan 1985, pp. 181–2).

And at first glance this theory appears not only to be plausible but also well supported by solid evidence. For most of this century households in developed countries have been subject to intense technological change. Houses have been electrified, running water connected, toilets and bathrooms moved inside. Gas or electric ranges have replaced fuel stoves, and the washboard, mangle and copper have been displaced by washing machines. Irons no longer need to be warmed on the stove and even produce their own steam. Some synthetic fabrics require no ironing at all. Carpets are vacuumed and not beaten. There are small electric motors to help us open cans, chop and blend food, sharpen knives, remove facial hair and even clean teeth.

Iiris Niemi, in a recent survey of changing patterns of time use, noted a tendency for time spent on housework to diminish in a number of industrialised countries (Niemi 1988, p. 15). The relevant Australian data will be presented in this chapter, but it also shows a small change in the average time devoted to housework.

So what could be wrong with this vision? Obviously not its assumption of technological change in the home. However, despite this veritable 'industrial revolution in the home' (Cowan 1985, p. 181), the aggregate time spent by *full-time* housewives in housework has not significantly altered. Joann Vanek (1974) compared the findings of the US time use studies of housework from the 1920s to the late 1960s. She argued that the aggregate time spent on housework by non-employed women had changed little (52–55 hours per week) since the 1920s. Vanek also found that employed women devoted about half as much time (26 hours per week) to housework. As women's participation in paid work has increased, time spent in housework has fallen. Since the households of non-employed housewives were, if anything, better equipped than the households of employed wives, these findings cannot be explained by the diffusion of technology.

There has been, according to Vanek, some redistribution of time between individual tasks. While time spent in food preparation and home care has diminished, time spent on shopping and managerial tasks, and time spent on 'family care' has increased despite the trend to smaller families. The introduction of domestic technology often has counter-intuitive effects. Time spent on laundry, for example, has increased, despite the introduction of running water, detergents, automatic appliances and wash and wear fabrics (Vanek 1974, p. 117).

But these difficulties highlight a deeper flaw in reasoning behind the technological conception of the future—its faulty understanding of the relationship between technology and the division of labour. It ascribes to technology unwarranted, if not mystical, abilities to change the course of history. The model for this mechanisation and automation of the household is the shift from cottage handicrafts to mechanised factories during the industrial revolution. This shift, which first occurred in the textile industry, was thought to be a consequence of the impracticality of anything but a centralised power source. The difficulty is, however, that the first factories used more or less the same technology as the handweavers in their cottages (Clawson 1980; Marglin 1982). What was distinctive about the factory was the gathering together of craftworkers, and the new forms of cooperation and division of labour instituted between them. Far from being the result of some mechanical imperative, this detailed division of labour reduced the process of production to very simple elements. Given the factory owner's desire for control of output and profit (Bruland 1985), it was a short step to substitute machinery for the repetitive and highly simplified motions of the worker. Ernst Mandel, in describing the industrial revolution, notes that whereas in 1859 it took 1437 hours to produce 100 pairs of men's shoes manually, in 1895 it only took 153 hours to manufacture them using machines (Mandel 1968, p. 138).

Precisely because it is blind to the significance of the social organisation of labour, the technological conception of the future also fails to see that the development of domestic technology has been fundamentally different. The housewife is the last of the unspecialised workers—the contemporary housewife is a 'veritable jane-of-all-trades' at a time when the jacks-of-all-trades have disappeared (Cowan 1985, p. 198). The introduction of machinery into the household has, if anything, reduced the number of specialised workers since it has been associated with the demise of the domestic servant, the cook, the laundress, the nanny and the chambermaid.

Furthermore, because the handicraft nature of housework has basically remained unaltered by machines, attempts to apply the logic of Taylorist 'scientific management' to the household have foundered on the nature of this form of organisation. Not only is production small scale but, most importantly, in this sphere of work 'the manager and the worker are the same person'. This has meant that the 'whole point of Taylor's management science—to concentrate planning and intellectual skills in management specialists—is necessarily lost in the one-woman kitchen' (Ehrenreich & English 1979, p. 147). Intensification of household labour takes the opposite path to industry, eschewing cooperative application of labour, specialisation, and increase in scale, and instead imposing a pattern of simultaneous time use. In this sense the automatic washing machine is the prototype modern domestic appliance because its 'set and forget' quality allows the operator to undertake another activity while the washing cycle is completed. Busy time use diaries have many short activity episodes as a result of the pursuit of simultaneous tasks, all of which interrupt each other, so that eventually the whole day assumes the texture of a continuous interruption. It is interesting to note in this connection the close link between the contemporary concept of time and the commodification of human labour (Thompson 1967), and the absence of this concept in the domestic setting.

There has been little division of labour between households, indeed they may be even more homogeneous since World War II than they were before it (Cowan 1983, pp. 196–201). While some tasks have been abandoned and mass-produced substitutes purchased in the marketplace, most notably canned and frozen goods substituting for home preserves, others have been handed back to the household. Housewives have paid for the time they saved in preserving in the growth of time spent shopping, particularly in travelling to shopping. As Cowan aptly puts it:

> Several million American women cook supper each night in several million separate homes over several million separate stoves—a specter which should be sufficient to drive any rational technocrat into the loony bin . . . Out there in the land of household work there are small industrial plants which sit idle for the better part of every working day; there are expensive pieces of highly mechanised equipment which only get used once or twice a month; there are consumption

units which weekly trundle out to their markets to buy 8 ounces of this nonperishable product and 12 ounces of that one . . . (Cowan 1979, p. 59)

It is ironic that such emphasis should be put on technology when the data clearly indicate that so much of the growth of housework this century derives from care of children. This is true not only for cross-sectional comparisons, as we have seen in Chapter 4, but also historically. In this area, the effect of technology has been peripheral and the effect of cultural changes profound (Reiger 1985; Ehrenreich & English 1979).

In summary, one could say that the evidence tends to support the idea that it is the form of social organisation of the family, particularly ideas about how women should relate to men and the cultural value placed on the care of children, that will determine the shape of the household technology of the future. Without the requisite changes in these forms it is unlikely that domestic technology will liberate women or men from housework.

Changes in sex-role attitudes ('lagged adaptation')

There is a sociological theory of change that emphasises the development of new attitudes. This theory conceives of social structures as composed of roles. Roles, as the name suggests, are scripted parts for the social actors to play. The script consists of social expectations which define the relationship between any one role and other roles. These expectations are backed by both positive and negative social sanctions. Conformity to roles brings approval and transgression brings opprobrium of varying ferocity depending on the significance of the non-conforming behaviour.

Roles are learnt. Generally role theorists favour a model of learning based on contemporary theories of 'operant conditioning'. In contrast to the theories of Freud, operant conditioning reduces learning to stimulus–response relationships. In classical conditioning theory, dogs are 'taught' to salivate at the ringing of a bell. This learning is achieved by associating the new stimulus—the sound of the bell—with an existing stimulus—food, so that the response of salivating in the presence of food is transferred to the sound of the bell.

This 'learnt response'˙ must be reinforced by rewards (the food).

Operant conditioning, while making minimal assumptions about the interior states of organisms, assumes that organisms learn by making new responses which are either rewarded (positively reinforced) or not (negatively reinforced). It is a short step to conceive of human learning, especially socialisation, as a process of operant conditioning where the rewards are provided by the agents of socialisation (parents in the early years) in the form of approval and disapproval.

The infant may learn to make new responses, which elicit approval or disapproval, on the basis of imitation. This leads to the conception of the importance of 'role models' and an emphasis on the expectations implicit in educational materials, television shows and so on.

While role theory generates no explanation of historical change, it nevertheless acknowledges that change occurs. Change is introduced externally and must initially take the form of deviance (transgression of expectations). In order for this deviance to continue and eventually supplant earlier expectations, there needs to be a favourable climate of evaluation. Changes in attitude are indications of this shifting evaluative climate.

Recently, Jonathan Gershuny and co-workers have extended an idea developed in 1956 by Alva Myrdal and Vera Klein. The kernel of this idea is that married women's increasing participation in paid work creates strains in the pattern of gender relations within the family. Myrdal and Klein pointed to the recent emergence of the 'career woman'. 'The acceptance of this feminine role', say Myrdal and Klein, 'shows that it is possible for women to envisage the idea of work outside the home as a career for life without any feeling of self-denial or resignation'. They note that this ideal 'has until recently been held by women only—and a very limited number of women at that'; and 'men have, for a variety of reasons, found it difficult to adjust themselves to the idea of a wife who so radically differs from their mothers'. Faced with two other 'ideal' feminine roles—'hard-working housewife' and 'lady of the salon', young women with a paid job still envisage marriage and motherhood as the centre of their ambitions. As Myrdal and Klein argue, 'in this case, there is an unusually long time lag between the emergence of new realities and relationships and the acceptance of their full implications' (Myrdal & Klein 1968, pp. 8–9).

Gershuny and his collaborators claim that key studies of the distribution of household work (especially Hochschild 1989), are based on people who were in their twenties or thirties in the late 1970s and early 1980s, that is people born and raised before the 'second wave' of feminism. The implication of this statement is that these respondents were socialised in the traditional sexual division of labour where men are breadwinners and women are home-makers. Gershuny et al. approvingly quote Hochschild's description of individuals' subjective 'gender strategies', noting that:

> to pursue a gender strategy, a man draws on his ideas about manhood and womanhood, beliefs that are forged in early childhood and thus anchored to deep emotions. He makes a connection between how he thinks about his manhood, what he feels about it and what he does. It works the same way for a woman. (quoted in Gershuny et al. 1994, p. 154)

Since the generation observed by Hochschild (and most others) 'must confront and uproot the emotionally charged gender images of their childhood', Gershuny, Goodwin and Jones argue that the process of translating women's greater breadwinning into more sex equity in unpaid work will only occur after a considerable delay. They note 'we could only expect it [sex equity] to be complete and painless once all adult members of households were themselves children in households with unchallenged egalitarian models—that is, a very long time into the future' (p. 155).

According to Gershuny et al. the process of lagged adaptation works like this:

> The couple's division of domestic labour is a function of both early socialisation of the partners, and of the wife's employment experience. Starting from an initial position where the husband is generally employed and the wife generally non-employed, both partners may have a traditional gender strategy and the household has a stable and non-conflictual division of domestic labour. Women start to enter the workforce, and the influences of socialisation and employment experience at first push in different directions: socialisation

tending to maintain traditional female responsibilities for unpaid work, but the time-use consequences of the women's job leading to a 'dual burden', and hence pressure for change . . . [These] changed patterns of domestic labour, must then feed back into the socialisation of the next generation. Children growing up in an environment that has been affected by these processes observe patterns of behaviour which are less encouraging to the traditional gender strategies: their socialisation will encourage more of them towards interme- diate or egalitarian gender strategies. So in this generation the influences of early socialisation and the consequences of work experience will be less opposed, and change in the domestic division of labour will thus be easier. (Gershuny et al. 1994, pp. 186–7)

Regardless of the slow pace of progress, Gershuny and his co-workers are confident that 'this process of confronting and uprooting inherited gender ideologies is really taking place' (Gershuny et al. 1994,. p. 155). Using data from the Social Change and Economic Life Initiative (which studied six local markets in the United Kingdom), as well as time use information from the United Kingdom and seven other coun- tries, they produce evidence which shows an association between wife's paid employment, including her employment history and husband's greater share of domestic duties. They declare that this evidence may 'reflect some historical shift in the actual domestic division of labour' (Gershuny et al. 1994, p. 175).

They find that the actual domestic division of labour is influenced by couples' current attitudes to the sexual division of labour and their reports of their parents' attitudes on this issue. If a couple accepts traditional attitudes, favouring the pattern of husband as provider and wife as home-maker, then their actual division of labour is likely to reflect these views. Such couples, moreover, are likely to have had parents who practised a traditional domestic division of labour. Conversely, couples with egalitarian views about the domestic division of labour are more likely to actually share housework, childcare and shopping and to have had parents who did the same (Gershuny et al. 1994, pp. 168–75). Gershuny and his col- leagues comment that parents' influence on the domestic division of labour parallels the 'well-known influence of parents' party political allegiance on current behaviour and attitudes' (Gershuny et al. 1994, p. 174).

But they are still puzzled. 'If couples do indeed adapt their distributions of domestic work to compensate for changes in the pattern of paid work', they ask, 'why is it that husbands of full-time employed women still do substantially smaller proportions of the total work of the household?' (Gershuny et al. 1994, p. 179). Gershuny and his collaborators answer their own question by arguing that 'households adapt gradually'. Until the wife enters paid employment, the household pays little attention to the domestic division of labour. Employment puts considerable pressure on the wife and draws the attention of the household to this problem and the household acts to reduce this pressure. However, couples may still find it difficult to establish an equitable partnership because the couple may 'not know how much work they themselves do, they may similarly not know how much work their partners do' and therefore 'the adaptation of the division of domestic labour may, in short, lag behind the change in paid work pattern' (Gershuny et al. 1994, p. 180).

At first sight it would seem that Gershuny and his colleagues have assembled a persuasive case for the process of lagged adaptation. 'Our findings so far are themselves at the least consistent with the "adaptive partnership" view' (Gershuny et al. 1994, p. 174). First, there is the evidence that husbands' proportion of unpaid work rises (slowly) in response to wives' length of attachment to the labour force. Second, they document 'a regular steady, and substantial growth in men's proportional contribution to the unpaid work total' rising from 25 per cent in the 1960s, through 30 per cent in the 1970s and reaching 40 per cent by the 1980s, a period when women's labour force participation has increased steadily. Third, they point to evidence of greater parity in 'total work' load (the sum of paid and unpaid loads). Finally, there is the evidence that current attitudes are connected to parents' behaviour and that both influence the actual domestic division of labour. These points, they argue, 'add up to a clear case for a model of gradual and lagged adaptation' and 'while women's paid work increases faster than the men's substitution of unpaid for paid work, ... nevertheless a process of adaptation is clearly under way' (Gershuny et al. 1994, pp. 183–5).

The lagged adaptation thesis is open to a number of objections. First is the problem of the relationship between attitudes and behaviour. As we shall see in Chapter 6, there may be little association between attitudes and behaviour. Even where a correlation between a particular set of attitudes and relevant set of behaviour can be established, it is far more difficult to show that attitudes cause the behaviour. It is equally plausible to argue that attitudes change to justify the actions currently being taken.

A second problem has to do with tracing change by following movements in the relative shares of unpaid work done by husbands and wives (Gershuny et al. 1994, p. 151). In this chapter we will try to demonstrate that most of the adaptation to women's increasing labour force participation has come from women reducing the time they spend in unpaid work. Even without any absolute change in the time men devote to unpaid work their 'contribution' to the total of household time devoted to such tasks increases if their wife reduces her time. In other words, unless husbands actually reduce the time they spend in domestic labour, it appears as though they are compensating for wives' greater paid work demands. These changes in the relative shares of unpaid work are more often the result of women's adaptation, while men remain rigidly inflexible.

Using parity of total work time (the sum of time spent in paid and unpaid work) as a measure of equity in the partnership between husband and wife also has a major flaw. As the authors freely admit, parity in total work time can be achieved by one partner specialising in paid work while the other specialises in unpaid work (Gershuny et al. 1994, p. 188). Such an arrangement hardly addresses the social disadvantages accruing to the partner who specialises in unpaid work that were canvassed in the last chapter.

A third criticism relates to the interpretation of comparisons between husbands of full-time employed wives and those whose wives work part time or are not in paid employment. The problem here is that the comparison is most useful when these categories of husbands are alike in every respect except the employment status of the wives. This condition is not met.

In all probability we are being asked to compare the behaviour of young men in childless couples to men with dependent children who are at the peak of their labour force commitment and consequently working long hours. The effects of wives' employment would be easier to gauge if the comparison controlled for the effects of husbands' hours of paid work, age, the number of children and so on.

Finally, establishing that a process of lagged adaptation is taking place requires longitudinal data, that is information gained from tracking couples as they change over time. As the authors acknowledge such information has not been available to them and they have been obliged to use less than perfect data for their purposes. However, there is one form of analysis—cohort analysis—which is appropriate in the situation and which is used in this chapter. Cohort analysis follows information about people born in a particular year. For example someone who was twenty years of age in 1974 is 33 years of age in 1987 and 38 years in 1992. Perhaps more importantly, this kind of analysis makes it possible to examine the issue of generational change.

The theory of lagged adaptation explicitly predicts that each successive generation of men will move further towards equality in domestic labour. The authors of this theory argue that the generations before 1970 will be capable of only small adjustments over their lifetimes, whereas the young adults of the 1990s, born to mothers in the vanguard of these changes, will exhibit not only egalitarian attitudes and altered gender identities, but will also manifest more egalitarian behaviour. In the remainder of this chapter we will see that behaviour of this cohort gives little indication of this prediction being fulfilled.

Change, gender and the domestic division of labour

Few social changes since World War II have aroused such emotion as the large-scale entry of women, especially married women, into the paid labour force. The economic historian Graeme Snooks sees change in women's labour force participation as the fulcrum of 'the new economic revolution', comparable in scale and significance to the industrial revolution of the late eighteenth and early nineteenth centuries

(Snooks 1994, pp. 14–15). The American sociologist Arlie Hochschild links the revolution in women's earnings to the problem of the division of domestic labour. Hochschild, among many others, believes that the traditional family division of labour by gender, which assigned men and women into the segregated roles of breadwinner and home-maker, is now a thing of the past. She argues that women are now sharing the breadwinning but coined the phrase 'the stalled revolution'[2] to describe men's failure to participate more fully in the activities of home-making (Hochschild 1989). There is even a literature about how it is possible to successfully re-negotiate the domestic division of labour (see for example, Goodnow & Bowes 1994).

All of this discussion, however, has run ahead of information available. Until now the only information we have had about the domestic division of labour in Australia has been cross-sectional information, that is information about one point in time (Bittman 1992; Baxter 1993; ABS 1994c; ABS 1994d). Cross-sectional material does not tell us about change over time; to talk confidently about change we need information from at least two points in time.

A new data resource—an opportunity to study change

The Australian Bureau of Statistics' 1992 Time Use Survey[3] provides a major new information resource. By analysing this national 1992 Time Use Survey in conjunction with earlier, non-national time use surveys collected in 1987 and 1974, it is possible to study just how the amount of time women and men allocate to unpaid work has changed.

This offers an unparalleled opportunity to study change at the heart of family households; it is the sociological equivalent of the Hubble telescope. Unfortunately, like the Hubble it needs some correction to its lens before a clear picture can be obtained. Neither the 1987 nor 1974 time use surveys were national in scope and they were collected in autumn and winter. So when we compare the raw results of these surveys we are never sure whether to attribute any differences to regional variation, seasonal variation or to historical change. To alleviate these difficulties, a method of mathematically standardising the three surveys is used so that all results are given in terms of Sydney, May–June.[4]

Another fact which also needs to be taken into account when considering change is that over time the composition of the population alters. The population of Australia has become significantly older in the past two decades. We know that age affects time use, so that average times in 1992 are affected by the larger proportion of older people in the population. By comparing change within narrow age bands we remove this source of confusion. A by-product of the division of the population into five-year age bands is that it opens the way for analysing generational change by following groups born in the same year through each successive survey. This kind of analysis is called an analysis by birth cohorts.

Types of change

Any observable change may be the compound of three logically distinct effects (Gershuny & Brice 1994, p. 34). The simplest kind of effect is the change that occurs within a single generation over a person's life course: the kind of change we examined in Chapter 4 (that is, leave the parental home, marry, become a parent, divorce, become a single parent, see all one's children leave home, retire, and become a widow/er). As we saw, all these life course changes have major effects on the time spent in unpaid work, especially for women.

Another kind of change results from a cohort effect. When a whole group enters a particular state (being born, starting work, getting married) at the same historical point there is a relatively constant effect on each member of this cohort. Birth cohort effects, or generational change, occur when a daughter's experience is different from her mother's experience at a similar life course stage.

The third type of change can be called a 'period effect', which occurs when all respondents, irrespective of life course phase or generation, experience a change because of the year of the survey. An example of a person's savings illustrates the distinction between these three effects. A person's savings may vary with their position in the life course, so that those who are mid-career and have no children find it easier to save. There may be a cohort effect on the savings: those who

Table 5.1 Changes in mean time use Sydney, May–June 1987–92 (hours per week)

	Difference: males	Difference: females
Domestic activities	0.00	−2.57***
Housework	*−0.35*	*−2.92****
Garden/lawn/pool and pets	*−0.35*	*−0.23*
Home maintenance and car care	*0.23*	*0.35***
Miscellaneous domestic work	*0.93*	*−0.23*
Childcare/minding	0.35*	1.40*
Purchasing goods and services	−0.12	0.35

Notes: * When age is held constant, the difference in mean times is statistically significant at $p < .005$ ** significant at $p < .005$, *** significant at $p < .001$
Source: Bittman 1995 p. 10

reached their prime earning years during the Great Depression, for example, may have saved less. In a period of economic recession everyone, regardless of life course phase or generation, may save less—this is a period effect.

Gender, segregation and change: mean time spent in unpaid work, 1987–1992

Table 5.1 sets out the change in the mean time devoted to household productive activities, with the national data standardised to Sydney, May–June, 1987–92.

With all the breathless talk about 'revolutionary' changes in gender roles, the extent of this gender segregation and the pace of change might be considered disappointing. Were a revolution underway, it might have been expected that the distinction between 'women's tasks' and 'men's tasks' would have become more blurred and that the rate at which this change was occurring would be more rapid. Men's share of indoor housework tasks is still small. Perhaps even more surprising is the fact that most of the improvement in the relative shares of housework comes from women reducing their time spent in unpaid work rather than men increasing the time devoted to housework, childcare or shopping, as we anticipated in Chapter 4.

The most conspicuous change has come in women's housework time, which in five years has fallen by nearly 3 hours per week. Any convergence in men's and women's time spent in housework since 1987 has occurred because women are behaving more like men rather than because 'new' men have discovered how fulfilling housework can be.

The next largest change is the increase in women's time spent in childcare. Smaller increases are found (0.35 hours per week) in the average time men devote to childcare and child minding and in the average time women devote to home maintenance and car care.

Only the increase in time spent with children is a bilateral change, that is, where there is a change in the average time for both sexes. Otherwise the apparent dilution of sexual segregation comes from changes in the average activity time of women. Apparent changes in the time devoted to other activities are not statistically significant and could be due to sampling error. A closer, more disaggregated examination of the data reveals that the main arenas of change are cooking, laundry, home maintenance and car care, childcare and travel to shopping. We will examine each of these in turn.

Indoors

Our examination of time use survey data shown in Figure 5.1, reveals that the phrase 'stalled revolution' describes, more aptly than Hochschild could have imagined, the changes in men's domestic participation over the last two decades. Practically all the changes in men's cooking time occurred in the thirteen years between the 1974 and the 1987 surveys, and there is no evidence of significant change since that time. This finding of 'no change' between 1987 and 1992 not only applies to the aggregate of all men, it also applies to men in each and every age group. A physicist contemplating the rate of change in men's cooking time would describe it as moving from acceleration to deceleration. In lay language we would describe the change as moving from 'slow motion' (Segal 1990) to 'no motion'.

Most of the change which has occurred is as a result of the period effect rather than a cohort effect. Consistent with the pattern of 'stalled revolution', there was a tendency for men, regardless of their birth date, to increase their cooking time in the 1970s and early 1980s, but by the early 1990s, this enthusiasm for more cooking had exhausted itself. For all men

Figure 5.1 Men's time spent in cooking—1974, 1987 and 1992 (hours per week)

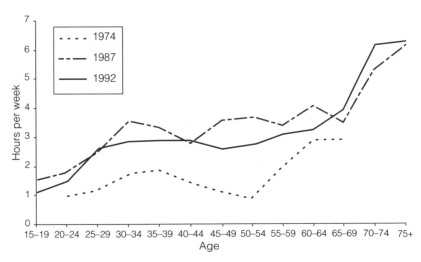

Source: Bittman 1995, p. 14

born in 1953 or earlier there has been an increase in their cooking time between 1974 and 1987 and either no increase or a very small decrease over the five years from 1987 to 1992. Among those born in 1953 or after the picture is considerably more complicated. It shows traces of generational change together with evidence of changes in the timing of life course transitions. Cohorts born after 1957 exhibit average cooking times that are slightly higher than those born before 1952 at similar ages. However, in more recent times there is little evidence that successive age cohorts have started from a higher plane. Indeed, the 'stalled revolution' is nowhere more evident than in the failure of younger men, raised in 'post-feminist' households, to increase their contribution to cooking.

In contrast to the changes in men's time spent in cooking, the change in the time that women devote to cooking has never been more evident than in the last few years. Strangely, while much has been written about women's expectations of men, the actual change in women's own domestic labour times, independent of the actions of men, has gone largely unnoticed.

Not only is the magnitude of the change in women's cooking time the largest of any of the changes in housework

Figure 5.2 Women's time spent in cooking—1974, 1987 and 1992 (hours per week)

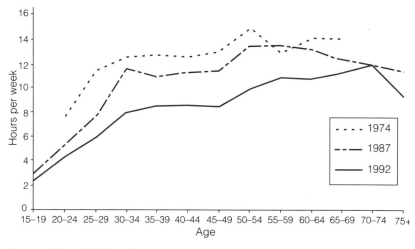

Source: Bittman 1995, p. 16

activities, but the rate of change has increased markedly. While no one can confidently claim there have been changes among the very old and very young women, across the broad span of adult women's life course, from the ages of 25 to 64, there has been a significant (p < .01) reduction in women's cooking time in the last five years. The magnitude of this change has been least (1 hour 37 minutes per week) among those aged 25 to 29 and greatest among 30- to 34-year-olds and 50- to 54-year-olds (3 hours 31 minutes and 3 hours 37 minutes per week respectively). For those aged 35 to 49 and 55 to 64 average cooking time has reduced by around 2 hours 19 minutes between 1987 and 1992. With the exception of 25- to 29- and 35- to 39-year-olds, the extent of the reduction that occurred in the five years between 1987 and 1992 is double that which occurred in the thirteen years between 1974 and 1987. In what, historically speaking, is a short period of time, both the order of magnitude and the acceleration of these changes in women's cooking behaviour has been astounding.

The analysis of the age cohorts of women uncovers a pattern which is in many respects the opposite to that for men. Once again it is the result of a combination of period effects, cohort effects and life course effects. For women born in 1947 or earlier, there appears to be no pattern of generational change but a powerful period effect in the last five years. Among these women there has been a sharp fall in cooking time over the period from 1987 to 1992. For those born in 1948 or after there may have been a generational change. After this date each younger cohort has a lower cooking time than women of an equivalent age in the cohort before.

The pattern is complicated by the effects of a dramatic rise in high school retention rates among women, greater participation in tertiary education and a continuing pattern of postponed marriage and child-bearing (ABS 1994d, pp. 32, 90). Participation in tertiary studies lowers women's time spent in housework, and marriage increases it (ABS 1994d, pp. 121–2; ABS 1994c, p. 58; Bittman 1992, pp. 53–5, 108–9). All these factors contribute to a lower average cooking time for those born after 1947. Nevertheless there is continuing evidence that young women at home spend more time in cooking than their brothers (ABS 1994d, p. 124; Bittman 1992, pp. 38, 108–11). If sex roles were predicted to dissolve among the younger generation it has not happened yet, not even among groups whose mothers were young enough to have their child-rearing practices influenced by feminism. On the other hand, in more recent times it makes much more sense to talk about all women's behavioural rejection of the idea that 'their place is in the kitchen'.

A number of possible explanations spring to mind for this steep decline in the time women (and therefore households in aggregate) devote to cooking. Perhaps the most commonly offered explanation is the diffusion of the microwave. There were practically no households with microwave ovens in 1974 but by 1987 more than one-third of Australian households owned a microwave. Between 1987 and 1992 the proportion of households owning a microwave oven had risen to more than two-thirds (Ironmonger, personal communication).

Presumably the microwave oven yields greatest time savings in cooking when combined with food purchases tailored to maximise the advantages of the appliance. Analysis of the patterns of expenditure on food items shows there has also been a shift away from raw foods towards convenience foods, which require minimal preparation (Bittman & Mathur 1994). Of course, many of these food purchases would reduce meal preparation time even using conventional food preparation appliances. This observation immediately raises the possibility that food preparation time can be reduced by greater resort to the market, in effect substituting the labour of an employee for that of the unpaid 'home-maker'.

Certainly the same analysis of expenditure shows that households are increasing their outlay on restaurants, take-away meals and school lunches (Bittman & Mathur 1994). All these tendencies may take place within the framework of changing norms about what constitutes nutritious home cook-ing, or who decides what should be eaten. This would not only license the purchase of more convenient foods, especially if stir-fry and prepared vegetarian pasta are seen as healthier than home-made suet pudding, but also alters the idea that a mother's love and devotion is judged by the hours she commits to preparing home-cooking. Perhaps the modern parent can demonstrate affection by sanctioning the purchase of a pizza!

One of the most astonishing findings reported in Vanek's celebrated article 'Time Spent in Housework' (Vanek 1974) was her claim that the time spent in laundry had not decreased since the late 1920s. Of all the domestic tasks to which technology has been applied, the tasks of laundry, ironing and clothes care would seem to be the ones where appliances had 'saved' most labour. Most people would agree with the American social historian Ruth Schwartz Cowan when she says, 'The change from the laundry tub to the washing machine is no less profound than the change from the hand loom to the power loom' (Cowan 1985, p. 186). Vanek's finding that women's time spent in laundry initially increased slightly in response to each technological innovation associated with laundry produced widespread shock and disbelief (Vanek 1974, p. 17). 'Surely', the doubters maintained, 'a "set and forget" automatic washing machine saves washing time when com-pared to the copper, wash board and wringer?' Much ink has been expended in seeking to refute Vanek's findings or to explain them (Gershuny & Robinson 1988; Cowan 1985). Whatever the reason, laundry, ironing and clothes care con-tinue to occupy a substantial proportion of time.

In the period 1974–1992, there has been little technological innovation. Washing machines were found in over 90 per cent of households in Victoria between 1980–87 and the proportion of these machines that were not automatic was small. Eight per cent more Victorian households acquired clothes dryers between 1980 and 1987 (Lewis, Nicholas & Smith 1987, p. 27; ESV & GFCV 1987). Paradoxically, with such little technological innovation, the recent Australian evidence shows that there have been some significant changes in the time spent in laundry. Once again these changes are largely due to significant alteration of women's activity patterns and not from the appearance of a new generation of eager 'laundry capable' men.

Indeed, laundry remains the touchstone of sexual segregation. In 1992, as in 1974, it is a task predominantly done by women. While men's laundry time has increased since 1974 it is still a small fraction of the average time spent by women. Life course events have remarkably little influence on the quantity of time men invest in laundry. The exceptional influences seem to be independence, employment and loss of spouse. There is as yet no detectable cohort or period effect for men's time spent on laundry.

Before 1987 it was not unusual for women to spend between five or even six hours a week in laundry activities. In recent times, however, there has been a reduction in women's laundry time of up to two hours a week. The contraction of the amount of time women spend in the laundry has been the second major reason for the decrease in their overall housework time. Across all age groups, women's time spent in laundry activities has decreased by 44 minutes per week.

The distribution of women's mean laundry time by age shows a progressive diminution of an early adult peak, which was quite a pronounced feature of women's laundry pattern in 1974. The general pattern of the change over the eighteen-year period has been for this peak to be to be postponed and lowered until ultimately becoming a plateau stretching from the mid-thirties into the fifties. This pattern of decline is consistent with the reduction in family size and the postponement of child-bearing that has occurred between 1974 to 1992. The effects of this change in women's laundry time are quite

Figure 5.3 Women's time spent in laundry—1974, 1987 and 1992 (hours per week)

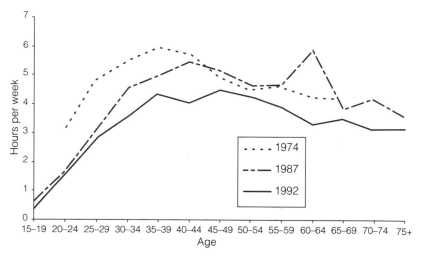

Source: Bittman 1995, p. 20

age-specific. The largest changes occurred first among 20- to 29-year-old women (a reduction of more than a third between 1974 and 1987) and then among 30- to 44-year-old women (a reduction of 10–20 per cent between 1987 and 1992).

The analysis of women's laundry time by birth cohorts shows a pronounced period effect, which leads to a decline in laundry time from 1987 for women of all ages. This has been combined with a gradual generational shift which compresses the age range of peak laundry times. This is evident at both ends of the age distribution, with each younger cohort taking more years to reach the age of peak laundry time and beginning their descent from peak times at a younger age. Those born between 1948–52, for example, did less laundry than older cohorts in their twenties, reached their peak of laundry activity in their thirties, and their laundry time declined in their forties. The mothers of these women did a similar amount of laundry into their fifties. In many ways the generational changes, which mirror the shrinking of child-rearing years, are more easily comprehended than the period effect. It is difficult to think of an event or an innovation in the years 1987–1992 which should so affect the time of women of all ages.

Figure 5.4 Men's and women's time spent in home maintenance and car care—1987, 1992 (hours per week)

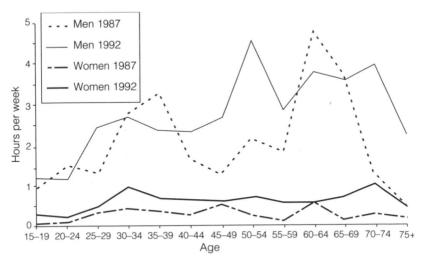

Source: Bittman 1995, p. 26

Perhaps the most promising explanation of this change is a normative one, that is, one that relies on more relaxed standards of clothes care. If one were to believe fashion magazines, the 1980s was a period of change in fabric preferences, with a return to natural fibres, especially cotton and linen, both fabrics that crush and require ironing. This development was perhaps offset by the growing popularity of tracksuits as all-purpose leisure wear, especially for children. All this may have been accompanied by normative changes about presentability, that is by changing ideas about what garments and manchester required ironing. Current standards about ironing and presentability will be presented in the next chapter.

Outdoors

Home maintenance and car care remain the most 'masculine' of all the household productive activities. On average men spend much more time in this category of activities than on laundry and cleaning put together. As we saw, the amount of time women devote to this category is small and readily comparable to the time that men devote to laundry. However, there has been a statistically significant (p < .005) 21 minutes per week increase in the time women devote to home maintenance and car care activities. This seems to be spread thinly across all ages, since the only significant (p < .05) age specific increase is among women aged 70–74 years. By 1992 the gender gap in home maintenance and car care had narrowed to 1 hour 36 minutes per week.

Does this reflect a 'feminisation' of do-it-yourself home renovations? This is certainly an area where individuals can substitute their own labour for market services (especially painting). Such substitution could either be the product of households' response to recession or it could be part of a long-term change. If advertising material is taken as an index of social attitudes, the increase in the depiction of women pushing lawn mowers and painting walls may indicate a process of feminisation. The cohort analysis of potential changes here is not particularly revealing because the mean time for these activities is small and the measurement error is relatively large.

Shopping

Shopping is one of the less sex-segregated unpaid work activities, as we saw in the previous chapter. Although men's mean shopping time is only two-thirds the mean shopping time of women, men spend more time on average in this unpaid work activity than any other. Australian men spend almost as much time (4 hours 5 minutes per week), on average, in shopping as they do in cooking, laundry and cleaning combined (4 hours 19 minutes per week). The time men devote to shopping is also greater than that spent either in yard work (3 hours 30 minutes per week) or in home maintenance and car care (2 hours 20 minutes per week) (ABS 1994c, p. 8).

Some have argued that while the aggregate time spent in housework has remained constant since the 1920s, the allocation of time between the tasks has changed (Vanek 1974; Cowan 1985). 'Perhaps trends affecting the household', Vanek suggests, 'have created as much work as they have saved' (Vanek 1974, p. 117). Although preparing food and meal clean-up continues to be the most time-consuming aspect of housework, it has fallen tangibly over the century. However, Vanek found a compensatory increase in the time spent in shopping and household managerial tasks. On the basis of this reasoning we would expect that, because food preparation time has fallen so dramatically, time spent shopping would have markedly increased. This study did not find an overall rise in time spent shopping but it did find that an increasing proportion of shopping time is spent travelling to and from the shopping complexes and finding parking space.

Childcare

A small but nevertheless startling change has been the increase in time that Australian parents, both female and male, devote to the care of their children. The modest increase in childcare time is startling because (a) it goes against the predominant trend to reduce time spent in unpaid work and (b) it flies in the face of the expectation of increasing neglect of children that has been created through the mass media.

The decline in fertility, the growth in women's paid employment and the increasing use of childcare might all be expected to lead to reduced time spent in childcare. The views of commentators such as Penelope Leach (1994), who suggests that working mothers must be careful to ensure that they give their children their personal attention, seem to be based on the assumption that parents' time spent with their children is shrinking. Yet data from the time use surveys suggest that women's time spent in childcare has risen for all age groups by an average of 1 hour 24 minutes per week between 1987 and 1992.

Almost all of this increase comes from more time devoted to the physical care and minding of children and not from increased time spent in teaching or playing with children. The age at which mean childcare time peaks for women has shifted from 25–29 years in 1974 to 30–34 years in 1992. An analysis of cohort effects shows that it is especially among women born after 1948 that the tendency to spend more time with young children has taken hold.

Among fathers the story is similar with a small but measurable increase of up to 2 hours per week in the five years between 1987 and 1992. Again almost all of the change comes from extra time devoted to the physical care and minding of children. There are clear indications that men are taking greater fatherly interest in very young children. In 1974 the age at which men's engagement with their children was most demanding was 35–39 years whereas in 1992 it was 30–34—a full five years earlier. There is a progressive trend among men born after World War II for higher childcare times among younger men, although this appears to be reversing among men born after 1959, revealing the effects of postponed child-bearing.

Given this unambiguous evidence of rising time devoted to fewer children it becomes tempting to think of the concerns about children being deprived of their parents' attention as moral panic, perhaps occasioned by the large-scale entry of women into the labour force. Another explanation suggested by this paradox is that, perhaps under the influence of popular psychology, expectations about how much time parents should devote to their children are rising faster than the actual increase in parental care. According to overseas studies, time spent in childcare has been increasing for most of this century and these Australian findings should not come as a surprise (Vanek 1974, p. 117).

Conclusion

This analysis of time use surveys shows that there have been some important changes in the organisation of domestic labour. These changes are not those anticipated or debated in most discussion about these issues. On the whole, the process has been one of women 'doing it for themselves', reducing the time spent in the kitchen and in laundry, ironing and clothes care. Women are also increasing their activity in the traditionally masculine area of home maintenance and car care. These changes have been purchased at the cost of increased 'travel to shopping' time. The only area where men have increased their activity has been in childcare. Both mothers and fathers are spending more time with their children.

It seems justifiable to conclude that many of the theories that have been used to aid our understanding of change in the domestic division of labour need some significant revision. Perhaps policy-makers also need to concentrate on the supports that will allow women to have domestic responsibilities similar to those of men rather than expect that men will assume the domestic burdens of women.

6

Pseudomutuality: the disjunction between domestic inequality and the ideal of equality

The theme of this book is that the family has a double life. In one respect, family life is simply what people living in families do. But as we saw in Chapter 2, whatever people do in families is oriented by their beliefs about how family life should be. People's experience of families is therefore conditioned by these beliefs and their attachment to them. In Chapter 3, we saw how families were seen as vehicles of self-fulfilment, as ways of achieving meaningful intimacy. This intimacy in turn rested on the apparent decay of pre-industrial patriarchy and the rise of a notional equality between men and women.

This chapter is organised around a discussion of what happens when the normative beliefs about the family are in stark contradiction to people's actual behaviour. We shall see that this tension can be resolved in a myriad of unexpected, even mysterious ways.

The paradox

Domestic work remains women's responsibility even though most people believe that housework should be shared. The 1983 Australian Values Study showed that 87 per cent of Australians agree with the statement 'Men and women should share the household jobs' (Holmstrom 1985, p. 4). By contrast, the extensive evidence presented in Chapter 4 shows that in 1992, women's labour accounted for 70 per cent of the total time devoted to unpaid work. This suggests a trend emerging with an overt disjunction between belief and action. In other words, while there is now a broad subscription to the 'new' values of gender equity, there is continued evidence that in the practical world of family life, the 'traditional' sexual division of labour in the allocation of time and tasks has shown virtually no change at all. How is a phenomenon of simultaneous conformity to the discourse of egalitarian values *and* to these inequitable practices to be explained? This quite obvious disjunction between attitudes and practice cannot be accounted for by the classical theory of sex roles (Connell 1987; Connell 1995) and 'lagged adaptation' examined in Chapter 5.

This chapter suggests the discrepancy may be described as 'pseudomutuality' (Wynne et al. 1967). Pseudomutuality is a faked or a false complementarity, where the actor may deny or conceal evidence of non-mutuality in order to maintain a sense of reciprocal fulfilment. Pseudomutuality, as we explored in Chapter 3, is a characteristically 'modern' form of the exercise of domestic power. Modern couples subscribe to some version of romantic love which in principle must involve an intimate relation between equals. No man should order his wife about today—they make shared decisions. Yet all the evidence suggests that despite the rise of intimacy, women are still waiting on men and taking the major responsibility for bringing up children. Pseudomutuality is a possible way of explaining how the hurt and exasperation is shuffled off the family stage in various ways.

Studying how couples respond

Our analysis of the Australian Bureau of Statistics Time Use surveys, presented earlier, shows that marriage, children and retirement—in short, the most important life course phases—have the greatest influence on time spent in unpaid work. So, in trying to investigate the problem of a disjunction or contradiction between people's beliefs and their actions, a study was carried out in 1991.[1] The study selected 130 heterosexual couples (by using a quota sampling technique) in three life course phases.[2] The life course phases of interest were couples with no dependent children living at home; couples with pre-school children; and couples with dependent children of school age living at home. The sample was small scale because of the emphasis on how the subjects interpreted and responded to discrepancies.

The couples surveyed were asked to describe the allocation of 28 household tasks in their household, and also to nominate the main users of a number of typical household appliances and market services. Their responses to a well-established sex-role attitude scale and the background characteristics of the respondents were also collected.[3] Each partner was also interviewed separately on issues such as cooking, cleaning and laundry, childcare, shopping, gardening, and house, pool and car maintenance. Each respondent was asked about their view of the domestic division of labour, what kinds of decision-making took place, estimates of their own activity and their partner's activity, the history of the relationship, and financial control and management in the household.

How strongly do Australians believe in domestic equality?

Results from the survey of Sydney couples show a general commitment to egalitarian attitudes, although women in the sample are more strongly committed than men.[4]

While men's attitudes are less egalitarian than their partners', they nevertheless broadly accept egalitarian values. Only one in eight men gave any support for the 'traditional sexual division of labour', while the overwhelming majority (81 per cent) expressed overall support for an 'egalitarian' position. Most responses were skewed towards the egalitarian end of the scale. The chief difference is between the strength of views, since a smaller proportion of men than women are likely to 'strongly agree' with the statement affirming egalitarian values.

Extraordinarily high support was found for the statement 'If both husband and wife work, they should share equally in the housework and childcare', with 97 per cent of women and 89 per cent of men expressing agreement.[5] Only 9 (mostly men) of our 130 respondents disagreed, and not a single person strongly disagreed. The more unconditional statement

'Men should do an equal amount of work in the home' also called forth an astonishing level of agreement, with almost as many men (86 per cent) expressing agreement as women (88 per cent), and only two respondents (both men) strongly disagreeing.

Elsie Holmstrom, in a study of opinion surveys to 1985, reported on this egalitarian shift in Australia (Holmstrom 1985, p. 3). She found that by 1983 most Australians (80 per cent of women and 71 per cent of men) opposed the traditional view that 'women should take care of running their homes and leave running the country to men' (Holmstrom 1985, p. 4). Comparing data from the 1984 and 1990 National Social Science Survey, the number of Australians who believe that 'All in all, the emotional life of the family suffers when the woman has a full-time career' has fallen by more than 16 per cent over this relatively short period of time, regardless of gender.

An important point that Holmstrom makes, in relation to attitudes about the family suffering if women work full time, is that whenever the words 'family' and 'children' are included, we may be conflating two separate opinions. One concerns the sexual division of labour between adults and the other, the relative importance of the life of paid work and the life of family and children. In a poll taken by the *Age* in November 1981, respondents were presented with the statement 'A woman should put her husband and children ahead of her own career', and a clear majority (67 per cent of men, 75 per cent of women) agreed. But when, after some mild criticism, the pollsters re-ran the item asking whether a man should put wife and family ahead of career, a similar majority agreed (men 78 per cent, women 68 per cent), indicating that 'most women and men regard their spouse and children to be more important than their career' (Holmstrom 1985, pp. 9–10).

In the Sydney couples survey, the answers showed strong support for women's labour market participation. The statement 'There should be satisfactory childcare facilities so that women can take jobs outside the home' stimulated 94 per cent of women and 89 per cent of men in our sample to agree, and only one woman and one man disagreed strongly. Few thought 'It would be better for Australian society if fewer women worked in jobs outside the home', while 89 per cent of women and 85 per cent of men disagreed that women's (paid) labour force participation threatened the Australian social fabric. Male respondents were less enthusiastic about the statement 'Ideally there should be as many women as men in important positions in government and business', with over one-quarter disagreeing, and over one-third disagreeing with 'A woman who works can be just as good a mother as one who does not'. Women's assent to these propositions remained at high levels (above 88 per cent). In summary, women and men subscribed to the same attitudes but women held their views more strongly.

Most textbooks argue that the scaling of attitudes is bedevilled by the problem of social acceptability, that is, respondents may misrepresent their 'true' attitudes in their earnest desire to win the social approval of their interviewer (see for example, Madge 1967, p. 244). In this instance, however, such 'interviewer bias' could be a methodological advantage, a direct source of data in itself, since conformity with what the respondent presumes to be the socially acceptable answers makes the prevailing social norms more plainly visible. Clearly the respondents think the answers about sex roles that are acceptable to the community should be 'egalitarian', and they are eager to show the interviewer their knowledge of community standards. The advantage in this survey lay in the fact that attitudes were only a part of the investigation: the other part was about their actual practices. Similarly, although the sample consisted of people who were more highly educated than the population at large, this had the unexpected advantage that egalitarian attitudes are more prevalent among the highly educated (Baxter et al. 1990). We could assume, therefore, that these people would be the most likely to imbue their daily practice with egalitarian attitudes.

Disjunction between belief and action

Eighty-nine per cent of men in the Sydney couples study agreed that 'they should share equally in the housework and childcare' if both husband and wife were in paid employment. By contrast, as shown in Chapter 4, the amount of time husbands spent in housework and childcare did not increase in response to their spouses' increase in paid work. A husband whose partner had a full-time job in the paid workforce in fact did no more than a man whose spouse did no paid work. Acceptance of the unconditional statement 'Men should do an equal amount of work in the home' is similarly gainsaid in practice. The only stage in the life course when men do spend comparable time to women in unpaid work at home, is when they are retired and living alone. In all partnered phases of the life course, the average time men spent in these activities was less than half that of their partners.

The overwhelming majority of people in the Sydney couples survey agreed that 'A woman who works can be just as good a mother as one who does not', and rejected the statement 'It is better for the family if the husband is the principal breadwinner outside the home and the wife has primary responsibility for the home and children'—but it is still women who interrupt their careers to provide full-time care for pre-school age children (Young 1990, pp. 17–26, 110). Moreover, as we have seen in Chapters 4 and 5, household tasks remain highly segregated by gender.

As noted previously, analysis of time use based on ABS data revealed that educational attainment of neither women nor men affected time spent in housework, childcare and shopping. When marital status, number and age of children, age, labour force characteristics, wage rates and occupation are held constant, education has no systematic effect on the time women and men spend in unpaid work (Bittman 1991, pp. 36–7, 72). In the Sydney couples study, high educational attainment increased the likelihood of the individual endorsing strong egalitarian values (see also Baxter et al. 1990, pp. 58–9).

Some serious policy implications flow from these findings about education, attitudes and practice. Education, it would seem, is highly effective in changing the attitudes of both women and men. Attitudes among the young and highly educated (as in this sample) are beginning to approach the egalitarian limit of the scaling instrument.[6] It is doubtful if the attitudes of the highly educated can get much more egalitarian. If not from general cultural changes, the community education campaigns have succeeded in achieving their goal of changing attitudes first, especially among the young. This has not, however, led to a congruent redistribution of domestic labour, or substantially altered the inhibiting effects of family responsibilities on women's labour market participation. What *has* changed is the normative context of the exercise of power, so that the subordination of women in the family occurs in the moral framework of an *apparent* commitment to equality, that is, within a framework of pseudomutuality.

How people make sense of the disjunction

There are two opposing assumptions that we can make in trying to interpret this disjunction, and consequently, two approaches to the dilemma of the relation between social change and the clash of values and actions. Let us look at the logic of each of these positions in turn.

Assume domestic instability: social change and the theory of 'behavioural lag'

Sex-role theory assumes that people's behaviour is motivated by learnt normative expectations (Baxter et al. 1990; Percucci et al. 1978; Pleck 1985). A disjunction between egalitarian expectations and behaviour, clearly our problem here, is therefore a difficulty for sex-role theory. The gap between beliefs and behaviour is often explained away as a mere by-product of rapid change. Eventually, according to this view, behaviour will catch up with these new attitudes, but just at the moment behaviour is merely lagging behind attitudes because of the sheer pace of the change.

The theory of behavioural lag requires us to recognise that we are in a period of rapid change: there is a bewildering reformulation of expectations and roles, hence respondents' discourses and practices are unstable and temporarily out of synchronisation. Changes in discourse have run ahead of changes in practices. Such a theory of 'behavioural lag' is often associated with the prediction that the family will in time become more 'symmetrical' (Young & Wilmott 1973). There are, however, a number of difficulties associated with this interpretation.

First, there is the implicit (unstated) theory of social change and the ambiguities concerning the direction of causality in the association between changing cultural values and changing cultural practices. In Ogburn's (1950) famous theory of 'cultural lag', the introduction of new technology is the force that imposes changes in practices, and cultural values eventually adjust. In other words, 'machines make history' in that new practices are apparently 'caused' by new technology and lead to changes in values. It is, however, far more plausible to argue that domestic technology is shaped by cultural values than the other way around (see Chapter 5, and Wajcman 1991).

Second, there is substantial evidence of stability in domestic labour despite apparently dramatic changes in household technology. In 1974 Joann Vanek argued that, among non-employed housewives, time spent in housework had not diminished since the late 1920s. As we have already discussed, the time may stay constant and the segregation remain similar even though the tasks have changed (Vanek 1974). Since that time controversy has raged about the applicability of what some of the specialists call the 'constancy of housework thesis' (Robinson 1980; Gershuny & Robinson 1988). Evidence for any redistribution of labour from women to men is patchy and changes are weak, slow and relatively recent, as we saw previously.

More important perhaps, are the political implications of the 'behavioural lag' explanation. Since Australia became a signatory to the ILO Convention 156, 'Equal Opportunities and Equal Treatment for Men and Women Workers with Family Responsibilities', the argument revolves around the disadvantageous effects of family *responsibilities*. But the privately negotiated solution being promoted through community education programs must be credible rather than merely economically expedient. This requires evidence that men are indeed moving beyond merely 'helping' their partners, to accepting responsibility for major tasks and thus that education programs will just speed up this process. No proponents of 'behavioural lag' have produced such an analysis as yet.

The small increase in men's domestic work times between 1974 to 1987 had slowed to a complete halt by 1992. There is a persistent pattern showing that, on average, Australian males will transfer indoor housework to their wives upon marriage, and devote any increase in time spent on domestic tasks to traditionally 'masculine' outdoor activities. The appearance of infant children will produce a strengthening of the pattern of sex segregation in domestic tasks. It would certainly be safe to say that the influence of 'new men' as committed fathers and mutual supporters had not subverted the traditional sexual division of labour in Australia by 1992, despite more than a decade of fanfare for the contrary position (Russell 1983; Wheelock 1990).

Assume domestic stability: the management of contradiction

If the domestic division of labour has, therefore, been stable throughout this century, other explanations for discrepancies in beliefs and practices must be sought. Festinger and his colleagues proposed that when strongly held beliefs are contradicted by evidence, people experience what they called 'cognitive dissonance'. Cognitive dissonance is psychologically awkward, even painful, because cherished beliefs are constantly subverted by contrary experiences. This leads to a tendency to reduce cognitive dissonance. One response to the problem of cognitive dissonance is where people manage to maintain their conviction by effectively blinding themselves to disconfirmation, that is, by reducing, concealing, or denying the all too obvious contradictions (Festinger et al. 1964, p. 26). Berk and Shih's (1980) study of domestic labour indicates the presence of such dissonance. They found high levels of agreement among couples regarding who 'generally' (meaning more than 50 per cent of the time) did sex-stereotyped tasks. Comparing one partner's report of their own contribution to a particular task with the other partner's, Berk and Shih found that on the whole, they tended to reduce the subjective difference by 'underestimating' each other's contribution.

Three ways of pinpointing the possible discrepancies were devised for the Sydney study. First, respondents were asked to say whether 28 separate tasks were performed by: self always; self mostly; self and partner equally; partner mostly; partner always; neither. Second, respondents were asked to indicate whether each of 27 household appliances 'were mostly used' by themselves, their partner or both. Finally, in a semi-structured interview,[7] respondents were asked to estimate the time they spent on housework, childcare, shopping, gardening, and house and car maintenance, and to give an estimate of the time they thought their partner spent in these same activities.

Table 6.1 Reported use of appliances

Agreed: wife uses mostly	Agreed: husband uses mostly	Agreed: mostly used by both	Disputed: husband says both, wife says wife mostly*
Auto-oven	Computer	Fridge	Stove
Food processor	Power saw	Microwave	Clothes line
Auto-washer	Electric drill	Freezer	Dishwasher
Twin tub	Power sander	Waste disposal	
Dryer	Screwdriver	Coffee-maker	
Iron	Lawnmower	Camera	
Vacuum		Hi-fi	
Sewing machine		TV	
		Video	

Note: * Husbands thought the video camera was mostly used by both husband *and* wife, whereas wives thought this appliance was mostly used by the husband.
Source: Bittman & Lovejoy 1993

Wives believed that they did a higher proportion of tasks ('always' or 'mostly') than their partners were willing to concede.[8] Although husbands maintained they did about half as many tasks ('always/mostly') as their spouse, their wives thought they did significantly less.[9] Husbands also consistently claimed that more tasks were 'shared equally' than did their wives.[10] A similar pattern is found for the proportions of tasks women and men say they do 'always'.

Overall, after we balance the effects of women's extreme underestimation of their own and their partners' time spent on domestic tasks (to which we will return later in this chapter), the figures point to a tendency among men to view their contribution to the domestic division of labour as being closer to equity than their partners report. This is a pattern consistent with the expectations established by cognitive dissonance theory.

A strikingly similar pattern is found in the way the use of domestic appliances is described by the Sydney couples. The list of appliances set out in Table 6.1 indicates the level of agreement between the majority of both husbands and wives on who mostly uses these items.

The list of 'feminine' appliances, used mostly by women, are found in the kitchen, the laundry and the sewing room. The highest levels of agreement were found for 'masculine' appliances, chiefly power tools which are rarely handled by women who live with men. Perhaps the segregation in the use of these appliances helps create the male domain of the shed, as an area of retreat for the 'sheddy'. Computers are more ambiguously 'masculine', being used by men in ten of the twenty couples that had one at home, with 6 agreed cases of sharing, and in the remaining cases being used mostly by women. Apart from the disputed case of the video camera, there was strong agreement that most 'leisure' appliances— television, video recorder, hi-fi and camera—were shared.

The pattern of agreement about husbands' involvement with kitchen appliances, indicates a role of 'helping' with food handling—that is, food storage (refrigerator, freezer), heating (microwave) and drink preparation (coffee-maker)—rather than meal preparation. Husbands dispute this minor role and view themselves as contributing equally, as indicated by their characterisation of the stove and dishwasher as appliances that are in neither husband's nor wife's domain. The dispute over the use of the clothes line is slightly comic, given men's notorious avoidance of laundry. This impression is reinforced by the fact that six husbands claimed the family possessed a twin-tub washing machine or clothes dryer that their wives denied any knowledge of, and one individual even claimed that he 'mostly' used both!

As with the perception of participation in household tasks, the reports on the use of domestic technology conform with the pattern of reducing cognitive dissonance. The men maintain their sense of an equal contribution to domestic labour through a tendency to maximise the size and importance of their own contribution and to minimise the contribution of their spouse. Selective attention, selective perception and selective ignorance are all mechanisms which aid men in the accomplishment of this feat.

Compared with women's estimates of their own weekly time spent in domestic tasks, the majority of husbands underestimated their wives' weekly hours. In contrast, women's estimates of their partners' time spent in domestic tasks were more often in agreement with those of their partners.

This draws our attention to a series of more profound difficulties. Up to now, we have been exploring the proposition that men's underestimation of their partners' domestic activity reduces the cognitive dissonance that stems from their endorsement of egalitarian domestic values and their inequitable participation in practice. However, men estimate that their partners spend 19 hours 20 minutes per week on domestic work. Their estimation of their own activity is 10 hours 10 minutes per week. In other words, even after men have underestimated the activity of their partner and possibly even overstated their own hours they are still, by their own admission, on average doing half as much as their partners despite their own commitment to fairly sharing all domestic tasks. Clearly, if men are to reach cognitive consonance they have some further work to do.

Women, as was shown previously, are more committed than men to an equal division of domestic labour between the sexes. The theory of cognitive dissonance suggests, therefore, that such a disparity of effort should be even *more* uncomfortable for women. The estimate of hours spent in domestic work for women in our sample was an average of 20 hours 54 minutes. The expected time for a comparable group of women, calculated from the more accurate ABS time use data, was an average of 33 hours 57 minutes per week (ABS 1994c). In other words, this suggests that women substantially underestimated the time they spent in domestic work. These women also underestimated the time spent by their male partners in domestic work, by a margin of 11.4 hours. The net effect on women of these twin inaccuracies is to reduce their subjective impression of the extent of the average gap between men's and women's hours,[11] while they retain an awareness that men's contribution is proportionately about half the size of their own. In other words, although the subjective estimate of hours is wrong, the estimate of the proportion of time spent by each sex is roughly correct. Cognitive dissonance theory does not lead us to anticipate this result because it would predict that women would use selective perceptions to make the proportions more equal.

Typology of strategies for minimising inequality through re-interpretation

Nevertheless, the desire for a faultless family life can be propped up in numerous other ways. Alternative methods of reducing the subjective experience of a gap between upholding the value of equality while flouting it in practice, hinge upon strategies of redefining the scope of the value of 'equality' and its content (see also Dempsey 1992). An analysis of the Sydney couples survey suggests that such strategies include defining equality as mutual participation; displacing the issue to the terrain of differing standards; insisting that equality should be interpreted in a framework of difference (using optimisation of preferences, competence or both); and trivialisation. Each of these strategies is discussed in more detail below. Each of these strategies is made more effective by the power of 'nondecision-making'. This implicit form of power arises from the ability of one partner to keep discussion of an issue off the agenda, making it difficult for the other to raise key issues for decision-making. It appears that no power is exercised because no overt decisions are ever made (Bachrach & Baratz 1962).

The strategy of claiming mutual participation

The strategy of defining equality as mutual participation involves simultaneously inflating the significance of occasional participation and denying that the regular burden of responsibility for the execution of domestic tasks such as childcare and housework remains with a partner. In other words, this is the familiar defence that the distinction between 'helping' with household tasks and 'accepting responsibility' is intended to unmask. Material presented from the Sydney couples survey on whether tasks were done by one partner 'always', 'mostly' or 'equally', conforms to this pattern. One man says he does vacuuming, washing up, and takes out the garbage. His female partner says they both do these tasks 'equally' adding that he does these things 'maybe once a month' (vacuuming) and 'once or twice a week if I'm lucky' (washing up). He agrees 'Men should do an equal amount of work around the house'. The woman in another couple who said they shared equally, commented that when her husband helped her with the cooking, she only saved about half the time he spent cooking, because she had to instruct him about which utensils to use, how high to set the oven, assemble the ingredients, and interpret the recipes for him.

The strategy of claiming differing standards

Evoking the issue of differing standards is probably the most commonly used justification for unequal labour. It is used by men to explain why they are still contributing equally even though their partner is doing most of the work. And it is used by women to explain why they end up doing (what they consider as) their husbands' tasks for them.

Men claim that their standards of hygiene, cleanliness and order are considerably below those of their spouse. In mild form this is stated as a difference in taste but more typically, differing thresholds are reconfigured by men as the virtue of superior tolerance. The idea here is to claim that women have a low threshold to levels of dirt and untidiness, or even that they are too fussy. This creates the subject position of the misunderstood and unappreciated husband who may eventually be totally discouraged from participation. One respondent said he 'keeps clear' of the laundry 'because they [women] always find fault with the way you do it'. His partner said 'I think his laundry ended up being done with mine for the simple fact that his clothes would start to walk 'cause he'd never do it'. However, they seemed to agree that tasks are left by one until the other is irked enough to perform. The male respondent said, 'usually she breaks before I do: I can tolerate a mess a lot longer'. Another woman commented that although her partner would put a lot of emphasis on the fact that he cleans up, she does not agree that this is proper cleaning, as she 'has to go and do it again'.

Different ways of talking about things establish definite speaking positions, both for the person doing the speaking and the person being spoken about. The discourse of the 'superior tolerance' of the male subject implies a view of the other as the opposite, establishing a female subject position of irrational, fetishist intolerance to dirt and disorder. While women may accept the male attribution of pathological personal characteristics and describe themselves in this way, this does not automatically mean that women uphold men's standards as rational. A female respondent says of her partner: 'He thinks I'm obsessive . . . He lives in a pile of shit'.

Women often assert that 'men's superior tolerance' verges on blindness, because they are so insensitive to the demands of household and children. 'He does not notice that things need doing', said one woman, 'that's the difference'. 'His standards are not as high . . . he doesn't care . . . it's easier and quicker to do it myself' claimed one woman resignedly. One male respondent adopted the subject position of inattentive man with lower standards: 'I don't know who does the bathroom, she must do it, 'cause I don't'.

A digression on gender differences in standards of housework

Since the claim that there is a gender difference in standards of housework is so frequently encountered, in 1995 a subsequent study was undertaken to investigate these issues (Bittman & Pixley 1995).[12] Standards are a set of normative expectations about how things *should* be done. The survey aimed to measure a variety of dimensions of normative expectations about housework—(1) the level of tolerance for tasks left undone, or how frequently respondents think tasks should be done; (2) the level of awareness of the intricacies of the task—their stock of knowledge and skills or 'competence' in labour process terms and, (3) which tasks are considered to be most important or urgent.

In relation to norms about frequency, respondents were asked to decide how often a particular task should be performed. For example, respondents were asked 'When do you think the washing up should be done?' and were then offered various set responses: 'straight after a meal', 'at the end of the day', the 'next day', 'when you run out of dishes' or 'at another time'. Similar questions were posed about cleaning floors, the bathroom, oven, fridge and curtains; vacuuming under the furniture; making beds; doing the laundry, and ironing; and preparing fresh home-cooked meals. It is presumed that frequency is related to the stringency of standards, so that the greater the frequency with which it is believed that a task should be performed, the more demanding the expectations (standards). Conversely, responses indicating that tasks need only be performed at the lengthiest intervals reveal the lowest standards.

With regard to awareness, competence and skill, respondents were asked to comment on some statements of laundry folk wisdom by indicating the level of agreement on a 5-point

Table 6.2 Women's and men's views on the frequency with which tasks should be performed

Task	Frequency	% Women	% Men
Fresh, home-cooked meals	At least once daily	87.5	84.7
Wash up	After meal	75.0	69.3
	At least at the end of the day	92.4	85.3
Vacuum	At least once a week	92.9	85.3
Clean behind furniture	At least once a month	57.0	63.0
Clean bathroom	At least once a week	94.4	77.3
Clean oven	At least every 3–6 months	88.6	87.7
Laundry	At least once a week	82.4	77.0
Iron	At least once a week	54.8	44.6
	When you want to wear	39.2	33.2
Make bed	Daily	83.3	76.0
Clean curtains	2–6 months	39.4	37.1
	Once a year	40.1	35.7
Clean fridge	At least once a month	71.4	47.3

Source: Bittman & Pixley 1995

scale. In the time-honoured tradition of scaling, some items are reversed to inhibit automatic responses. Respondents were invited to comment on the following statements.—(1)'These days clothing standards and modern washing machines mean that very little can go wrong in the wash'; (2) 'Before doing the laundry it is important to check the pockets of clothes for tissues'; (3) 'When doing the laundry, it is important that towels and other items are washed separately'; (4) 'Handwashing anything today is unnecessary'; (5) 'When doing the laundry, it is important that light colours and dark colours are washed separately'.

Respondents were also asked to rate the completion of each housework task on a four-point scale ranging from 'very important' to 'not important at all'. To provide more depth in the analysis of expectations about items that should be ironed, respondents were asked to indicate which specific items on a list of common household articles they thought it was 'important to iron'. The articles, which were designed to represent various levels of presumed fastidiousness included trousers, shirts, skirts, jackets, tablecloths, pillowslips, bedsheets, and even socks.

The most striking finding of the study is the level of consensus about the frequency with which tasks should be performed. The results are shown in Table 6.2.

Broadly speaking, Sydneysiders, regardless of sex, have very similar ideas about how often tasks should be done. Generally, both men and women share very high expectations. Thus, more than three-quarters of respondents believe that beds should be made daily, at least one meal a day should be a fresh home-cooked meal, and more than two-thirds believe the dishes should be done promptly after this meal. Less than 3 per cent of respondents think the washing up can wait until the next day. A high proportion, over three-quarters of respondents, expect that the laundry should be done, the bathroom should be cleaned and the carpets should be vacuumed at least weekly. And it mustn't be a superficial clean either, since more than 60 per cent of the men and 57 per cent of the women think you ought to move the furniture at least once a month when you vacuum. In any interpretation of this survey, it is important to remember that respondents are *not* answering about their own behaviour, they are merely indicating how often they think these tasks *should* be done. This does not imply that they think that they should have to do them personally. Indeed it may well be the case that they are describing standards they expect someone else to fulfil— that is, husbands may be describing the housework standards they expect from a wife; flatmates might be outlining the expectations they have of each other; prospective in-laws may be prescribing what they expect of a prospective daughter-in-law; or the very same prospective daughter-in-law might be second-guessing what her future in-laws might demand of her. Nevertheless there can be little doubt that these 'standards' are both high and widely shared.

There is some evidence that men were less aware of what could go wrong in the wash. The vast majority of women (83.3 per cent) disagreed or strongly disagreed with the statement that handwashing anything these days is unneces-sary, whereas fewer men disagreed or strongly disagreed (65.3 per cent) and a higher proportion of men were uncertain.[13] Men were more likely than women to have no opinion on such questions as whether anything can go wrong in the wash these days, and were even less opinionated about whether towels should be washed separately. Women were far more adamant that one should check pockets for tissues before washing, perhaps having experienced more than once in a

Table 6.3 Importance of task by gender

As ranked by women	Very important %	As ranked by men	Very important %
1 Do dishes	63	1 Do dishes	48
2 Clean bathroom	58	2 Do laundry	36
3 Home meals	48	3 Home meals	32
3 Do laundry	48	3 Clean bathroom	32
4 Make bed	33	4 Make bed	24
5 Vacuum clean	30	5 Vacuum clean	20
6 Clean fridge	26	6 Ironing	19
7 Ironing	22	7 Clean fridge	14
8 Oven	13	8 Oven	9
9 Curtains	6	9 Curtains	1

Source: Bittman & Pixley 1995

lifetime the irritation of having to remove minute flecks of tissue paper from every garment. Bearing in mind the high degree of sex segregation in the performance of laundry tasks, the marginal differences between men and women in normative standards about how often laundry needs to be done, could hardly be the explanation for why actual measured participation is so clearly assigned according to gender. Whereas 42 per cent of women, compared with 28 per cent of men, strongly agree that whites and colours should not be mixed in the wash, 23 per cent of men, compared with 13 per cent of women, deny the importance of separating them.

Table 6.3 compares the numbers of men and women who ranked tasks as 'very important'. In general women are more likely than men to rate the performance of tasks as 'very important' but there is a great similarity in men's and women's ranking of tasks. The chief divergence is confined to women's higher overall rating of regular cleaning of the bathroom and the fridge.

Richard Glover gave an amusing account of the different meanings associated with cleaning the bathroom when he described his efforts in the *Sydney Morning Herald*, 2 December 1995. After admitting that nobody likes doing boring jobs such as the bathroom, he somehow found himself becoming involved in the job. 'There are some grey bits in the grouting which I get off with a scratchy pad . . . Then there's the toilet, which to be cleaned properly needs the whole seat assembly unscrewed and removed, which I find pretty easy, especially using my battery drill, fitted with its screw-driver attachments . . .' There he is found, 'hunched over my toolbox—the bathroom a disaster, the taps on the floor, the toilet disassembled—wearing my toolbelt and, in order to use the acid, my full-face safety breathing apparatus. "I can't believe," said [his partner] Jocasta, genuinely aghast, "the way you've managed to turn the ultimately ordinary job into a show-off bloke's job."' In response, '"Well, I don't know who's been trying to clean this bathroom for the past ten years," I said, rather gamely, "but they haven't been doing a very thorough job." A week later . . . [he says], I now can see this comment was a mistake' (Glover 1995).

Despite men's actual low participation in laundry tasks, they share women's high ironing standards. More than 90 per cent of men believe it is important to iron trousers (and 93 per cent of women agree). Strangely, fewer men (75 per cent) than women (91 per cent) thought it important to iron skirts. Only 44 per cent of men, compared with 71 per cent of women, thought it important to iron jackets. These results may reflect men's lack of experience in ironing for the whole household rather than men's lower standards. In general, however, men and women both seem to be quite fastidious about what they would like to see ironed. About half of both men and women thought it important to iron T-shirts. Rather fewer men than women considered that tablecloths were important to iron. A significant fraction of people (over one-third) thought ironing pillowslips was important, while 13 per cent of men and 10 per cent of women also iron bedsheets. Practically everybody completely dismissed the idea that one would ever iron socks. Even so, if people actually did what they said was important to do, both women *and* men would be ironing fairly often.

In his book, *In the Shadow of the Silent Majorities*, Jean Baudrillard develops the term hyperconformity to describe an 'uncontrollable', 'excessive', 'ever-escalating' conformity with social injunctions (Baudrillard 1983, pp. 46–7). Our results do show that when asked, many people subscribe to remarkably high household standards which are, one might say, unrealistically high—or even a 'simulation'. People do not seem prepared to admit to interviewers anything but a high level of fastidiousness. The numbers prepared to suggest their standards were truly 'slack' were very low. Both men and women seem to have listened to every 'injunction' about hygiene, cleanliness and possibly fashion (Cowan 1983; Hoy 1995; Reiger 1985). Minor gender differences in standards that were revealed at the margins were, we also argue, more related to folk skills, ordinary experience and simple avoidance, rather than to differing standards of housework.

The strategy of defending equality in a framework of difference

Returning to strategies used to alleviate cognitive dissonance in our survey of couples in Sydney, one strategy not yet explored is that of redefining equality within a framework of difference. Some couples argue that equality is a question of parity. Parity or reciprocity, it is suggested, can occur in a division of labour among distinct individuals with differences in talents and preferences. Specialisation, this strategy assumes, increases household productivity and satisfactions through what economists call 'the gains of trade'. Implicit in this notion is the proposition that it is wrong to judge specialised workers as only achieving equality when they do exactly the same things. Equality, in this view, is too often identified with sameness, when equality can also co-exist with difference, such as 'femininity' and 'masculinity' or separate skills. An appropriate judgement of equality, it is implied, exists where mutual benefit derives from a separate activity, rather than more benefits going to one party at the expense of the other. In this view, an egalitarian partnership is possible where the partners are separate but equal.[14]

It is interesting to note in this context that very few of the people interviewed in the Sydney survey of couples resorted to the sex-typing of tasks as a method of claiming parity. Rarely did the justification for non-participation in a particular task take the form of saying 'I don't do that because that's women's work' or vice versa. In other words, the interviews provided further evidence that few people think a male breadwinner and a female home-maker is a sound basis for parity between the sexes. In the couples surveyed, most men used the notions of competence or preference instead: women specialise in doing the housework and childcare because they are better at it or because they like it more than their husbands.

A male respondent gave a prototypical answer in terms of competence—'19 times out of 20 she cooks because she's better at it'. Just how this specialisation is supposed to advantage wives as well as husbands is unclear. A female respondent addressed this directly when she said 'I really do the cooking because he cooks so terribly. He thinks he's creative, because he's a male, and all the great chefs are male, so he puts peanut butter in meat stews and it doesn't improve them at all really—it wrecks them—so I don't let him do the cooking.'

Female respondents often implied male 'incompetence' was a transparent form of resisting demands. 'He'd be a great help . . . out at the [clothes] line', said one woman ironically. 'In fact, he'd hang out dirty clothes!' Another woman made tactful suggestions to her partner as to the nature of the work to be done. She said, 'I sort of try to set the priorities, 'cause he loves sitting there polishing a brass stand'.

Men also refer humorously to manipulative strategies of feigned incompetence. One man kidded along with his female interviewer, in the manner of male to male banter: '. . . a good trick . . . if you burn the fry pan and smoke the place out, it's amazing how she'll start cooking afterwards'.

Perhaps the most bizarre forms of male legitimation derive from the discourse of optimising preferences. This can involve claims that women derive great pleasure from housework, such as when one man said of his partner that 'she loves straightening out the cupboards and drawers'. Another man, who scored as very egalitarian on the attitude scale, claimed his partner 'likes cooking, so she prefers to do it. I don't cook much at all, I'd rather eat food that doesn't have to be cooked. But [she] likes cooked food, so she cooks and I eat it.'

The strategy of trivialisation and discounting

A strategy of trivialisation was often revealed directly by a respondent's reaction to the interview situation. Male respondents would often try to draw the interviewer into a collusive dismissal of the significance of housework and childcare. The basic thrust of this communication was an attempt to place all subsequent events within the frame of play (Bateson 1973, pp. 150–66), which has the effect of saying 'none of this is serious' and 'nothing which is said within this frame can be taken to mean what it appears to mean'.

A surprising number of women discounted their own domestic activities. One respondent provided an exhaustive account of a day packed with domestic labour but in response to the question of how long she spent in these activities per week, and in the face of instructions to do otherwise, began by listing substantial activities such as childcare and shopping which she said 'you can't [in fairness to males] count'. The resulting estimate of her time spent in domestic work was less than those with minimal household responsibilities—teenagers living with their parents. The discounting of domestic burdens by women was widespread and resulted in a comprehensive misrepresentation of length of time required for their activities.

Some implications for domestic power: pseudomutuality

Since Lukes (1974) published his celebrated book on power, sociologists have been preoccupied with what he called the third dimension of power—that is, the ability to shape people's thoughts, ideas and beliefs in such a way that they do not even acknowledge their own grievances. In the three-dimensional view there is a latent conflict of objective interests which does not surface. This idea of 'hegemonic power' has been enthusiastically employed by sociologists in the 1970s and 1980s. Developed in the context of analysing politically dormant class struggles, few theories have attempted to analyse struggles along different lines, such as gender, by using any other concept of power but the idea of hegemony (see for example, Connell 1987, pp. 107–11).

However, inequities in the domestic division of labour, as we have already noted, were rarely justified by reference to the 'masculinity' or 'femininity' of specific tasks. Despite the energetic attempts of sociologists to explain men's domestic power in terms of the construction of hegemonic 'masculinity' (Segal 1990), in the study of Sydney couples, the participants' legitimations of the pattern of allocation and avoidance were rarely based on an appeal to gender. Despite the *beliefs* in equality, there can be no doubt that in practice domestic labour is assigned according to gender, and its quantity is determined chiefly by women's, and not by men's, responsibilities to others (spouse, children and elderly partners) (Bittman 1991).

In relation to struggles over the social disadvantage arising out of domestic organisation, it may be more appropriate to refer to what Lukes calls the two-dimensional view of power, exemplified in the work of Bachrach and Baratz (1962; 1963). Their central theoretical innovation was to highlight the significance of 'nondecision-making'. As they point out: '[to] the extent that a person or group—consciously or unconsciously—creates or reinforces barriers to the public airing of policy conflicts, that person or group has power' (quoted in Lukes 1974, p. 16). Unlike hegemonic forms of domination, the two-dimensional view of power assumes nondecision-making to be an event that occurs in the context of observable conflict, where participants (rather than the analyst) define their interests as being opposed. The most celebrated analysis along these lines is Creson's study of how air pollution failed to become a political issue in cities such as the steel-making town of Gary, Indiana, until the 1960s (Lukes 1974, pp. 42–5). In the case of domestic power, 'potential issues' over the allocation of domestic labour, and the distribution of the goods and services produced by it, are suppressed.

Respondents in the couples study were asked a series of questions about the process of allocating responsibility for unpaid work. They were asked whether they ever discussed housework and childcare with their partner; how decisions were made about who did which tasks (and were prompted to talk about each task in turn). Further questions concerned how disputes were resolved; and what would/did happen if they were unable, or they refused, to do a certain task (i.e. went on strike).

A majority of respondents, both women and men, suggested they had never discussed the allocation of unpaid tasks. A male respondent answered: 'We didn't discuss household tasks—it was never an issue—no, it just happens—I'll do this, I'll do that, none of that sort of crap'. 'It just happens . . . sort of automatically', said a female respondent, who then went on to say 'everyone just pitches in'. She sustained this view in the face of its increasing implausibility, so that when asked about whether she had ever refused to do unpaid work, she replied that she had, and that the domestic organisation had collapsed.

Sometimes when a dispute about household chores arose, the couples discussed the problem, in an overt form of negotiation, but when no decision was reached the stalemate was broken by one partner, usually the woman, terminating the discussion. After raising the issues many times with no response, one woman said, 'I don't bang my head against a brick wall anymore'.

Other couples, where they were able, have sidestepped the issue by employing outside paid help. 'I decided to get someone in so we wouldn't argue' said one wife. 'If no one feels like cooking', said another woman, 'we eat out or get take-aways'. Strangely, many of the paid services involved 'help' with traditionally 'masculine' tasks. The most frequently used services were cleaning (used by 20 per cent of couples), lawnmowing and gardening services (12 per cent of couples), household repairs and maintenance (10 per cent), and ironing services (9 per cent). Ten of the 48 couples with children living at home (33 of whom had children below school age), used full-time childcare. Nine used part-time childcare, four had occasional childcare services, and only one couple used a nappy service. Male partners were sometimes unaware that paid services were used.

Negotiation followed by an apparent but reluctant compliance was another way to avoid taking an effective decision. One female respondent earns a lot more money than her partner (more than $70 000 per year compared to his $18 000 per year), works long hours, owns the house they live in, but still does most of the housework. When asked why, she replied: 'because it's easier to get things done than to put up with someone who procrastinates for a week over unpacking the dishwasher'.

Just as illuminating are what might be called the off-stage or back-stage noises, (see Goffman 1959), made by respondents outside the frame of a recorded presentation of self. We have referred to the 'good-natured' taunting of female interviewers by male respondents. Most interviewers also encountered anxiety, especially from men, at the prospect of separate interviews.

One interviewer said of this experience, '. . . before I had even started the interviews he said: "She's going to lie, she's going to lie—I better have a talk with her!" Then after the interview he desperately asked his wife: "What did you say?".' There were many reports that arguments broke out between couples after the interviews were conducted. More generally, major cracks in the women's presentation of self were seen in their inability to maintain a plausible impression of harmony and unity in domestic labour. Powerful feelings of unacknowledged toil, of unequal exchanges, of less than total resignation, surfaced through careful presentations of unrehearsed family harmony. Many of these feelings were expressed openly, as can be seen from the material already presented. Many women signalled their amusement, irritation and even exasperation with the manoeuvres of their male partners, and few women unreservedly adopted a patriarchal definition of their interests.

This off-stage noise suggests that discussion of the domestic division of labour is practically taboo. An outsider, not bound by the constraints of continuous operation within a particular domestic terrain, disturbs the delicate arrangement that prevents the half-concealed conflict from erupting. It is difficult to see why the concept of hegemony is here required by theorists because, unlike class, struggles over gender inequities arising from domestic sources are neither dormant nor completely covert.

We suggest that these struggles currently exhibit many of the characteristics of nondecision-making. Many of the practices described here are strategies concerned with reducing pressure towards negotiation, circumventing grounds for discussion, subverting discussion through pseudomutual concord and finally, by raising the costs of discussion, and other forms of threat.

It seems that many commentators on the rise of the companionate form of marriage, such as we discussed in Chapter 3, have been misled by the absence of signs of a formal status hierarchy, and by the apparent intimacy of contemporary heterosexual marriage. We would suggest that much of this is 'pseudomutuality', both in the general sense of being a miscarried search for genuine reciprocity and agreement, and in the narrower psychiatric sense (Wynne et al. 1967), as a technique which denies differences in order to defend power. Such forms of the exercise of power in the domestic setting are congruent with Carole Pateman's analysis of the form patriarchy takes in the contemporary welfare state, committed as it is to equality for all citizens (Pateman 1989, pp. 179–209), as we consider in Chapter 8.

Contemporary patriarchy is about the subordination of women *within* the framework of equality. The suppression of the contradiction between overtly stated values and privately maintained practices is an apparently stable arrangement, but not one which completely conceals the exercise of power. Wherever power is seen as not legitimate by the powerless and by those exercising power, it is most open to challenge. Domestic labour remains a site of struggle, a political issue of some weight in the Australian community precisely because of this contradiction.

Conclusion

The pseudomutuality that surrounds the domestic division of labour is perhaps the clearest example of the theme of this book, because in it is captured all the tensions associated with the double life of the family. The couples (like many commentators) speak as though they were children of the revolution in intimate life. What we have seen in this chapter is how this strong commitment to the value of equality and companionship in intimate relations is combined with the inability to live out these precepts. This contradiction results in a situation where it is difficult for either partner to acknowledge the inequalities in the relationship in any sustained way. Communication miscarries, the participants fudge their circumstances, and the actual and perceived inequities of family life cannot find an effective form of expression. All the various justifications for the unequal and currently disadvantageous responsibilities are frequently barely credible to a third party and yet they are made by people who are more committed to egalitarian relations than most. These forms of pseudomutuality, false reciprocities, of discounting or even trivialising the work done, serve to manage the tensions but not to banish them for ever. The commitment to an equal, pure relationship barely masks the visible relations of power and the result is frustration, guilt and pain. The inability to speak out has led to a growing number of women eventually turning to divorce.

In the following chapter we consider how the modern system of employment helps to set up this pattern of familial inequality. We will suggest that the tensions in family life are only partially resolvable through personal effort, however much improvements are desirable. All the marital counselling and child guidance clinics in the world will not change the modern market in labour that in principle recognises only single adults. Anyone with family responsibilities is doubly handicapped in the market race and in the dynamics of family life. The market has a profound impact on family life—and it is governments, not individual family members, that temper market rules.

7

Economics, breadwinning and family relations

The experience of paid work is a key element in understanding the tensions between our normative expectations of family life and the ways in which families manage in practice. Economists' efforts to explain family life are both contradictory and mystifying. Economics has been called the 'dismal science' and indeed, economic concepts such as 'utility', 'preferences' and 'human capital' do sound very far removed from our hopes for reciprocity and mutual comfort in family life. Orthodox economics assumes 'utility' maximising behaviour, and has conventionally argued that housholds are merely sites of consumption—production only takes place in 'the economy'. Efforts to improve on this narrow view within the framework of economics are, as we will see, largely unsatisfactory. Yet economics is currently so predominant that much of social and thus family life is subordinated to economic principles. So it is essential to ask whether the reality and expectations of families, *and* the actual operations of the market can be satisfactorily understood in these terms.

Families in contemporary industrial societies depend for their daily sustenance mainly on the links that individual members can make with the labour market. In most Western countries this simply means that to obtain material resources to set up and maintain autonomous households at a socially acceptable standard, at least two family members need to earn salaries or wages for considerable periods. Although personal property in the form of home ownership might appear the biggest asset of many families, it pales in significance compared to access to employment. 'The investment in career assets is by far the most valuable property owned by couples' (Okin 1989, p. 156). How the labour market affects families is clearly important, although the dependence of modern markets on families is just as important but rarely acknowledged.

This chapter explores the relation between working for money in the market and working for nothing in the household. We will evaluate the prominent explanations of how the labour market is said to be shaped by household 'preferences', and how labour demand—the employment system—shapes a range of family relationships and needs. Questions about labour supply—employees—will also be considered, by looking at whether the needs (not just the preferences or 'wants' as revealed in market transactions) of individual members of families, from children to the elderly, affect the shape of the labour market.

Economists' explanations of family relations

In addition to the fact that families may become wealthy or be rendered impoverished by labour market processes (for example, unemployment due to the introduction of technology), these same employment patterns may also exert considerable influence on the internal workings of households. The extent of this impact is a highly contentious issue. There is a widespread belief that partners reach household decisions by mutual agreement. In economic terms these 'mutual' decisions are described as 'revealed preferences' or choices of individuals. Important decisions over fertility and who should forgo all or part of their income to do unpaid housework and caring when children are born are, in this view, purely private matters within each family. The contrasting position is that the impersonal structures of the labour market heavily influence decisions about child-rearing responsibilities. The idea that families and individuals make unconstrained choices at such vital moments is in this view an illusion. Indeed, employment opportunities may even determine the division of domestic labour, the dignity and respect attached to these roles, and power relations within households. The simplified economic question at stake here is whether families get what they want, or must adjust to what they can get on the labour market (Schor 1991, p. 127).

Gary Becker: superior male wages cause domestic division of labour

One of the most influential views in recent economics, and a view also held by many people with no exposure to economics, is that taken by Gary Becker of the Chicago School of Economics. Becker gives an account of the sexual division of labour in households as an outcome of pay differentials in the labour market (Becker 1974; Becker 1981). This approach has been called the New Home Economics.

In contrast to orthodox economics, Becker argues that households are more than just units of consumption which 'graze' (like cattle) on items purchased from supermarkets. In other words he recognises, as we saw in Chapter 4, that households produce a stream of valuable goods and services that never reach the market.[1] Becker insists that 'a household is truly a "small factory": it combines capital goods, raw materials and labour to clean, feed, procreate and otherwise produce useful commodities' (cited in Berk 1985, p. 22). He assumes that households are part of a non-market but highly productive sector. Becker also revises the assumption made in orthodox theories of labour supply that individuals make trade-offs or choices *only* between work and leisure, adding that there is also the further 'option' of unpaid, non-market work (Becker 1974, pp. 301–2).

So how do households, in Becker's view, allocate their resources of time and money between these spheres of market work, non-market work and leisure? Becker assumes that households seek to maximise their welfare by dividing their labour. Thus individuals specialise in those tasks for which they have a 'comparative advantage' (Becker 1981, p. 21). The decision about who should do what, according to Becker's New Home Economics, is based on relative productivities (Becker 1974, p. 303). Men are said to be more productive in market work because men's wages are generally higher than women's, and any extra allocation of men's time to housework would oblige them to forgo a greater amount of income. By contrast, the 'shadow price' or opportunity cost of women's time spent in unpaid work at home is lower because the cost in income forgone is smaller. Decisions are made on this basis: women rather than men will quit work to have children and care for them for some years, because the loss of income from a female wage is less than the loss of a male wage. New parents frequently refer to this calculation of relative wage rates.

In addition, frequently it is claimed that women are more productive than men in household work. This claim is based on women's 'on-the-job' training (Gronau 1977, p. 1113), or in other words, greater experience in housework and childcare built up from women's supposed biological advantages in child-bearing *and* child-rearing (Becker 1981, p. 21).[2] This reasoning allows the New Home Economics to claim that men have a 'comparative advantage' in paid work, while women have a 'comparative advantage' in unpaid work. Because each member specialises in activities where their advantage (productivity) is greatest and they pool and exchange the rewards of these separate activities, the household is said to benefit from 'gains of trade'. Collectively, the household that specialises, says the New Home Economics, is better off than the one that does not.

Becker's argument has been criticised by many (see for example, Ben-Porath 1982; Berk 1985; Jacobs 1989; England & Farkas 1986). As Sarah Berk has pointed out, however, Becker's theory is certainly an improvement on neoclassical economists' neglect of the family, particularly his recognition of the extent of household production (Berk 1985, p. 25). Moreover, few dispute that employment opportunities for women are more restricted and that male wage rates are generally higher than women's.

Women's lower pay

In 1996, 52.9 per cent of all women (and 52.5 per cent of all married women) and 74.1 per cent of all men participated in the Australian labour market. As a share of the labour market, 43.2 per cent of all workers were women and 56.8 per cent men (ABS 1996b, pp. 6–8). Yet, except for a handful of industries and types of occupation, the employment opportunities available to women are far less than those of men. After nearly two decades of equal pay legislation and some subsequent efforts to counteract discrimination, little, if any, overall change seems to have occurred since 1911 (Mumford 1989 p. 20). The Australian labour market is highly segregated by sex, with women concentrated in a small number of industry sectors (health and community services and education, with more equal shares in the hospitality, finance and retail sectors) and occupational classifications. That is, in the mid-1990s women are still segregated in a small number of industries—60 per cent in wholesale and retail, community services, recreation, personnel and other services. Likewise, women are working in a narrow range of occupations—clerical, sales and personal services—that pay relatively lower wages. Only 25 per cent of women are managers and administrators and 10 per cent are tradespersons. Even among the professional and para-professional occupations, women have the less prestigious jobs, such as teaching and nursing, and fewer senior positions. As well as earning less, women are far more concentrated in part-time and casual work than men, with 75 per cent of women and 25 per cent of men classified as 'part-time' (Women's Bureau 1996; Baxter, Gibson & Lynch-Blosse 1990, pp. 62–3; Mumford 1989, pp. 18–30).

Women still earn substantially lower rates of pay in the 1990s, although Australian women's wages are much closer to men's than in most Western countries. The average total average earnings for female full-time workers in 1995 was $585.10, and of male counterparts $703.90 (Women's Bureau 1996). In the public sector, female full-time workers earned $647.20 ordinary time and male full-time workers $736.40 ordinary time (which excludes overtime, penalty rates etc. which again advantage men). Average weekly earnings of ordinary time in the private sector were $546.20 for women full time and $690.80 for men full time (ABS 1995a, pp. 2–4). Within different occupations, the wage difference is over $130 per week more for male labourers ($430.90 male and $294.50 female full-time weekly earnings), and in the case of full-time managers and administrators (where nearly 80 per cent of managers and administrators are male), men are earning an average of $992.70 a week while their female counterparts receive $801.50. Full-time professional earnings are the most disparate—from an average $905.10 male adult to a mere $625.70 female adult weekly salary—and only slightly less so in para-professional occupations. With tradespersons, men full time earn over $200 more per week than women full time. Female part-time workers across all occupations earn an average $25.10 more per week than male part-timers (ABS 1995b, p. 9), however, the male part-timers are mostly students and young adults in unskilled temporary jobs. While substantially more adult women of all ages work part time, men dominate in working overtime, but even full-time, 'ordinary wage' comparisons still show marked variations, let alone comparisons that include overtime. In Australia, and even more in most OECD (Organization for Economic Co-operation and Development) countries with the exception of Scandinavia, there is clearly a structure of gender differences in job opportunities and earnings that lends plausibility to Becker's claims.

Nevertheless, Becker's argument has been criticised as circular and apologetic. It is circular because lower wage rates are used to explain why women are responsible for unpaid work at home, and women's commitment to domestic responsibilities is used as an explanation for lower wages (Ben-Porath 1982, p. 53). A similar criticism can be made of the explanation of men's comparative disadvantage in household productive activities. Men's inexperience in doing housework and childcare tasks is used as an explanation of why they do not engage in such activities, and therefore they are inexperienced and less productive! The accusation that this theory is an apology for a currently unjust situation arises from the apparent 'justification' of a one-sided division of labour as a rational optimising of costs and benefits. As Berk says: 'Kipling himself could not give us a better just so story' (Berk 1985, p. 33).

Altruism or individual gain?

The supposed advantages of specialisation by gender also rest on the assumption that family households pool and transfer resources. This raises the problem of the collective welfare of households, a problem which has been addressed theoretically in a variety of less than satisfactory ways. Perhaps the best known of these theories is the one that assumes all members of the household simply conform to the preferences of the head of the household. This has often been the assumption behind welfare benefits and industrial doctrines such as the 'family wage'. (Such family policies are discussed in the next chapter.)

Becker suggests, however, that the arbitrary selection of one, usually male, individual to represent the interests of all is inequitable (Becker 1974). Orthodox economics assumes that humans are primarily motivated by the least effort for the most gain. They maximise their 'utility' by making trade-offs between work and leisure. Hence if the female and younger household members 'conform' to the utility of the male household head, their 'utility' or 'welfare' must be completely sacrificed. Becker argues instead that family households are characterised by 'altruism'. Because family members 'care' for one another, one member's welfare is affected by the welfare of other members. If, as Becker says, 'the "head" . . . cares enough about all other members to transfer resources to them, this household would act *as if* it maximised the "head's" preference function, even if the preferences of other members are quite different' (Becker 1974, p. 331, emphasis in original).[3] Transfers or exchanges between members would eliminate the conflict between different members' wants and needs (Becker 1974, p. 343). This line allows Becker to invent the concept of a 'single family utility function'.

There are at least two problems with Becker's argument about altruism. In retaining the concept of utility maximisation, it is technically suspect, and it neglects more plausible and simple explanations. As Killingsworth and Heckman have pointed out: 'The difficulty with this claim [of a family utility function] is that it is not generally true' (Killingsworth & Heckman 1986, p. 131). Acting so as to maximise my spouse's welfare is not the optimum solution to my wants and needs, and acting in a way that maximises my own welfare will not ensure the best possible solution for my spouse's wants and needs. In other words, within the framework of orthodox economics, utility is gained only by individuals and 'altruism' or a collective household or 'single family utility function' are technically dubious. As a consequence, one can either adhere to the notion of 'altruism' or retain the concepts of orthodox economics, but one cannot do both.

Putting these internal difficulties with the New Home Economics aside, Becker also neglects the obvious point, that power relations rather than altruism and selflessness within the family explain the pattern of family transfers in cash and kind. An alternative explanation along these lines is provided by England and Kilbourne (1990).

Marital power through superior male earnings

England and Kilbourne offer an explanation of how men's higher earnings translate into greater marital power.[4] The corollary of this statement is that women's 'specialisation' in domestic work disadvantages them and puts them in a comparatively less powerful position within the household. Their explanation has four propositions. Women have less marital power because first, 'cultural forces devalue traditionally female work and encourage women to be altruistic'. Second, 'the beneficiaries of much domestic work are children rather than men'. Third, 'some domestic work involves making investments that are specific to a particular relationship', rather than general and fourth, 'even "general" investments in domestic skills are less "liquid" than earnings because they do not ensure survival until one finds another partner' (England & Kilbourne 1990, p. 163).

Power is defined by England and Kilbourne in the following way:

> One's power depends on how much one contributes to a relationship, the ease with which one could leave the relationship and take the fruits of such contributions, the extent to which one is inclined toward self-interested bargaining, how much one's contributions are valued by the partner, how this compares to the value the partner places on what could be had outside this relationship, how one compares what is had within the current relationship to what could be had outside it. (England & Kilbourne 1990, p. 170)

We have noted in Chapter 4 that domestic work has often been overlooked by economic and social theorists, a fact symptomatic of its general cultural devaluation. England and Kilbourne also argue that socialisation predisposes women to adopt 'connective' and nurturing values and an altruistic orientation whereas men's socialisation predisposes them to the kind of selfishness presumed by economic theory. Women's connective values, they suggest, affect their capacity to bargain, even in conditions where their earnings are as high as those of their male partners (England & Kilbourne 1990, p. 171).

Orthodox economics looks at specialisation within the family household very narrowly as an 'exchange' between spouses of earnings for housework. Its potential credibility is gained only if children do not exist in families, for infants cannot make exchanges. Obviously, children are the chief beneficiaries of women's child-rearing work. Moreover, England and Kilbourne suggest that women's work on behalf of children militates against giving women any leverage in the marital bargain:

> First, an exchange or game-theoretic perspective implies that something one offers one's partner creates power on the assumption that offering it implies the ability to retract it. But since women usually retain custody of children in divorces, any benefits men perceive from what women do for their children will not be lost even if the marriage ends. Women cannot derive power from a credible threat to stop taking care of the children when men know that the women's bond to and commitment to the children transcends the relationship to the men. (England & Kilbourne 1990, pp. 172–3)

A crucial step in England and Kilbourne's argument is to draw attention to the 'asymmetry of relationship-specific vs. portable investments' in marriage (England & Kilbourne 1990, p. 173). Following the standard economic practice, investment is defined as incurring a cost at an earlier time that yields a benefit at a later time. This is a 'human capital' framework, which suggests that employers' possession of *capital* (tangible investments) is much like everyone else's possession of 'natural' capacities, motivation and the 'investments' made in gaining skills, qualifications and experience, called 'human capital', which they sell on the labour market.

The authors argue that in marriage, men mostly invest in their capacity to earn—through time spent in education, job-search, on-the-job training and career development. In so far as training is specific to the conditions, organisation and machinery found in a particular firm, this leads to the creation of firm-specific skills, which are valuable to that firm but not valuable to another. In contrast, the investment in education and career development is portable or 'general', that is, applicable to any firm in that industry. England and Kilbourne believe that men's investment in their own human capital is comparatively general, and this is supported by much of the evidence (e.g. Jacobs 1989, pp. 44–7).

In contrast, 'relationship-specific investments' in a family are more comparable to firm-specific training. As the authors explain, 'both employer and employee have invested in an asset (firm-specific human capital) that pays off to either party only if the employee continues to work there' (England & Kilbourne 1990, p. 174). This means that the firm and individual both have power over each other.

The 'marriage market'

England and Kilbourne consider how the search for a mate is comparable to a market exchange. Individuals search for the optimal partner (given their preferences), in a market where the partner one can 'catch' is 'limited by the attributes one has to offer (given the preferences of those on the other side of the market)' (England & Kilbourne 1990, pp. 174–5). So much for mate selection in economic terms, but for marriage to remain analogous to a market situation, each party would behave as though in a perpetual marriage market, so that if a better deal came along they would leave the relationship. If this situation were to prevail, England and Kilbourne say that marriage would be comparable to a 'spot market' of continuous turnover. Despite rising divorce rates, marriage 'turnover' does not justify this description.

A characteristic of relationship-specific investments is that, like the employee and the employer in the firm-specific investment, one's propensity to stay in the relationship usually increases and therefore lowers 'turnover'. One reason for this is the psychic and pecuniary 'search costs' of finding a new partner (England & Farkas 1986, pp. 36–42). But even ignoring the costs of constant search, a personal relationship is highly valued over the relative impersonality of being continuously in the 'rating-dating game'.

> In marriage or cohabitation once such [relationship-specific] investments have been undertaken, both partners are likely to be better off within this relationship than they would be were they to start over with someone else. Marital investments that transfer poorly to a new relationship involve learning to deal with the idiosyncrasies of one particular partner, such as learning his or her preferences and personal history, forming attachments with in-laws, learning this partner's sexual preferences, learning how to resolve disagreements with this partner, or contributing to the felt solidarity of the marriage by investments in children. (England & Kilbourne 1990, p. 175)

These authors argue that marriage is best described as an implicit contract. They contrast implicit contracts with formal contracts and suggest the following reasons why marriage is usually an implicit contract:

1   formal contracts entail transaction costs, such as lawyers' fees, divisiveness in drawing them up, the fact that contracts may need to be ludicrously specific and enforcement costs could continue indefinitely;
2   formal contracts undermine trust; and
3   there are legal restrictions on what matters can be subject of binding marital contracts (England & Kilbourne 1990, pp. 175–6).

Implicit contracts refer to the long-term, informal understandings between spouses. These understandings are 'grounded in each party's incentive to remain in and conscientiously contribute to the marriage by virtue of past relationship-specific investments' (England & Kilbourne 1990, p. 176).

Women, according to England and Kilbourne, make greater relationship-specific investments than men. For example, women contribute substantial emotional work in catering to the psychological needs of their partners, they devote more effort to forming emotional attachments with in-laws, and to the socialisation of children. None of these relationship-specific investments can be turned into assets on the so-called marriage market, whereas men's general investments in earnings are usually more portable.

> This asymmetry . . . contributes to men's power in marriage. Both sociological exchange theory and game theory suggest that the better one's alternatives outside the relationship, the worse one's partner's alternatives, the more one can afford to risk the other partner leaving by bargaining harder within the marriage. (England & Kilbourne 1990, p. 177)

Game theory describes positions in a bargaining situation as 'threat points'. Threat points are invoked by the pressure of one party threatening to walk away from the relationship. In bargaining over how to allocate the surplus from relationship-specific investments, threat points, according to game theory, predict what each person would 'walk away with' (and without) were the relationship to break down. 'Thus, one's threat points are more advantageous the more one's investments have been portable' (England & Kilbourne 1990, p. 177).

For women who make more relationship-specific investments, there is a cost. Women forgo important opportunities for making general investments in their earning power. Time spent out of the labour force to care for young children, relocations to advance a husband's career and the energy devoted to maintaining the image of a sociable couple, all represent time devoted to relationship-specific investments— time which is no longer available for advancing one's own education, on-the-job-training and career prospects. This lack of 'portable investments' disadvantages women in marital bargaining since they have forgone opportunities which would improve their threat points.

There is, however, some 'general' investment in marriage, analogous to investment in earnings, which consists of domestic skills such as 'keeping an attractive house', budgeting money well, developing the best in children, being a good listener and lover, and being 'a gracious entertainer', which is potentially transferable to other marital relationships (England & Kilbourne 1990, p. 178).

Such general investments in domestic skills should theoretically lead to increased desirability on the marriage market. However, they are less 'liquid' than investments in earning power. As England and Kilbourne point out, 'If one leaves the marriage having made general investments in earnings, one can survive without another marriage. But if one has made general investment skills as a marital partner, one needs to find a new partner on the marriage market to "cash in" these investments' (England & Kilbourne 1990, p. 178).

England and Kilbourne argue that the marriage market should be compared to an 'imperfect capital market'. Capital markets are institutions in which money can be borrowed against future returns. Economists have long acknowledged that 'human capital markets' behave 'imperfectly'. For example, there is no fierce competition among lending institutions seeking to advance loans to students to cover the university costs of developing their human capital. Indeed in Australia, the state, through the medium of the Higher Education Contribution Scheme (HECS) is obliged to substitute for private capital markets. HECS advances money (invests) against the expectation of higher labour market earnings in the future. Unfortunately, there are neither private capital markets nor state agencies prepared to invest in the acquisition of women's domestic skills or, even more disheartening, in child-rearing skills. Unlike returns on investment in education, which are realised by many graduates in higher, postponed earnings, the returns on most domestic skills can only be realised through the marriage market.

Human capital theory views the search for better employment as an investment. The cost of this search in labour markets is the income that unemployed people forgo as they look for a job. By analogy, realising one's general investment in domestic skills requires a period of search. Since these general domestic skills are only appropriate in a marital relationship, divorced people must search in the marriage market for a new partner. Searching the marriage market has its costs too but, unlike lending against education, there is no provision whatever for lending against one's future marital prospects. Divorced people with investments in general domestic skills (mainly women) are doubly disadvantaged compared with those who invest in future earnings. As England and Kilbourne point out, '[u]nderlying this argument is an assumed hierarchy of needs; one can go without emotional benefits of marriage for a while during search, but one cannot meet even the most basic needs of food and shelter without earnings' (England & Kilbourne 1990, p. 178). In human capital terms, the result is a very 'limited liquidity' of women's general domestic investments. Furthermore, within a marriage, it means that compared to general earning skills, women's threat points and the ability to bargain are adversely affected (England & Kilbourne 1990, p. 179).

Exit, voice or loyalty?

In the contemporary context, however, women whose general skills are purely limited to 'domestic' are a minority. Many women today have also invested in their earning power through job-search, schooling, on-the-job training and career building. This earnings investment is also portable back into the marriage market. How does women's increased labour force attachment affect their marital power?

To deal with this question, England and Kilbourne draw on Albert Hirschman's framework from his increasingly popular work, *Exit, Voice and Loyalty*, first published in 1970. In discussing the relationship between organisations and their customers, Hirschman canvasses three basic options of customers—exit, voice and loyalty. If they are dissatisfied, customers can leave an organisation and take their custom elsewhere, an option Hirschman calls exit. Alternatively, customers may remain with the organisation but express their dissatisfaction in a variety of ways, with a view to improving the firm: this option is called voice. The third option, whether customers are satisfied or dissatisfied with the organisation, is to continue passive allegiance, which Hirschman calls loyalty (Hirschman 1970, pp. 15–20). For example, if parents are unhappy with their local state school, they can remain passively loyal to the school (in the hope that it may get better), they can exit by putting their child in a private school or move house so that their children can enrol in another school or they can give 'voice' to their concerns through complaints or activism in the Parents and Citizens Association and other public agitation. Only 'voice' can effectively improve the organisation.

Both England and Kilbourne (1990) and Castles and Seddon (1988) argue that this framework can be usefully applied to marriage. Disregarding, for the moment, violent and coercive options, individuals dissatisfied with a particular marriage can exit through divorce or desertion, or voice their dissatisfaction by drawing attention to their unhappiness, by attempting to diagnose the problem or through criticism and attribution of blame.

Loyalty is a more complex issue. England and Kilbourne point to the recent changes in women's workforce participation as a potential source of increased marital power for women. 'During the 1950s', they claim, 'women's limited marital power meant that even those deeply dissatisfied with their marriages generally chose loyalty because their only option was destitution' (England & Kilbourne 1990, p. 181). The result was a low divorce rate. Men were in a position to voice their dissatisfactions without fear of being divorced.

Since that time, England and Kilbourne suggest, women's increasing employment has given them the capacity to leave unsatisfactory marriages or to voice their dissatisfactions. Were women to exercise the voice option, these authors suggest that women would most want to change the degree to which men provided emotional intimacy, listened to women's feelings and increased their participation in domestic work. As we have seen in Chapters 4 to 6, studies of domestic labour suggest that women still find it difficult to exercise the voice option effectively and to change the behaviour of men. This leaves divorce (exit) as the most probable alternative.[5] Statistics on divorce rates are consistent with this theory, since far more women initiate divorce, and younger women (with higher earnings) are more likely to divorce (England & Kilbourne 1990, p. 182; Castles & Seddon 1988, p. 124).

A variety of cultural explanations for men's resistance to any change in their marital roles are given by England and Kilbourne. Amongst the cultural factors are the devaluation of women's traditional activities, the argument that men sharply define their identity in contradistinction to the feminine and women's alleged 'altruism', which inhibits their bargaining. This means that men fiercely resist any alterations in their behaviour, but curiously are less concerned—in contemporary times—about women entering the formerly male preserves of paid work. The increase in women's power has paradoxically reinforced the masculinist values of the marketplace.

England and Kilbourne sum up by saying:

Given the continuing division of labour in which women do more domestic work and men have large earnings, these factors explain why men have more marital power than women, while employed women have more marital power than homemakers. However, power implies a potential to either leave a relationship or bargain for change within it. As women's employment has brought them more power, it appears they are using this power more to leave relationships than to change them. (England & Kilbourne 1990, p. 184

England and Kilbourne's analysis shows the signs of their American origins. Divorce in some US states has been liberal for some time, and women's increased employment coincided with rising divorce rates. Strangely, they do not consider the impact of one of the few welfare payments in the United States not conditional on previous paid employment, that is paid to single parents, namely Aid to Families with Dependent Children (AFDC). In contrast, the Australian analysis of Castles and Seddon ignores the increasing financial independence women have derived from their labour force participation, focusing instead on Australia's Family Law Act of 1975 which substantially liberalised divorce, and on the increase in payments to sole parents in Australia at that time.

Castles and Seddon propose an interesting interpretation of the relative absence of women's 'voice' in the traditional marriage before these changes. They argue that 'the relative weakness of voice in the traditional marriage has been misinterpreted as an absence of overt dissent where in reality it may well have represented the only possible mode of opting out of an otherwise intolerable situation'. Instead of interpreting a lack of 'voice' as loyalty or even feigned loyalty, Castles and Seddon suggest a fourth option—partial exit, often called 'the empty marriage'. This option, they claim, is most likely to arise in the face of one partner's discontent with the other, under circumstances 'where full exit [divorce] barriers are high and moral sanctions discourage the articulation of voice as effective disloyalty' (Castles & Seddon 1988, p. 122)—that is, in a traditional (pre-1970s) marriage. As they say:

> [T]he range, extent and seriousness of such withdrawals varies enormously, from spending more time at the pub than with the kids to finding more fulfilment in work than in the other partner's company, from missing out on an expected endear-

ment to vacating the marriage bed altogether and so on through all the multiple activities that comprise a marriage . . . [I]n marriages perceived to be in crisis, there is a strong tendency for both partners to have withdrawn to what they severally consider to be the irreducible minimum activity consistent with a continuing relationship; wives focusing more or less exclusively on the role of mothers and husbands seeing themselves almost wholly as breadwinners. (Castles & Seddon 1988, p. 120)

The novelty of Castles and Seddon's approach is that it allows us to see how damaging 'partial exit' is to those members of an organisation who are unable to exercise the 'voice' option. Full exit terminates marriage whereas partial exits are 'inimical to recovery'. In Hirschman's terms, partial exits do not help the 'organisation' to improve because 'they involve a further deterioration in performance without any overt signal of the character of performance lapse, especially since minor or gradual withdrawals can readily be confused with the normal evolutionary process by which marital expectations are transformed' (Castles & Seddon 1988, p. 125).

Children in market societies

Up to this point, we have chiefly considered the effects of labour markets on the family relations between spouses. Superior wages and possession of more 'portable' career assets are associated with unequal power relations, where one partner (usually a male) is in a stronger bargaining position than the other, who has fewer of these assets. The effects on the person (usually a woman) who is the powerless partner are not just loss of self-esteem, confidence, and leisure. They also include a weakened capacity to improve the relationship, to share the family tasks of earning and caring and therefore to turn the hopes for shared comfort and personal fulfilment in family life into practice. Yet, other important household members that everyone associates with families—namely children—need further consideration. For the rest of this chapter, children are central to our analysis. How does economic theory cope with children?

Neoclassical economics inherited the legacy of Thomas Malthus' prediction, when the industrial revolution was beginning in England, that rising incomes would lead to an increase in fertility until the population increased to the point where agriculture could no longer sustain it. Thus economists were completely confounded by the long-term fertility decline over the last century that accompanied rising incomes. This decline cannot be explained by new technology (e.g. contraceptive pills) since fertility levels declined permanently long before any of the array of ancient fertility control techniques were superseded. In all industrialised countries, total fertility dropped steeply in the 1890s, from an average of six births (that any woman would expect over her lifetime) in the 1860s, to two births per woman by the 1930s (Hugo 1992, p. 7). Except for the post-war 'baby boom', the fertility rate of 1.8 children (in 1994) has now stabilised below the level of population replacement (ABS 1994e, p. 1).

Explaining fertility decline

Orthodox economics did not attempt to explain fertility decline until the 1950s. Working from the individualist model of the rational agent who makes choices, economists set up a framework where children are assumed to be 'purchases' by parents who make initial calculations about the long-term costs and benefits of children. A leading proponent of this framework, Theodore Schultz, proposes that contemporary child-rearing is highly labour-intensive and children's human capital investment costs are large. To this is added the idea that the 'net flow' of resources between children and parents had reversed by the twentieth century, from one where children brought in earnings and contributed labour to the household, to one where parents must provide for their children over a long 'childhood'. There is also an opportunity cost in forgone earnings for the parent who cares for children. Hence, the decline in fertility is associated with 'the rise in price of human time', specifically a mother's, over the past two centuries (Schultz 1974, pp. 3, 12; Willis 1974, pp. 25–6). Apart from these market metaphors being so inappropriate for babies and children, there are also problems with economists' explanations.

Classical economics was developed at a time when industrial society was emerging out of a pre-industrial past. In trying to come to grips with fertility decline, economists now argue that if today's children must be seen as 'consumption' items of families, this is because in pre-industrial societies, children were 'the poor man's capital' (Schultz 1974, pp. 6–21), or 'production' items. However repulsive the terms, it is conceptually more plausible to explain fertility as rational economic preferences of the pre-industrial past. Whether on peasant farms or in artisan workshops in towns, children provided some economic benefits to families from a relatively early age. Children over about seven years old were needed in an immediate sense for a family's survival and continuity. Their early contributions to household or kinship economies took numerous forms across societies and classes. They did not necessarily work for or with their biological parents; and they were trained 'on the job' by men and women (variously), and were expected to undertake productive (e.g. dairy work) and reproductive tasks (e.g. caring for younger siblings). Women were not isolated into exclusively caring for children, rather children went everywhere. By the age of eleven, most children, if they were not occupied on the family holding, had left home to join another household as apprentices or domestic servants (Laslett 1965, pp. 14–21, 104). The marriage of children was an opportunity to consolidate or increase the wealth of a family through alliances with other families and, as we saw in Chapter 3, this was the prime consideration when making a match. Children were also a great hedge against the time when parents became too old or infirm to sustain themselves. Before the introduction of universal pensions, parents hoped to be able to rely on children for economic security in their old age.

In Schultz's terms, today's children, unlike their counterparts in pre-industrial times, provide none of the 'economic return' (Schultz 1974, pp. 6–21). Now children increasingly remain dependent on their parents into their adult years, and are not expected to contribute either income or domestic labour to the family household—this is described as 'wealth flows'. By the 1920s the transition in most Western countries was complete, in that wealth flowed from parents to children instead of the reverse (cited in Berg 1988, p. 66). This means that in the course of this transition, households lost the income brought in by children. Apart from the direct costs associated with children (Australian families spend on average $9932 per year for a one-year-old, $11 798 for a teenager: AIFS 1995a, p. 17), such as expenses on food, clothing, schooling and transport, there are indirect costs. The indirect costs, which overwhelm the direct costs, are the opportunity costs associated with raising children. In 1986, Beggs and Chapman calculated that the lifetime costs in forgone earnings of raising a first child were close to half a million dollars (Beggs & Chapman 1988, p. iii).

On the basis of these economic theories, one might expect that fertility would decline to zero, that is, people would simply calculate the economic consequences and avoid having children. Predictions in the early 1970s were as follows:

> . . . the marginal opportunity cost of time has risen secularly with the rise in real wages and with the growth of human capital. It is natural for economists to connect to this basic fact both upward trends in labour-force participation of women and downward trends in fertility [and] changes in the family. (Mincer & Polachek 1974, p. 428)

Such a logic would also dictate that, since utility maximising behaviour in the market is the primary motivation of any rational agent, and interpersonal relations are apparently irrelevant to this behaviour, familial relations might become less prominent and the unequal division of household labour would decline. It also means that there would be hardly any children left to populate future societies. This obvious conclusion from the model poses a problem for these economists. The New Home Economics' theory of fertility assumes that households *do* maximise some utility function in having children. Since it is plain that utility maximisers would be irrational if they persist in seeing children as commodities who will bring future production benefits to the household, the task is to switch children into consumer items!

Even then, the number of children depends on 'resource-constraints' or the costs in 'producing' such consumer items as children (Ben-Porath 1974, p. 189). Put in plain language, however, it simply means that the more they cost, the fewer children people will have. These economists have been forced into some tortuous conceptualisations and contorted expressions in trying to explain why people have children. Take, for example, the following passage: '[c]hildren are viewed in this model as home-produced durable assets from whom parents consume a flow of services. This flow varies with both biological units of children (numbers) and with the resource intensity (quality) with which children are raised' (De Tray 1974, p. 92).

But even *within* such an economic model, the question arises as to what 'services' children could possibly provide their parents. Theodore Schultz virtually admits that, given the opportunity costs of children in modern societies, human capital theory cannot really explain why people have children at all, except for 'future personal satisfactions' or psychic rewards (Schultz 1974, p. 6). Schultz views children as forms of human capital, that is, in relation to their future *employers*, not their parents.

Children as 'commodities'?

In contrast, Gary Becker's description of households as 'home factories' emphasises the view that children are produced as 'commodities'. Like the others, Becker also makes a distinction between quality rather than mere quantity of children, one item referring to how many children are born or 'purchased', the other to the 'quality' of commodities imbued with more or less intense efforts in rearing to adulthood. Sue Donath argues that the distinction between quality and quantity of these two 'commodity items' is necessary, because with the declining birthrate (or reduced 'demand' for children), a focus only on the quantity of children would have to describe children as an 'inferior' commodity (Donath 1994, p. 18) on a declining 'market'. Economists of course have only themselves to blame for this terminology. The focus on 'quality' moreover, only highlights how, given the human capital invested in them, children become ever more costly and time-consuming.

The New Home Economics rightly demonstrates the vast expenditure involved in modern child-rearing and the economic disadvantages for women. Dependency, needs, and the obligation to give care vanish from sight, however, for households are seen only in terms of a 'single family utility function' of individuals making choices and exchanges. Donath suggests that the model is inaccurate since young children have nothing to exchange but are helplessly dependent on gifts of care (Donath 1994, pp. 20, 39). A parent does not 'exercise a preference' to care for an infant. By using a single household utility function, the model removes all the differences between individual members of the household. As Donath says, 'the effects of the economy cannot be disentangled from effects on other household members (particularly children) and the effect the household has on the economy cannot be assigned to the different household members' (Donath 1994, pp. 20–1). Women's caring for children, even cast as an exchange of care for 'pleasure', or just as nonsensically, children's 'utility' derived from simply surviving until more or less independently 'viable', become subsumed in the single household utility function. The theory suggests that all choices are possible and equal, so that those who are obliged to provide care are usually portrayed as making a 'free' choice of a poorly paid job to accommodate their 'preference' for caring for children (Donath 1994, p. 39).

Thus, contemporary economic theory has shown how, on the assumption of rational economic actors who maximise their utility, there is no economic incentive to reproduce in contemporary industrial societies. Accordingly, households respond 'rationally' to the costs of children and income forgone, as female wages have risen and children's education lengthened, by refraining from having children (which actually shows that the labour market still fails to accommodate child-rearing). The fact that children continue to be born and raised remains a weakness in the theory. Despite their efforts, economists have not explained the 'baby boom' of the 1950s, nor why fertility did not continue to decline from the 1970s to the present day, but has levelled out. In sum, they are no closer to an explanation of why family life has taken the forms it has, nor why families persist at all, given that the model is unable to go beyond individual preference and choice.

Whose 'utility' are children?

To press this point, let us start from Schultz's proposition that today's children, unlike their counterparts in pre-industrial times, provide no 'economic return' (Schultz 1974). Children are obviously economic liabilities (even if personal pleasures) for families, mainly for mothers, but it is ridiculous to suggest they do not provide an 'economic return' to the wider economy as future consumers and producers. Furthermore, in their adult working roles they also maintain the older generation's pension or superannuation funds. With no children, economic life—all life—will eventually cease. Orthodox economics conveniently does not incorporate this elemental fact. It treats the family as if it were an individual, either embodied in a male household head, or as a 'single household utility function' which 'produces' babies and altruism, health and cooked dinners. One may purchase a cooked dinner on the market or cook it oneself and in consuming it gain individual utility either way. Babies and altruism are fictitious commodities—if they were 'consumed' they would cease, because in practical terms babies need care and altruism expands with practice and reciprocity.

Economics usually makes a distinction between macro-economic functions and micro-economic functions. At the macro-level of aggregate supply and demand, the total marketed output and total expenditure is examined. These aggregates are seen as the result of the activities of millions of adult individuals at the micro-level. Diane Elson (1994) points out that while some economists have introduced a middle level or meso-economic analysis, they do not include the family here. The meso-level describes private sector institutions of market mechanisms, businesses and firms, and public sector services such as hospitals and schools, that is, all the social institutions that bring people together and mediate between them as micro-level individuals to produce macro-level results. Elson suggests that the family is also a 'social institution that brings people together and mediates between them', yet orthodox economics assumes the family is a micro-economic unit. Furthermore, only the micro-level is acknowledged to be gendered, not the meso and macro levels (Elson 1994, pp. 34–36).

By regarding the family as a micro-economic rather than a meso-economic unit, orthodox economics is relieved of the problem of explaining 'how the economic agents who are the subjects of mainstream economic theory are reproduced' (Donath 1994, p. 39). As previously discussed, women's work on behalf of children does not provide women with any leverage in the marital bargain because the family unit involves an implicit contract where caring for children gives mothers little or no bargaining power with fathers (England & Kilbourne 1990). Similarly, the assertion that families are micro-economic units gives women no leverage to have their contribution of bearing and rearing children included at the macro- and meso-economic levels. That is, the trade-offs between mothers and the society as a whole are virtually impossible to discern in orthodox economics because the family is not seen as a 'meso-economic unit' in a relation with other such units. The crux of Donath's argument is that very few economists, even feminist economists, have entertained the idea that there is a 'public goods' aspect of children (Donath 1994, pp. 39–41).

As mentioned previously, a typical example is Gary Becker's view that children are private commodities 'produced' entirely for individual pleasure and benefit. Given that children are personal economic liabilities today, a more consistent solution would be to argue that women are 'irrational' in wanting babies, except that such prejudice might highlight Becker's failure to acknowledge the utterly obvious social or public gains from children, namely the continuation of the society. An 'individual' motivation for reproduction, in contrast, lends support to Becker's argument that parents should pay for all their costs (Donath 1994, pp. 46–7). As Daly and Cobb point out, however, Becker's search for individual gain as the sole reason for children's existence is weak (Daly & Cobb 1989, pp. 38–9). So Becker refuses to follow orthodox economics in consigning women to irrationality. Instead he tries to argue that a parent might gain a 'utility' from bequeathing his or her capital or human capital to future and distant descendants. This search for an individual utility in having a child leaves Becker in further difficulties. This is because:

> [t]he farther in the future is the hypothetical descendant, the greater the number of co-progenitors in the present generation, and consequently the more in the nature of a public good is any provision made for the distant future. To the extent that you are concerned about the welfare of your descendant, you should also be concerned about the welfare of all those in the present generation from whom, for good or ill, your descendant will inherit. (Daly & Cobb 1989, p. 39)

In one attempt to prove an individual parental motive for reproducing, Becker adopts 'the obvious if extreme expedient of assuming asexual reproduction!' (Daly & Cobb 1989, p. 39). An obvious conclusion is that economists never learned the 'facts of life'.

'Public goods' aspect of children

What are 'public goods' in orthodox economics? Lighthouses, roads, immunisation programs and street lighting are examples of the 'purest' public goods because they cannot be supplied to any one person without being automatically available for everybody (the non-excludability principle), and their individual users cannot be made to pay for them. Thus a ship-owner wants a lighthouse to protect *his* ship, but once built a lighthouse cannot exclude offering to all other ships protection from foundering. Other, less 'pure' public goods, like 'freeways' can be turned into 'tollways' under a user pays principle, which means that some motorists can be excluded from using them.

Public goods which do not easily exclude many people from freely using them (e.g. lighthouses) are treated in economics as 'market failures' on the grounds that markets only produce goods for which those producers who bear the costs can also capture the benefits. That is, market goods are 'ownable' or transferable in some way, whereas public goods are not. If the market prevails—such as the view that government investment (via taxation) 'crowds out' private investment—public goods will be chronically underproduced. The general properties of public goods are their 'non-excludability and non-rivalness' (Caporaso & Levine 1992, p. 93). First, it is difficult to find practical ways of forcing the beneficiaries to pay, thus they become 'free-riders' who enjoy the benefits without paying the costs, and second, my use of the lighthouse or the public park does not rival your use of these goods (Caporaso & Levine 1992, pp. 93–4). There is no firm demarcation between many public goods: too many people in the park or on the freeway may cause overcrowding and thus rival everyone's use of the public good. In contrast, my use of my toothbrush or my eating a hamburger entails my purchase, my right to exclude and to rival your use of the 'good'.

The concept of public goods was developed in the 1950s by Paul Samuelson to explain the inefficiencies of an under-supply of public goods. He argued that self-interested maximisers want to grab as many public goods while paying as little tax for them as possible. His prescription was that governments were misreading public demand, because although people grumble about taxes they also understand the significant benefits of 'quality' public goods. Therefore governments actually tax and spend too little (Stretton & Orchard 1994, pp. 54–5). The idea was popularised by J.K. Galbraith's concept of 'private affluence and public squalor'. Since the 1970s, however, the prevailing economic view is that public goods should become more squalid—and even water supplies should be privatised.

The aspect of 'public goods' entailed in children is a most interesting, but most neglected case. Here some curious reversals seem to operate. It is easily understood that an underproduction of many public goods is common, and without state intervention public streets would be dark at night and contagious diseases would abound. The decline in fertility can be explained as another case of 'market failure'—through a macro-level and meso-level analysis of fertility *rates*, not individual motivation: as children cease to provide a 'private' return to their parents, fewer children are 'produced'. Children are less marketable or transferable 'commodities' than they were in previous eras. In modern societies, children are not meant to be bartered in marriage, or indentured to local warlords or aristocrats or variously sold off as child labour, slaves or prostitutes. Indeed, in recent times there is anxiety about the ethical implications of 'hiring' or paying to use a woman's womb, as in surrogacy cases.

The point, however, is that in modern societies children do provide a 'public return' to our collective futures. In addition, like the environment which is taken as an outside 'given' by the private sector rather than a resource whose costs of tending and replacing should be internalised as a cost on profits, children are liable to be treated as 'externalities' at the macro-level. Parents pay directly for the costs of children, and mothers pay in forgone earnings and in effort (however enjoyable). Mothers in particular have received virtually no economic benefits from this heavy investment. More precisely many women have been doomed to poverty for making this provision in modern societies. Yet all elderly people (where pensions and superannuation are universal) are the free-riders on this effort of bearing and raising children. As Nancy Folbre points out, many old age security programs are 'based on transfers from the working to the retired population, which means that all the elderly depend on other people's children' (cited in Donath 1994, pp. 41–2).

Gains for employers

Employers are free-riders in a rather different way. Not only do they want a supply of workers already 'endowed' with human capital due to the personal expenditure of the parents and government expenditure in education and training, but they also want an oversupply of this public good, so that inflation may be restrained and employers' prerogatives can be maintained. Employers want to free-ride on the backs of mothers, whether within a nation or through migration and indentured schemes.

Those economists who support public goods have pointed to the fact that the concept of 'freeloading' refers to getting something you haven't paid for, and rarely refers to private freeloading from something that you haven't earned, that is, the 'unearned income' of wealth from share and property owning (Stretton & Orchard 1994, pp. 76–7, 54–7). Employers, by and large, use and further augment their unearned income (wealth or capital) from the use of 'human capital' which they do not bear the costs of producing. Parents and education authorities who have made the investment cannot 'exclude' employers from using the public goods aspect of children. On the contrary, in times of oversupply of labour, parents and governments are desperate for children to become employed, at least in the sense that the financial drain of providing for children is better ended at some adult stage. Tensions between unemployed adult children and their parents—many also suffering from unemployment—are often high in contemporary times.

In another irony, employers are not just freeloaders but covetous ones. Employers want a large, skilled workforce from which to pick and choose. Parents want their children to be 'chosen'—parents study the market in human capital carefully, from school subjects to university and TAFE courses. The workforce, however, must offer loyalty not to parents but employers. One employer's purchase and consumption of a worker's activities usually excludes most other employers', but in general the labour supply never excludes employers from using this public good. An oversupply of labour is useful to employers but as such it becomes part of the 'public squalor', in that only a few are 'chosen'.

So, economists' talk of the 'quality' of children avoids the fact that there is no economic justification for 'rational actors' (namely individual parents) to have children, but many reasons for employers to want a large number of highly skilled future workers without paying for any of the long-term costs of their 'production'. The decline in apprenticeships is a case in point (with few employers training their own workforce). The use of the term 'human capital' proposes a direct personal benefit to the 'owner' but not the supplier, that is the parents. Interestingly, HECS is a method of making the owners of human capital return some of the investment in tertiary education to government revenue. Even so, while some owners of human capital may be able to claim higher salaries (and thus should give some return to governments), employers benefit most from this investment. Thus, the claim that students should pay *all* their university and training fees is less convincing than the idea that employers contribute through corporate taxes or training levies.

If families were regarded as meso-economic units, similar to firms, the effect of families on the whole economy would be clearer. It is hardly surprising that economists are loath to explain why fertility has not declined to zero, and try to find an individual utility derived by parents from their children rather than admit to the public goods aspect of children. In the present situation, a fertility strike would need to be global to reverse the imbalance of employers' freeloading on such 'public goods'.

The idea of a fertility strike is improbable, however, mainly because the economic framework—that at best views children as 'public goods' and 'externalities' and at worst as commodities purchased on a 'market'—is a deficient understanding of social life. Orthodox economics begins and ends with the principle that every modern individual is equally able to act rationally in a situation of unconstrained choice. It rejects the possibility that humans are human because of their webs of mutual obligations, social recognitions and desires.

The reasons for having children are multifarious. To belabour the obvious, reasons and consequences are frequently different for men and women—the gendered and irrevocable aspects of children vary according to relative forms of sexual power, the social significance of children and the broader system of male domination. However, as Rebecca Blank suggests, one does not have to believe that economic incentives fully determine behaviour in order to accept that economic incentives matter 'at the margin' of behaviour (Blank 1993, p. 139). It is here that economists' predictions of fertility decline due to the costs of children are credible. By the same token, an economic analysis of the economic benefits of children shows that it is both a fallacy and an injustice to argue that mothers gain 'utility' from children and should personally pay for supposedly maximising this utility. Rather, employers derive utility from children and economic life continues and benefits from the existence of children.

The labour market and families

We have seen that economic theories misread fertility as a case of individual utility maximisation. They also miscast the care that infants and children *need*, as a personal choice of mothers. Once a child is born, this is not a choice at all, since a baby will not survive without institutional care from families, kindergartens and many others. Orthodox economics not only regards the direct and indirect costs of children as private and not public responsibilities, but when women are employed, their inferior market wages are also attributed to a so-called private choice to provide unpaid care for children. Within orthodox economics, 'choice' is in fact a basic calculation about women's lower pay: if women earn less, women will be responsible for all or most caring work. Yet choice is not only an inadequate description of the commitment to children, given that a 'preference' to withdraw care is usually judged criminal neglect. It also avoids the typical reality that fathers do not have to make a choice between paid work and 'having' children at all. Is it convincing to argue that women's lower pay is due to their own choice?

The human capital approach

In explaining women's lower pay rates, human capital theory concentrates on the supply of labour rather than demand by employers. Human capital theory maintains that the labour market is neutral towards all sellers (male or female) and their households. These theorists do not accept discrimination by employers, and focus on the behaviour of employees, or the supply side, to explain women's lower pay. On the supply side are workers who are motivated to maximise their lifetime earnings, and this is presumed to involve a lifelong rationality of choices in making 'investments' in studying and in acquiring skills. In answer to why women have continued to fare badly in terms of pay, security and promotion in comparison with men, the broad idea is that family responsibilities virtually 'cause' women's weak position in the market.

Human capital theory tends to explain wage differentials as the outcome of individuals' investment in their human capital and not the result of a labour market that discriminates against women or any other group. Employers are considered only as mere labour buyers, motivated solely to maximise profits. The possibility that employers, that is, the demand side, would discriminate (by gender or ethnicity) against certain groups of workers is implausible in this approach, because economic orthodoxy assumes that conditions of perfect market competition hold, as a rule, and prevent labour buyers from ever acting irrationally (in buying too 'expensive' labour) and thus threatening profits.

In this view the labour market is one vast pool where buyers treat men and women as interchangeable sellers of abstract labour, with more or less marketable skills—described as 'human capital'—which find a natural price across all competing market participants. The private relations and personal attributes of labour sellers, like their sex or parental responsibilities, are treated as irrelevant to their 'capital' in skills and job experience, or simply factors external to the operations of the labour market (Jacobs 1989, pp. 169–71; England & Farkas 1986, pp. 154–9; Mumford 1989, pp. 67–71). The theory suggests it all depends on effort, choice, motivation and ability. Any labour market differences, such as low pay, are simply women's own fault or, more mildly, because of 'attributes' women bring to employment. Those who 'choose' to gain the greatest amounts of human 'capital' do best on the market and gain most leisure or utility; the rest chose differently because of cultural reasons or expectations that they would spend little time in the labour market, too busy with 'motherhood' or other 'preferences'. Levels of motivation or scholastic ability are external to the market and result in different amounts of human capital, but each level of invest-ment (length of training) receives the same rewards. The difference between a salary and a wage is allegedly explained also by this theory. Men (some of them) have simply invested more time and effort to become professionals.

Each woman, according to this theory, takes a considered, lifelong decision, as a young adult, on the basis of future reproduction responsibilities and the persistence of lower female pay, to avoid lengthy training and to self-select into predominantly female occupations where 'intermittent' work experience is less penalised. Moreover, after children are born, women's family responsibilities are alleged to result in a lack of 'commitment' to their jobs. Meantime their skills have 'gone rusty' or 'depreciated' during their prolonged absence from the labour market (Mincer & Polachek 1974, pp. 404–15).

Do women 'choose' low pay?

A number of criticisms has been made about the extent that individual choice is responsible for female disadvantage. Given contemporary labour market upheavals, with structural unem-ployment, automation, the rise of service occupations and redundancies or 'downsizing', it would seem plausible to argue that 'going rusty' and the need for retraining are general phenomena across the labour force, regardless of sex. Thus the alleged 'depreciation penalty' faced by women leaving work to have children should be no more severe than for other workers, because depreciation is, according to England

and Farkas, 'no lower in female- than in male-dominated jobs' (England & Farkas 1986, pp. 157, 155).

Moreover, Jerry Jacobs disputes the imputation of a lifelong rationality of choices, on the grounds that individual behaviour is unstable and responds to changed social climates, new opportunities or labour market trends. It is worth remembering that fertility plans are quite unreliable in predicting behaviour even two years in advance. For example, Helen Marshall's study of voluntarily childless couples, that is couples who claimed to have decided that they would never have children, was dogged by the number of respondents who fell pregnant, and couples who split up (Marshall 1993, p. 138).

Similarly, when employment opportunities for married women rose from the 1960s onwards, women seized them. When high quality childcare places become available, women use these services with alacrity. Moreover, ABS estimates show a considerable unmet demand for childcare: nearly half a million children under twelve required additional formal childcare in the mid-1990s (ABS 1994f, p. 16; AIFS 1995b, p. 5). That is, give women a chance and they will take it. Occupational choices, similarly, are unlikely to be the result of a lifelong distaste for male-dominated occupations (Jacobs 1989, pp. 169–71; Curthoys 1986, p. 323). Why would women actively want lower paying 'female' jobs? If women are in 'female' jobs because they expect intermittent employment and allegedly self-select these occupations, the question arises, why are women who plan and actually experience continuous employment, not in the same high-paying jobs as men? Jacobs also argues that men who fought in World War II were not penalised on return to work for lack of commitment, but women who produce the next generation are penalised (Jacobs 1989, p. 47).

Supply-side theories insist that the labour market would be 'neutral' (with no wage differential between men and women) if the supply of labour were neutral, that is, if there were 'no division of labour in families' (Mincer & Polachek 1974, pp. 424–5). This is, regrettably, not an argument in favour of equal sharing of family responsibilities by men, but an argument for no families at all. Their view is that labour market competition always eliminates wage differentials that are irrelevant to productivity or efficiency (Jacobs 1989, p. 171).

Since the male–female wage differential still persists, supply-side theorists have sought new reasons for describing women as inefficient. Women (not men), according to them, must be deficient in some personal attribute or because of their familial responsibilities. The demand side is only interested in employing workers who behave as 'single' unencumbered individuals. Profits should not be threatened by women's absence (having babies).

The supply side is therefore 'blamed' for persisting in having families, although men are apparently not responsible in this respect. Supply-side theorists fail to account for substantial 'residual discrimination' even after all relevant attributes that are economically measurable are taken into account (Jacobs 1989, p. 172). When these economic differences—education, marital status, trade union membership, occupation and industry—are subtracted, women still earn 13 per cent less than men, facts strongly suggesting that employers do discriminate against women (Mumford 1989, p. 43). Statistics for contemporary Australian female employees also show their high efficiency, low turnover (or similar quit rates to men) and rates of absenteeism virtually equal to men's (Mumford 1989, p. 3).

The alternative to supply-side explanations of wage differentials in the labour market is demand-side explanations. Evidence about the demand side—about employers' behaviour—remains a formidable obstacle to human capital theory's expectation of declining occupational segregation. This suggests that the labour market is so structured against women per se, and equally against responsibilities entailed in rearing of children in general, that it defines women's weak family position. Not only is there a substantial wage gap but sex segregation also keeps appearing in new forms.

Labour market discrimination against family responsibilities

In relation to segregation in the labour market, Jill Rubery finds that while patterns of contemporary segregation differ across OECD countries, the sexual division of labour has neither decreased nor simply stagnated over the century. Equivalent levels of segregation or, in the United States with less sex-typing of jobs, simply lower female pay, were created anew in the 1970s when major changes occurred both in female workforce participation and in the structure of industries and occupations. Processes of substitution—the feminisation and downgrading of an occupation—have occurred around old and new technologies (Rubery 1988, p. 256).

Segregated markets

From this picture of revitalised and obstinate sex segregation, a group of theorists quite different from orthodox economics suggests that the explanations lie in the employers' court. Demand-side theories suggest that women's unequal employment is due not to employers' mistaken ideas about women's inefficiency, but to employers' 'informed' demand for different types of workers (Beechey & Perkins 1987, p. 134). Discrimination is systematic, or institutionalised in the structure of the labour market. As Karen Mumford points out, demand approaches assume that employers have a degree of power which is used discriminately and advantages arise for them from the existence of at least two or more labour markets which are only in limited competition with each other. The labour market is divided into segments and perfect competition does not prevail because women do not have the whole labour market available in which to compete (Barron & Norris 1976, p. 47; Mumford 1989, p. 78).

The result is a lack of opportunities for women, who are concentrated in a limited number of lower paying, lower status and less secure occupations and industries, compared with male workers. Many suggest that employers actively seek to maintain low-wage segments within and across enterprises where women and migrants predominate, and to use male workers' sexism and racism to keep the working class divided, in order to cynically manipulate and control workers. This points to the contradiction between control over the workforce and cheap labour, since it means employers pay higher wages to men. It may be in their interest to divide and conquer but it is also in their interests to minimise wage costs (Curthoys 1986, p. 325; Jacobs 1989, p. 174).

A more sophisticated approach here describes competition in which there are a very few, exclusive labour buyers in a powerful market position, sufficient to discriminate between particular groups of workers.[6] Such employers can set conditions, reduce the wages of the particular group and deny them job opportunities. This increases the number in the group seeking the few sources of employment, who are replaceable however many leave for child-bearing reasons. When, as in Australia, there are large numbers of women concentrated in a narrow band of occupations, female workers' market power is low due to high levels of competition, and paid maternity leave is difficult to claim (Mumford 1989, pp. 84–5).

The narrow range of occupations are, at one end, 'backstage' jobs such as cleaning, food processing and sweated rag-trade jobs, and at the other, frontstage 'sexualised' jobs (receptionists, airline attendants, bar workers) where women are management's 'adjunct control workers' who soothe male customers and businessmen with heterosexual forms of flirting (Tancred-Sheriff 1993). Among other forms of discrimination involved here, such as ethnicity, sexuality and 'appearance', women with family responsibilities do not fare well in either job category.

'Managing to discriminate'

These demand-side explanations describe the ways an existing labour market is not neutral to all members of families. Sex segregation is undoubtedly useful to employers in increasing their ability to hire cheap workers on the market. Theories that examine employer or capitalist power *within* the workplace, rather than just the market power of hiring and firing, can show that the dynamic nature of employment is more significant in explaining discrimination than the existence of market segments. The human capital approach cannot explain why markets throw up new forms of discrimination, because it focuses on market competition and ignores employers' efforts to establish and maintain workplace control.

Profitability is contingent not only on wage price but also on productivity. To speed up the work process, gain more control and enhance productivity, employers frequently rely on removing workers with more human capital and substituting them with cheaper workers less able to achieve recognition for their skills. Labour process theories suggest low-paid work is continually recreated by introducing machinery and deskilling the existing workforce. Women are often used as the substitutes because their labour is cheaper, not because they are less productive.

As for explaining women's low pay, however, we are no further ahead. During cycles of deskilling and reskilling, the short-term decisions and intermittent employment ascribed to women, on account of their child-rearing responsibilities, should be no more disadvantageous to women than men's long-term decisions, which provide far from 'steady' employment these days.

As Collinson et al. point out, the thesis of deskilling and substitution ignores rigidities in the labour market (such as segregation of women in secretarial jobs), and ascribes too much intentionality to employers and passivity to employees. In their study of how managers do in fact discriminate against women in workplaces where men and women perform similar work (e.g. insurance companies), Collinson et al. suggest that management tends to swing between harsh 'time-and-motion' strategies and 'soft' human relations approaches. Factional management interests often lead to contradictory strategies between seeking control over workers, and fostering initiative and quality of output. For example, management tries to use 'the career' to induce conformity among male workers, but this leads to competition for career opportunities and reduces management coordination (Collinson et al. 1990, pp. 25–38).

Collinson et al. suggest that employers' efforts to control the workforce result in job segregation as an unintended consequence of management's pursuit of other objectives (Collinson et al. 1990, pp. 52–4). They stress that most managements seek to maintain their right to make arbitrary decisions regardless of whether or not they are discriminating (and buying 'expensive' labour), especially in recruitment, because their primary concern is to seek ways to control employees after they are hired. In recruiting, therefore, employers try to predict where sources of control may lie. Line managers override Equal Opportunity policy to maintain control of hiring. Men less qualified than women are still viewed more favourably if they have 'mortgages, wives and children', because management assumes these men will 'stick it' no matter what the work conditions or where they are sent

(Collinson et al. 1990, pp. 58–61). Those same responsibilities on the part of women are viewed negatively for inducing 'divided loyalties' between work and home, and making them 'difficult' or unstable in careers, but useful as a casual work-force tied to one place.

Thus employers actively choose particular workers on the basis of their different family responsibilities, in order to treat workers discriminately inside the workplace as well. Caring responsibilities and lack of affordable or decent childcare put women at a disadvantage compared with male employees. Part-time female workers, as a 1993 study of Australian banks shows, were regarded as working for 'pin money', and were denied opportunities to take career paths despite their skills and *preferences* to move out of a 'mother's track'. The supposed flexibility of part-time work was gained by employ-ers, not employees, since work arrangements were not responsive to the women's family responsibilities. Yet in the long run this discrimination is costly for the banks. The part-time female workforce was more stable than the male full-time employees, yet banks invested in training the younger men, whose turnover rate was high (Junor et al. 1993).

Women do engage in informal resistance to obvious dis-crimination, Collinson et al. argue, but this is usually by resigning (to look for work elsewhere or, failing that, to have a child). This only reinforces the likelihood of further discrim-ination. Those who challenge managerial discrimination often risk everything. Without wide support, from their union, their EEO personnel and higher management commitment to EEO, formal resistance (especially in individual court cases) can often leave individual women unable to find any further employment (Collinson et al. 1990, pp. 188–91). Historically, women have rarely enjoyed any support from male unions, male co-workers or governments, rather the reverse, and often from those who pride themselves as 'family men', as the next chapter shows.

Conclusion

The idea that families do not 'get what they want' on the labour market and, rather, must adjust to whatever discrimina-tion and differential pay they may find (Schor 1991) is in our view correct. Nevertheless, some members of families do benefit from this labour market situation more than others, in a sorry story where marital power is derived from higher pay. Women, whether they are mothers or might be mothers or have been mothers, must adjust to what they can get on the market as well as paying for the costs of providing the future workforce. Even if employers have no rational interest in hiring expensive labour, their rational interest in controlling labour leads to contradictory and discriminatory practices. Nevertheless, employers derive numerous advantages from the privatised nature of family responsibilities. In times of high unemployment employers are also able to avoid training the future workforce.

Orthodox economics' claims about the neutrality of profit rationality rely on assuming lone adult individuals with neither past nor present ties and responsibilities (mother-free). That is, the family is fundamentally non-existent. In an attempt to provide a less discriminatory explanation than a single house-hold head who rules the family, another option is a single family utility function, but this is implausible. Economics cannot explain why people form families, and refuses to consider the dependence of the market on families. Orthodoxy neglects the public goods aspect of children, and the fact that employers will not pay for long-term future benefits they gain, by providing parental leave and family-friendly, non-discrimi-natory workplaces, unless they are forced to do so by universal government regulations. This would change the rules of com-petition for all. The only time that employers were required to pay for this 'public goods' aspect of children was the time of the family wage. We will now turn to government policies that may shape, make or break particular family forms.

8

How the family is a problem for the state

The requirements of market rationality create a modern dilemma for family life between the obligations of 'caregiving' and the necessity to gain wages, which is not resolved to this day. In trying to resolve this dilemma (for the state), governments dither between particular family models, mainly that of the male household head, but sometimes the gender-neutral, individual family member model. Embedded in policies, however, a particular model defines the basis of citizen claims. In contrast to the dominant male model, which leaves everyone else as non-citizens or lesser citizens, the individual model supports an egalitarian citizen status for each family member. While children's rights, the rights of women and the elderly are still contentious claims, the household head model, resurrected by some as the answer to everyone's dreams of mutual affection, welfare and self-esteem, is for others a nightmare of injustice. A question here is whether rights are a necessary, but not sufficient, condition of the kind of family support that would ensure everyone's wellbeing and mutual respect in a family.

Economic and social policies are more important to the family—for good and ill—than the 'family policies' that many Western politicians claim will now solve our worries about families. In practice 'implicit' family policies have been around a long time under the name of economic and social policy.

Many of these policies are marked by inconsistencies and double standards. Uneven development between government policies, economic life and the modern family has left major legacies. Nostalgic fragments and hangovers from unretrievable and inappropriate family models add confusion to our normative expectations.

We will explore the 'family wage' and measures to increase the population as implicit family policies through which governments earlier in the twentieth century supported the male household head rather than other household members. In contrast, today's social policies are more gender neutral, however, the market is again becoming increasingly important. Current economic policies are enabling market-generated income, age and gender inequalities to appear in different guises thus (as we saw in Chapter 7), putting new strains on many families. If, in order to 'get ahead', mobility and flexibility are essential, families become a hindrance to professionals and labourers alike, whether bankers, hotel staff or mine workers. But first, given that the market and the state depend on families as much as vice versa, why is the institution of the family such a problem for the state?

The state of the 'problem'

Liberal democratic states in principle rule under limitations. They are supposed to treat the family as a private entity like the business corporation, outside the realm of state control or any overt and explicit prescriptions about the shape or daily activities of households. Most of us, for instance, would be deeply offended if a modern government sent out a yearly duty statement to households. The idea is ludicrous. We like our privacy and resent nosy parkers, especially Big Brother.

Beyond a legal framework that sets boundaries on the permissible, this state-provided shell is not meant to prescribe any other normative content for the modern family. The legal framework has changed slowly over the years in many Western jurisdictions. Until recently, husbands could, if they wished, enforce conjugal 'right' against their wives' refusal but this is now legally defined as marital rape; male adults committed a crime if they had consensual homosexual relations in the 'private' sphere but this is now permissible. These are still contentious issues, however, one might reasonably assume the state is less prescriptive or biased about the private sphere than before.

We will argue that although today's liberal democratic state is relatively 'neutral' about the content and shape of all those households that lie within the contemporary normative legal framework, this neutrality is itself a normative expectation. The liberal state sets the legal shell within which the family is an entity free to make its own choices. If the wrong choices are made, then the family (or the unhappy family member) has only itself to blame. These normative expectations leave us all feeling that any trouble stems from personal inadequacies, even failures. Anxieties and tensions over child-rearing or parental control, and arguments over money, household tasks or unemployment, are taken as signs of a 'dysfunctional family'. If our family is not quite the haven we yearn for, then a family scapegoat must be found.

For the sake of the privacy of the family, liberal democracies assume that 'the family' makes decisions as if it were one rational economic actor exercising preferences on the market. This is most pronounced in English-speaking countries of the OECD. Although households are no longer legally subsumed under the category of 'male household head', on most issues governments assume that families make collective, mutually advantageous decisions. That is, families operate as if they were one entity trying to get as much as possible for as little as possible on the consumer and job markets, and governments merely provide the shell for the 'successful' families to get ahead. All the rest of us, with our secret tensions and guilts as well as achievements beyond market price, are failed families.

As we saw in Chapter 7, rational actors are defined by self-interest: those who make the most 'rational' choices are those free of encumbrances, with no responsibilities or obligations. Their choices are simply a sequence of preferences, with one better than all the others rather than any choice excluding the others. Family members do not have conflicting needs or desires but unite in a harmony of preferences to achieve collective market success, and governments rejoice.

This normative idea of the government–household relation entails a number of inconsistencies. In practice, governments cannot, for the sake of government interests, really accept that household members are self-interested actors with no obligations towards each other. It is not only brutal but also detrimental for the state. Western governments learned during the nineteenth century, when prisons for the destitute and foundling hospitals could not cope with the influx, that rational economic actors may often be forced to abandon infants and frail elderly people. Today governments are very concerned about child poverty, teenage homelessness, divorce and ageing, surprisingly similar problems.

So, in industrial market societies, governments have attempted to cultivate or impose different obligations on household members, mainly by regulating around the fringes of the market. Depending on government exigencies of the day, a stream of government policies celebrate the normative ideal of family life as a fusion of a market actor with freely accepted, intimate obligations. This amalgam is internally contradictory, for the liberal state only recognises obligations as individual choices of rational actors who are free from long-lasting obligations. Many obligations in modern market societies originate, at least, in a 'free choice', rather like purchases in a market. Unlike purchases, however, these choices conflict—they are not a sequence of preferences with one slightly better than the rest. As we saw in Chapter 3, labour is no longer assigned to a master but is free to search for any employer; marriages are no longer arranged but freely chosen; children no longer arrive, they are planned. Yet wherever an obligation exists, there is no 'choice' to say 'today I will exercise my other preferences and refrain from feeding this helpless child or looking after this ageing person'. To avoid this flat contradiction, the liberal democratic state tends to sentimentalise family relations in rhetoric and intervene in specific ways against some family members and in favour of others. Rarely have governments offered much in terms of genuine support.

In recent times governments have made great claims about their 'family policies'. These concern the laws (over divorce, adoption, domestic violence, for example), income policies (such as tax concessions or child allowances) and direct services (child health centres and home care) which are said to comprise the state's role in family life (Kamerman & Kahn

1978; Baker 1995, p. 5). The ideals shaping family policy may be egalitarian, liberal or conservative yet, as far as the amount of revenue expended on family services is concerned, it is trivial in comparison with defence expenditure, for example. A junior minister, usually female, is often given charge of family policy. Far more significant is the fact that most economic and social policies exercise a much greater impact on family life than so-called family policies. Very few governments openly admit this. Child poverty, for example, is not simply a family policy issue, unrelated to economic policy: if high levels of unemployment are promoted by Treasury to control inflation, many parents cannot get jobs and hence there is child poverty.

Explicit family policies are often better seen as code words for women and/or children. In family policies, women are frequently reduced to a single role as breeders and caregivers, and children's futures to a consequence, for good and ill, solely of their mothers' work. Departments for 'Youth Affairs' or 'Community Services' are often renamed to include 'Family' in their title when conservative parties take office, possibly because conservative parties place more emphasis on a united family and play down the potentially different needs and interests within families, such as the rights of children and women, or young people's futures as adults. Idealised models of the family, which are often claimed to be fostered or undermined by different family policies, are not only politically contentious but divert attention from the importance of economic and social policy. A case in point is the way that the male breadwinner model emerged.

The family wage

Labour markets only reached fully developed form in industrial societies. Although the fiction that humans are commodities with no family responsibilities may be advantageous to employers in the short term (as we saw last chapter), maintaining this fiction is not a long-term possibility, even for employers. On the one hand families and on the other, the modern liberal government, must deal with the consequences.

Jane Humphries (1977), writing about the British case suggests that the family wage represented a victory for the working class as a whole. By the mid-nineteenth century, the conditions of the working class were desperate. Thus, one way to improve living standards was through the family. At that time, she argues, a male 'family wage', a ban on child labour and the exclusion of female workers was the only option available to the working class. The struggle was conditioned by the legacy of pre-existing forms of subordination of women.

The strategy required both defending real wage levels of men and fostering domestic production. Protective legislation which restricted female and child employment in factories and mines was, according to Humphries, promoted by government officials (1988, pp. 98–9). Keeping women at home reduced competition in the labour market. Since women's wages were lower than men's, women's exclusion had the effect of raising male wages. Thus emerged the model for the breadwinner–home-maker family, an ascribed division giving rise to 'a modern feudal gender order' in Ulrich Beck's phrase (1992, p. 108).

Australia was one of the few countries to institutionalise the concept of the 'family wage' (though it was widespread in most English-speaking countries). In 1907, Justice Higgins, Chair of the First Commonwealth Court of Conciliation and Arbitration, handed down his famous Harvester Judgement which effectively established the idea of a family wage to be set by arbitration rather than the 'unequal' contest on the labour market 'with the pressure for bread on one side, and the pressure for profits on the other'. Justice Higgins' standard of a 'fair and reasonable wage' was that appropriate to 'the normal needs of an average employee regarded as a human being living in a civilised community'. The family wage was conceived as a minimum or living wage sufficient for a man to support himself, his wife and children in 'frugal comfort' (Commonwealth Arbitration Reports 1907–1908, pp. 3–4; Pixley 1996, pp. 43–4).

Gradually, Arbitration judges formulated criteria for determining the 'normal needs' for a man with a 'dependent' wife and three to five children. This became the base for all unskilled male labour, with skilled labour awarded 'margins' on top of that. Thus ensued the needs-based 'family' or Basic Wage fixed independent of profit—as Higgins said, 'If the profits are nil, the fair and reasonable remuneration must be paid; and if the profits are 100 per cent., it must be paid' (1907–1908, p. 5). Marriage bars on female public servants meant that women had to resign on marriage. General agreements that female wages could not be *less* than half this male Basic Wage, and only equal to it where women worked in 'men's work', also gave male workers further protection in these instances from female competition (Ryan & Conlan 1975, pp. 90–103).

Frank Castles has argued that compared to other nations, in Australia wages policy was *the* substitute for social policy, with the Harvester Judgement the early and major landmark. Although Australia is presently 'the lowest welfare spender in the advanced world', the whole system of 'social protection' is not necessarily inferior (Castles 1994, pp. 124–7). This 'anomaly' he attributes to the creation of a 'wage earners' welfare state' at the beginning of the twentieth century when an 'historic compromise' between capital, labour and government was enacted. The strength of the labour movement, but the rarity of occasions when the Labor Party held political power both conditioned this development. Instead of insurance schemes (based on employment) and a 'social wage' (with government provisions such as public housing) as in Europe, the Australian labour movement set its sights on the actual wage (Castles 1985, p. 76). That is, although workers did support a 'welfare state', the Arbitration Courts would be their chief 'welfare agency' (Jamrozik 1994, p. 165).

The family wage—triumph for the working class or for men?

Important criticisms of the family wage suggest, at the least, that it did not serve the needs of women and children as beneficially as is often claimed. For a start, the claim that male workers colluded with government officials to exclude women for reasons quite opposite to the family wage concept is just as credible, particularly when it involved denying women the civil right to bargain 'freely' over their terms of employment.

The dispute turns on whether the union strategy in seeking a family wage was a measure intended to increase the welfare of all working people or whether it was a strategy to ensure the continuance of male power. Cynthia Cockburn's celebrated study (1985) dismisses the idea that workers jointly struggled for a family wage. In discussing the introduction of new machinery in workplaces, Cockburn shows that technical divisions, skills, techniques and machinery are not neutral but embody male power as well as employer power. Male economic dominance, she argues, is based on 'material' and 'socio-political' elements.

Bodily physique and the way this is manifested in technology, buildings, clothes, space and movement, constitute 'material instances of male power' (Cockburn 1985, pp. 126–7). She stresses looking at 'the way in which a small physical *difference* in size, strength and reproductive function is developed into an increasing relative physical *advantage* to men and vastly multiplied by differential access to technology' (1985, p. 129, emphasis in original). Cockburn suggests that 'the political power' in designing workplaces that put women at a disadvantage, requires that differences do exist, such as bodily strength, but more importantly that these differences can then be 'made to matter' (Cockburn 1985, p. 138). Irrelevant characteristics of ascribed difference were installed as 'relevant' differences.

The idea that men and women came to an harmonious agreement to exclude women through the family wage is also at odds with the history of male union strategies. Male organisations and solidarity in institutions such as unions, churches, clubs and societies, according to Cockburn, were implicated in the whole discriminatory process to give men 'socio-political' advantages, especially in dealing with governments.

Heidi Hartmann agrees that male unions actively promoted women's inferior labour market position in collusion with government officials. The male guilds were traditionally more organised than women's trades; male professionals, such as doctors, also established themselves through organising to remove women from midwifery and other medical services (1979, pp. 215–17).

As industrial capitalism expanded, protective legislation was a major factor in female exclusion and job segregation by sex, which caused overcrowding in female sectors, forced women's wages down and allowed men's to be higher, according to Hartmann. She takes numerous cases of factory legislation in the United States and Britain that limited the hours of children's exploitation, where their supervision there-upon became a problem. Instead of demands for provision of nursery care, or for safety standards suitable for men as well as women, the overwhelming evidence was that male magis-trates, bureaucrats and unions wanted to send married women to domestic duties (Hartmann 1979, pp. 221–3).

Collective action by relatively well-paid female textile workers last century (notably in Lancashire) also counteracts the idea that women freely accepted the family wage. Between the 1890s and 1920s, these women successfully resisted gov-ernment efforts to impose the marriage bar and male family wage, mobilising around the line that their male co-workers were 'rivals'. They also agitated with bourgeois feminists for the vote (Benenson 1991).

Ryan and Conlan show a similar pattern in Australia of male exclusion of women by governments and unions, although segregation was more marked because centralised arbitration formalised the family wage for men, and set women's wages at 54 per cent of male wages. The edifice thus incorporated the belief that women never had anyone to support, but all men did! (Ryan & Conlan 1975, pp. 62–3). Higgins' family wage concept assumed this human being to be a white married man with 3–5 children, and all women to be dependent on husbands or fathers. Yet in the comparatively prosperous year of 1911, over 45 per cent of men were unmarried by the age of 30 (Ryan & Conlan 1975, p. 108). In sum, centralised arbitration basically legalised what had been standard procedure in the past, that women should earn half except when skilled male workers wished to exclude them (Ryan & Conlan 1975, pp. 84–5; Cass 1983, p. 55).

Consequences of the family wage

There were many consequences of preventing women from claiming this family wage. The level itself was so low that many working-class families could not afford a housewife. The record of the male Basic Wage (in Australia) shows that between 1907 and 1967 it provided, at best, a bare minimum standard quite separate from the community at large, and for many years it was below even that (Gill 1988; Ryan & Conlan 1975). In many countries, the 'family wage' ideology never prevented women from being used as a reserve army to weaken male workers' bargaining power. (Barrett & McIntosh 1980, p. 59) nor 'saved' all the women with or without dependants, who were single, deserted or with a husband on the Basic Wage or unemployed, from seeking even lower, 'female' paid jobs such as cleaning and food processing.

The family wage also left a legacy of male unions concentrating on trying to make employers acknowledge that men were *financially* responsible for families. Male patterns of overtime are still entrenched in the labour market, thus increasing the incidence of the absent father. It was not until the 1990s that unions began to campaign for employers to recognise that responsibility entails care for children and elderly relatives, for example when they are sick.

The notion of a family wage assumes that if sufficient income is directed to the family, the welfare of all the members will be guaranteed. Furthermore, it assumes that childcare takes place primarily within this family unit. The family (it is assumed) operates as a private self-regulating entity which delivers care and nurture to all in equal proportions. The assumptions of family altruism are reminiscent of the family utility function of Gary Becker in the New Home Economics.

Male control of money

Thus, one major issue is whether male control over virtually all income (via the family wage) is indeed exercised in a fair or altruistic manner, since the fact of control means that sharing is in principle a discretionary option. There have been a number of small-scale studies of the internal distribution of income between family members (e.g. Pahl 1989; Edwards 1984; Morris 1990) and more recent large studies, such as the British Household Panel Survey. This explored the financial distribution systems of over 6000 British couples in 1991 and again in 1992 (Laurie & Rose 1994).

Jan Pahl's pioneering work on household finances outlines four basic management systems (1989, pp. 67–77): the first is the 'whole wage system' where one or the other partner manages all household income; the second the 'allowance system' with the main earner handing over a set amount of money for housekeeping; third is the 'joint management' system or pooling and fourth and least common is the independent system where both partners earn and manage their own incomes. Each of these systems has its own potential for inequalities.

Meredith Edwards (1984, p. 132) and Pahl (1989, p. 68) agree that wives tend to manage the family finances in a 'whole wage system' when it is a case of stretching to make ends meet. Under the strain of inadequate household funds, along with a working-class pattern of male sociability around pubs, which protects male spending money, many contemporary wives are likely to take employment precisely because they cannot gain a fair share of male earnings. Lydia Morris also suggests that where male income is higher, there is a shift from female to male management, either the whole wage or allowance system. In both of these cases there is greater potential for secrecy about the amount of wage or salary, which is also likely to motivate married women into employment to escape conflict over financial distribution (Morris 1990, pp. 110–18).

In Pahl's study of 102 British couples' money relations, she found that while more than half her couples claimed to use a pooled or shared system, under pooling more wives than husbands had to justify spending to their partner (Pahl 1989, pp. 85). Even so, this greater accountability demanded from wives was not because they were the stereotypical extravagant wife, carelessly spending their husbands' income. Pahl found wives were more likely to be seen by themselves and their husbands as more careful with money than husbands: however the 'extravagant' working-class husband, she suggests, 'is still alive and still spending money at the expense of his wife and children' (1989, pp. 102–3).

In pooled as well as independent finance systems, wives rarely defined themselves as in control of finances. When interviewed individually there were disparities, for example, husbands perceived equality more than did their wives (Pahl 1989, p. 81), husbands overestimated the amounts their wives spent on leisure whereas wives underestimated their husbands' leisure spending. Both gave precedence to the husband's right to leisure (Pahl 1989, p. 148).

For those who argue that these surveys are too small, the British Household Panel Survey does not have this problem, with a sample of 6000 couples. The commonest form of management today, in agreement with the small studies, is pooled or shared management; however, allowance systems are most likely where women are not in paid employment. Moreover, nearly 30 per cent of respondents gave a different response to that of their partner about the financial system they thought was being used (Laurie & Rose 1994, p. 232), which suggests that negotiation here is limited. Although there is more sharing when women enter full-time employment, it does not automatically lead to more egalitarian management systems (Laurie & Rose 1994, pp. 220–1). By far the majority of the 6000 couples, about 65 per cent in both waves, said they had an equal say in 'big financial decisions', whereas in about 25 per cent of cases the man had the final say (1994, p. 228).

An English study of two-earner households found that men paid for 'the roof over the family's head' and women for shopping and childcare (Brannen & Moss 1987, p. 84). Also, women were far more responsible for expenditure incurred because of the two-earner lifestyle, such as childcare, running a second car and paid domestic help. These were seen 'as a charge on *women's* earnings rather than on household income' (Brannen & Moss 1987, p. 82). These outlays on recurring expenses reduce women's contribution to household capital investment, however there is a strong association between full-time employment of women and the use of a shared or pooled management system (Laurie & Rose 1994, p. 240) which could alleviate this division in spending. Supriya Singh's study of marriage and consumers' use of Australian banks found that modern joint accounts with electronic access and credit card statements have provided both husband and wife with access to information about the flow of money. This information can be obtained without having to ask each other questions about the cash flow (Singh 1994, p. 81). Indeed, questions about income inequality, power and control are not discussed but redefined as 'jointness' or 'sharing', 'trust' and 'commitment'. Those questions blocked during marriage, such as relative financial and non-financial contributions, only emerge as a central issue when the marriage dissolves (Singh & Lindsay 1996, p. 66).

It is clear, then, that the old family wage not only gave men more pay than employed women could ever hope to earn, but also men did not share it equally with their families. In cases of very low male wages, women had to manage the pittance. These traditions, the opposite of assumptions about family altruism, clearly persist to the present day, particularly for non-employed wives. Drawing on similar data from the United States, Susan Moller Okin agrees that even if married couples may share some material wellbeing, most housewives or wives with a part-time job lack access to very much of their own money. This can lead to mildly irritating problems or worse, to humiliating appeals for more money and devastating conflicts, even seriously affecting their physical safety because they lack the income to leave (Okin 1989, pp. 151–2).

Mother–child isolation—'all day everyday'

Another major consequence of the family wage was that for 50 years, the care of children became more private than in any culture at any other time in history. The notion of the mother–child bond is new (as we saw in Chapter 3), however, this bourgeois view became widespread with the family wage. It is often forgotten that working-class households never enjoyed the extensive support staff of nannies, servants and the governess of the bourgeois mother. The assumption that mothers are individually responsible for children's entire upbringing and nurture, and should be isolated with their small charges in private households 'all day everyday' (Brennan 1994, p. 52), severely curtailed the development of public childcare and other support earlier this century, particularly in English-speaking countries. In the 1950s, the controversial doctrine of 'maternal deprivation' gave a bad name to childcare centres which enabled mothers to take jobs. The doctrine was treated as 'gospel' by politicians and teachers alike. Yet most research on 'maternal deprivation' studied children in the huge, impersonal, understaffed orphanages of World War II, where their emotional, social and cognitive development was indeed likely to suffer; it did *not* examine children in childcare centres (Brennan 1994,

p. 59). There is obviously a stark difference between a kinder-garten—a garden where children can bloom —and orphanages or ill-equipped 'minders'.

Moreover, as Eva Cox suggests, exclusively private child-rearing tends to isolate households from the broader community links which can alleviate domestic 'problems of power and abuse, on the one hand, and loneliness and limitations on the other'. It has also led to 'inappropriate expectations that these small, fragile units can deliver a wide range of services through their limited personal resources' and rear children to be socially competent adults (Cox 1995, pp. 31–2). Such privacy is a 'deprivation' which has increased in past decades, as fewer parents permit children to play on neighbourhood streets now saturated with cars. Privacy deprives children of social contacts with other adults and children, and the training in sociability, trust and cooperation that occurs within dependable and quality childcare services. As Cox argues, the idea that 'bonding' of mother and child may be 'a continuous ecstatic experience' for the mother, does little to dispel concern that 'over-bonding' is more likely to create 'self-interested individuals in search of personal gratification' than competent and cooperative adults with 'civic virtues' (Cox 1995, p. 33). The effects on mothers—after years of isolated child-rearing with limited social contacts themselves, and the social pressures as the only person respon-sible for their children's entire development—are just as likely to be anxiety and feelings of inadequacy.

Decline of full-time home-making

Most evidence points to the fact that 'man the breadwinner' was a fairly broad reality only in the recent past. When factory work began, women and children formed the majority of early wage labourers in Britain (Berg 1988, pp. 64–5), and domestic service was the largest occupational category during the entire nineteenth century. In 1901, 31 per cent of all women were employed in Australia; although only 8 per cent of married women were so occupied, a far greater proportion of women (and men) were never married (by age of 40) than today. Since the 1940s, women's workforce participation has risen steadily (Mumford 1989; Kaplan 1996, p. 20).

The idea of a timeless and universal split between bread-winners and homemakers is even more untenable. Across all the OECD countries, such a specific division was widespread merely between about 1890 and 1940 (Pahl 1988). In Australia a dual breadwinning family began to consolidate after World War II as the majority of married immmigrant women joined the labour market. Since then, for example, two generations of Italian and Greek women have worked the double shift (Vasta 1995, p. 149; Kaplan 1996, p. 20). Australian-born women soon joined them: from a low point in 1947 when only 6.5 per cent of all married women in Australia took paid jobs, to the 1990s when over 50 per cent of married women participate in the labour force. In 1990, 72 per cent of all women aged 35 to 44, and an even higher percentage of women in their early twenties, were in the labour market, (Mumford 1989, p. 6; Bradbury 1996, pp. 15–18).

Nevertheless, for good and ill, the effects of the family wage policy on households have in some ways remained to this day. Conservative politics espouses the model as the ideal family. Economic theory disregards the state-imposed family wage when it suggests that women simply 'exercise a preference' for low-paid work to accommodate childcare. In principle, the family wage and more obviously the salary (which rises via promotion) becomes the chief mediation between the long-term collective, macro-level responsibilities for the future and past generations, and the privatised responsibilities of women. The labour market became rigidly segmented into women's and men's jobs. Women's pay has never caught up, even though Australian women won 'equal pay' in 1969, it was only much later that men's and women's pay rates became closer to equal in Australia than in many countries. Employers are now urged, but not required, to accede to workplace provisions for family responsibilities, whereas formerly they were required to pay for the costs of children and female dependency by assuming this in a wage to male workers. Women's low pay made the goal of marriage an economic necessity, and rendered home-making and exclusive responsibility for children a nearly compulsory path, not a choice.

Just as important, the family has become 'private'. With the policy assumption that welfare is exchanged within families, the non-intervention of the state in any further relations of individual members of families could be justified. Traditional male rule, with its potential for discretionary violence sanctioned by the state until the end of the nineteenth century, and the new power from superior earnings, continues within the modern family form.

The liberal doctrine of public and private spheres

The family wage is one of the most extensive family policies of the liberal democratic state (notably of the English-speaking countries), because it touched nearly all working-class households, so too the Factory Acts (1840s) and Education Acts (1880s) which protected children from exploitation. Yet liberalism is primarily a doctrine of freedom from state interference, as we noted earlier. One could assume that liberal doctrine might oppose these state restrictions, on women's freedom and civil rights at least, if not children's freedom to contract to an employer of their own choosing. In the case of children, William Blake and Charles Dickens could readily cast the nineteenth-century employer as villain. To counter the harsh, lonely world of selling oneself and one's child, the bourgeois family became the norm for policy. Traits of altruism and affection were newly ascribed to women in a normative sentimentalising of the family. Men found themselves free of these ascriptions.

In liberal political doctrine, as Carole Pateman points out (1979; 1983; 1988b), the inclusive 'public' sphere of state *and* market is governed by impersonal, conventional and universal criteria of achievement, interests, rights, equality and property, whereas the private sphere of family is governed by personal, natural (biological) and particular criteria: there is no place for equality, interests and rights in the family. Altruism reigns. Yet civil society, comprising both market *and* family, is not open to public scrutiny and the liberal state is not meant to regulate but to be a neutral umpire over the diverse interests of rational actors. Family members, in liberal doctrine, do not have diverse interests but harmonious unity.

There are, according to Pateman, contradictory principles for the two 'private' unregulated spheres, which entail two different kinds of relations. Governments must intervene in neither. The first is the free, self-interested market relation where a private property owner can exercise his opportunities free from state or personal paternalism. By contrast, in the non-liberal, self-sacrificial household relations, paternal power over children, for example, is justified as 'natural' (Pateman 1983, pp. 282–5), and until the 1890s, men had legal powers of property ownership and chastisement over their wives and children. Pateman identifies the dark side of the sentimentalised (bourgeois) family, showing how the sexually-ascribed subordination of women in the labour market and of wives to their independent property-owning husbands is usually played down by modern liberalism.

So, in the nineteenth century, *the citizenry,* or all those who freely operated as self-interested, rational individuals in the labour market *and* inside the family, was exclusively male. Even by the twentieth century, when governments could no longer ignore the fact that markets failed, the creation of a state-provided 'safety net' under this imperfect market was meant to ensure that men had a softer landing. The social policies of unemployment benefits, sickness leave and disability benefits began as gendered forms of state support. In Pateman's interpretation, these benefits were designed to prevent men from losing their independence and self-respect when they were 'undeserved exiles' from gainful employment. Governments looked upon women, by contrast, as 'natural' social exiles. Through the marriage contract they were financially the private dependants of husbands, subject to patriarchy 'behind closed doors' (Pateman 1988a, pp. 238–9).

Although most liberals do admit that the family is 'a structure of power', they claim it is also 'ennobled by sentiment' (Okin 1989, p. 121). But if the family is such a private affair, how can they know? Moreover, since marriage relations are entered into by contract between presumed equals, this free choice is meant to justify the subsequent subordination as well. A further sleight of hand occurs in extolling this questionable choice for women of the marital contract: children, of course, do not 'choose' their parents at all.

Economic policy or family policy?

For about forty years, until the 1970s, the normative assumptions about the unpaid home-maker family model were beyond much question. Particularly in the aftermath of World War II, when Keynesian economic doctrines provided the stability of full male employment, improved housing and community services, the model seems to have met with broad acceptance. Many formerly impoverished households managed to gain a relatively frugal comfort, with improved male wages supporting domestic consumption and production. The family was implicitly included as a 'meso-economic institution' (as outlined in Chapter 7). Since the 1970s, however, Keynesian macro-economic policies to regulate and coordinate public, private and household sectors within a nation-state have given way to increasingly internationalised markets in finance, labour, productive and property investment. Neoclassical economic policies have returned. In this new political and economic climate, it is hardly surprising that a number of different idealisations have emerged about the family.

One story is that feminism has captured 'family policies' with the dire result of 'destroying' the family. Far from a 'patriarchal welfare state' that previously seemed so entrenched in major government policies such as the family wage and breadwinner welfare, some conservatives claim there is a 'feminist welfare state'. The introduction of sole parent pensions, equal pay decisions, divorce reform, basic enforcement of existing laws against wife battering and child abuse, anti-discrimination legislation, childcare services and reproductive rights are variously said to foster selfish women who neglect their children and elderly parents by holding down jobs (e.g. Tapper 1990; Lyons Forum 1995; James ed., 1989).

Women are getting paid for some of the work they do. Also social policy in Australia now treats men and women as individuals in the pension and allowance system, rather than rewarding a sole male breadwinner. According to the conservative story, however, male authority in the family has been undermined and men are suffering. Also, only 'intact families' contribute to 'society's resources', but primarily as a 'negative contribution' by 'lack of depletion': it is claimed that they do not rely on public resources as much as 'separated families' (Lyons Forum 1995, p. 10). The welfare state is blamed for interfering in family life; its overspending has also resulted in the labour market being unable to clear. The safety net gives a soft landing—too soft for a flexible, disciplined workforce that should compete on the global labour market. The consequence is high unemployment as well as women denied the choice to stay at home. With the demise of the male family wage, women are apparently 'forced' into outside employment to make ends meet, to help pay the mortgage, and they are exhausted by the double shift. The answer is said to lie in restoring the self-regulating market and the self-regulating family.

These prescriptions are contradictory. The family wage in Australia involved one of the most striking attempts of any Western government to *impose* regulations on employers. That is, the labour market was required to support the family, however specific the family form. Unemployment, market-clearing wages, speculation on housing property are all detrimental to households (let alone diverse family members), and unnecessary when Keynesian national and international regulations were effective. Yet commentators and politicians of the Right in Australia urge that women (married women) be sent back home rather than seeking new institutional arrangements, particularly ones that would regulate the labour market to support family life in some way, indeed in any way, gendered or otherwise. Thus the Liberal Government in Australia in 1996 introduced family policies that operate through tax policies, that is, without a central arbitration system. Indeed, the Industrial Commission has been a central candidate for abolition. Although the Keynesian regulations and full male employment which supported post-war family life are gone, it is that unpaid home-maker *family model* which these commentators want to restore. They propose a 'solution' in which liberalism meets conservatism exclusively over the family, and economic liberalism (the unfettered market) reigns everywhere else (Pixley 1993a).

Comparative evidence about the major transformation away from the entirely dependent home-maker model suggests that state welfare does not have such a constructive or, depending on one's point of view, destructive effect on the family type. Obviously welfare provision may be ameliorative, but by the end of the 1980s, Jill Rubery's analysis of labour market trends led to the following conclusion:

> the striking fact that emerges in comparisons across countries is the lack of any association between *levels* of state welfare provision and either family structure or female participation

rates. Thus the US has experienced the fastest rate of break-
down in traditional family organisation and the highest female
participation rates against a background of very limited state
welfare support. (her emphasis, Rubery 1988, p. 279)

This raises important issues about 'family policy' or rather, the
precise ways that governments might be viewed as influencing
the earlier and currently predominant family forms. It suggests
that 'family policies' may either make family life more bearable
for all family members or only for the male household head,
but economic and social policies are far more important. In
the United States today, some couples holding down four jobs
between them cannot make ends meet, and 'non-elderly adults'
comprise an absolute majority (52 per cent) of all poor
persons. With minimum wage regulation increasingly limited,
average income on the lowest income scale has fallen by 23
per cent between 1973 and 1993 (Bluestone & Ghilarducci
1996, p. 40). In contrast, Australia's national system of labour
market regulation, for example, used to prevent women from
making wage claims as equals to men and then, after 1969,
enabled women to improve their relative pay rates more than
in most other Western countries. Full male employment turned
into full employment, with a social infrastructure that enabled
families to envision a bright future for their children. This dual
moment, of Keynesian regulations and women's further emancipation, was a brief episode in the story of government efforts
to reduce the baleful effects on families of full market societies.
Even more significant, the global market was stabilised to
enable many OECD countries to share wealth more equitably.

In the past, English-speaking liberal democracies rarely
pursued explicit and comprehensive 'family' policies. Debate
among specialists in comparative family policy has moved from
a defininition of *explicit family policies* as those designed to
support families, across class, for men, women and children,
with many other government policies operating as *implicit
family policies* for their indirect consequences (Kamerman &
Kahn 1978, p. 3). Now specialists maintain that family policy is
not a separate entity from broader social and economic policy
(Baker 1995, p. 371). For example, although the Australian
'family wage' of 1907 did shape a particular family form, it was
explicitly a policy for fostering industrialisation and increasing

the population. In our view, family policies (explicit and implicit) have often had other aims, such as controlling fertility and imposing caregiving on women, rather than supporting the various family members for their own sake.

Population policy

Any account of Australian population policies must acknowledge a history of racism. During the nineteenth century, Australian colonial governments were involved in warfare against Aboriginal populations and later, 'protection' policies directed at the Aboriginal population aimed to destroy their family–kinship systems. For Aboriginal people, these were not liberal democracies: the official position did not misrecognise Aboriginal family forms, it denied the existence of any 'family' whatsoever. Either Aboriginal people assimilated or they would probably die out on reserves or pastoral 'leases' of whites. Queensland governments only ceased removing children from Aboriginal families in the 1970s.

In contrast to this wide-ranging policy of the attempted destruction of Aboriginal society, colonial policy for white families was hardly far-reaching, if only because there were few 'families' at all. That is, the heterosexual couple was a rarity until the 1880s. The pastoral industry required a large pool of itinerant male workers which colonial governments supplied from convict gaols and immigration schemes. A gender imbalance among the white population remained so extreme that by the 1850s there were 'dire predictions of a homosexual society' (Jones 1980, p. 8). Governments encouraged religious reformers to scour the British Isles for families of 'respectable immigrants' and single women who were meant to begin as servants and then marry their job. Pastoralists continued to prefer importing single men 'with no encumbrances', and single male migration also swelled with the gold rushes from 1850 (Summers 1975, pp. 296–304).

Women as 'breeders'

In Australia by the 1890s, the demographic ratio between the sexes had finally evened out in urban areas. But ironically for governments' pro-family, natalist intentions, the new balance of the sexes heralded a pronounced trend towards the permanent decline in the birth rate that was occurring in most industrialising countries. Arriving into a white society of close mates (too close for governments), women found that employment, child-rearing and leisure opportunities were extraordinarily restricted. Infanticide is thought to have been widespread and 'foundling hospitals' became a charitable growth industry. The strong feminist movement of the 1900s vigorously opposed the large family of twelve or more children (and the male double standard that accompanied it) (Pixley 1991).

Western governments' concern about declining fertility was possibly the most marked at this time in France. Yet in comparison with Anglo-American factory protective legislation which excluded women from employment, France took a different path to promote fertility. By 1913 legislation provided for paid maternity leave for French women. Women were addressed as workers needing such leave for the health of infants, but the debates embraced parents per se. Men were regarded as needing an eight-hour day so that fathers could spend more time with their children (Jenson 1990, pp. 153–6). Today France is judged to have the best maternity leave and public childcare systems in the world, although Sweden, also historically concerned about fertility, has most pursued gender equality (Baker 1995, pp. 35, 361).

In contrast, Anglo-American countries have been more indifferent to the actual needs of women and children in pursuing pro-natalist policies, and have never suggested that fathers play more than a financial role. Australia's panic over the birthrate decline became widespread after Federation in 1901, when the infamous immigration restrictions banned the importation of 'cheap' labour. The new Federal Government aimed to develop a skilled, stable workforce after the male itinerance of the pastoral era. Women had a role—only in the new 'stable' family and only as instruments to other ends. But they were not 'performing' and population growth could not be fostered by immigration. Pro-natalist considerations were certainly a factor in government support of the family wage, to the disgust of feminists at the time. In arbitration courts, justifications were often made in terms of protecting mothers from harmful employment and from the 'practice of prevention' (contraception) (Summers 1975 pp. 338–9). It was argued that if women's job options were drastically reduced, women would be encouraged to produce large families. A Royal Commission on the declining birthrate restricted women's access to abortion and 'prevention', with the result that abortion became more prevalent but also more hazardous. Influenced by racism and eugenics, population control and pro-natalist policies became entrenched as a legitimate concern of government (Allen 1982).

Jill Roe suggests that the Australian political system has been little concerned with women's welfare as such. During the 1900s the only positive support for women's welfare was also about national efficiency and race propagation, by being directed only to mothers, but even this was always very limited (Roe 1983, p. 4). While the sums in no way compare with male wage levels, in 1912 the Federal Government began a system of 'baby bonuses' to white women, with a premium of £5 for 'viable births' only, not still-borns or survival of mothers. This universal maternity allowance even disregarded marital status, a tolerance uncharacteristic of that era due to fears of 'race suicide' (Shaver 1993, p. 6).

As the demographic trends make clear, Australia's efforts to 'populate or perish' met with no success until the baby boom after 1945, since fertility rates continued to decline in the 1920s and 1930s. Maternal mortality actually rose between 1910 and 1930. It accounted for one-sixth of married women's deaths during mid-adult life, possibly due to the medicalisation of childbirth (Roe 1983, pp. 6–8). As Maureen Baker points out, although the governments of France and Sweden actually made the *social environment* more conducive to child-rearing than did those of Canada, Australia or the United States, this may not have increased the birthrate either. Nevertheless, the generous Swedish and French policies, supportive childcare services and maternity allowances certainly improved the lives of parents raising children, and possibly slowed the fertility decline (Baker 1995, p. 366). Through egalitarian policies greater welfare was achieved for both women and children than was possible with 'separate spheres' policies, so rigidly fostered in Australia.

It seems fair to say that 'Motherhood' (the provision of babies to the society), defined how women made claims on the state as citizens until the 1970s, in Australia as in many other Western countries. The treatment of returned soldiers was both more expansive than civilian pensions or benefits, and civilian health and housing provision. It further emphasised how risking and destroying life was valued by governments so much more than creating life, also a risky business until recently (Wheeler 1989). War service enhanced the rights a man could claim on the state, an 'RSL-citizenship' unavailable to women and male civilians, particularly certain ethnic minorities.

Shared parenting?

Nevertheless, Australia was unusual in its universal old age pension of 1908 to men *and* women, which required no prior contributions from wages. In contrast, with the introduction of compulsory superannuation in the 1980s, today's women who take unpaid leave from the workforce to produce the future generation will have reduced entitlements to superannuation in their old age (Donath 1994). This shows the difficulties for women in the introduction of gender-neutral social security, for it fails to recognise the 'public goods' aspect of children in supporting the elderly population. It will mean that the people who lose income to provide the next generation are a major category who lose income in old age as well.

Today, women are paid workers in their own right and, however difficult to achieve, some reforms are occurring around pay discrepancies and male-defined workplaces. Women are less dependent on men. The marriage contract no longer explicitly defines male possession as a right to male domination. In Australia abortion is available through Medicare, as a last resort if the plethora of contraceptive methods fail. Choices for women have expanded and this should be reflected in familial relations.

Yet the new two-earner family has been less an improvement for women and children than hoped for by 1960s feminism. The model of a supposedly independent woman is insufficient, as is neutrality in family policy and the labour market. Women are now income earners, yet domestic abuse persists and domestic tasks have not been renegotiated. Instead women turn to divorce. Labour market provisions for family responsibilities are neither extensive nor secure.

Why, despite all the advantages of female employment, is family life still troubled? Many feminists suggest that the liberal feminist promise has become a hollow gain, made at the expense of women becoming like men. For Pateman, for example, legal equality has safeguarded women's bodily integrity, by removing legal sanctions on male domestic violence. Although this is an obvious gain, she argues that equality as a contracting 'individual' places women in a patriarchal category (Pateman 1988b, p. 231).

It also requires that women should treat their families as men have done, as last resorts, only of utility when comfort is needed. But then, who is left to provide comfort from loneliness, or to care for the children of the marriage, de facto marriage or whatever sexual liaison? The sexual division of labour and the modern private/public dichotomy has imposed on women a choice of career *or* children—only men and the 'exceptional woman' can have both. Thus the modern 'corporate woman' tends to buy her way out of domestic duties (Di Stefano 1991, pp. 182–5; Jaggar 1990, pp. 248–52). Career life increasingly destroys family life—the labour market assumes unattached singles.

Liberal democracies now provide equal rights for women to be like men, but the public/private split leaves women's either/or choices remaining in slightly revised form. The old 'non-interventionist' patriarchal state that allowed discretionary male violence in the family is technically gone. With reformed policies and employment opportunities, but still deep family tensions, the question then arises as to why women still marry. Who would want marriage (or cohabitation) if it is only about male sexual access, or even mutual access, and acrimonious disputes over male demands for domestic servicing?

The tribulations of 'reproductive choice'

It cannot be emphasised enough that the category of family embodies not merely a contract between a couple but usually children. Economic liberalism tries to avoid its own conclusions of the irrationality of reproduction for economic actors, as discussed in Chapter 7. Even debates about the development of a potentially 'pure relationship', where children are an 'internal drag' (Giddens 1991, p. 89), mainly question whether

a male-defined contract to sexual possession between heterosexual adults only subordinates women in a new way (Pateman
1988b). Children are mentioned in passing. Yet normative
expectations about children have been part of family policy
(and economic policy) for over a century. Children are predominantly thought of as personal delights, sacred, priceless beings
and as such, attention to their personal safety, development
and welfare has rightly expanded greatly, particularly in Scandinavia. We all tend to idealise children, although less so the
teenagers they inevitably become as, for example, in the use
of the term 'youth'. The British government recently found it
easier to increase parents' financial and other responsibilities
for children (even 'children' of 25) than to increase adult
children's responsibilities for their ageing parents. There is a
much stronger sense that we are personally responsible for the
younger generation than for the older (Millar 1996).

Policy assumptions that parents *indulge* themselves in
bringing children to the world and—as we noted last chapter—
do this for their personal utility, are nevertheless unfounded.
Everyone wants to love children but care takes time in a world
where time is money. If children are a personal indulgence,
women will gladly have many children and government pro-
natalism would be unnecessary. Pro-natalism has returned
mainly in Eastern Europe: in the 1990s Poland and Hungary
are trying to outlaw abortion, although in the former East
Germany young women are having themselves sterilised to
improve their job prospects (Einhorn 1993, p. 103). In countries
with no population panic, economic liberalism insidiously
undermines government policy that deep down knows that
societies can only continue with some population 'turnover', to
put it crudely.

In a climate of market-driven 'coordination', the biological
impossibility of sameness, that is, women's child-bearing ability, is cast in liberal terms as disability. Hard-won labour
market regulations such as maternity and parental leave are
attacked as fetters on competition. Workers can play the job
market only if mobile, career-obsessed and flexible, so women
delay child-bearing for as long as possible. Despite the sentimental rhetoric of liberal democracies about dependency and
caring for young and old, modern institutional arrangements
to foster society's responsibility for the future generation face

reductions when the market prevails. The responsibility for children is dressed up as women's free choice. This is a major reason why governments cannot devise consistent family policy.

Liberal democracies are inconsistent about the choice of whether to have children, which is supposedly private and yet remarkably public, given that abortion is a regular debating point of male politicians. With abortion legalised and contraception available, decisions about having children are in that sense a *choice*. Modern feminism has defended women's 'right to choose' as a principle in legislation, not without misgivings in using such a flawed legal framework that demarcates private from public and society from individual (Di Stefano 1991, p. 170), for conception is hardly an individual affair. The offer of the 'right to choose' implies that women be constantly available to heterosexual genital sex, a common 'first wave' feminist objection to abortion (Gordon 1982), and that only women are responsible for whatever children might be born as a result.

Those opposed to abortion frequently employ double standards. Fundamentalist and nationalist opposition to abortion wants the state to reimpose on women the burden of unwanted pregnancies but places no requirement on men to exercise restraint, take precautions or shoulder childcaring responsibilities.

There is, however, no doubt that the abortion issue is a fundamental ethical dilemma. Some people are opposed to all killing, however, this is a minority view. It is true that abortion does entail killing an unformed life, but opponents of abortion are rarely pacifists. That is, if killing in war may be justified, *on some occasions*, as a lesser evil—and governments have no 'conscience vote' about this—the same should apply for an unwanted foetus. Moreover fundamentalists say nothing about the enforced sterilisations and abortions performed on ethnic minorities, for example in the British National Health System (Williams 1989), which have more than justified feminist claims for reproductive rights.

Meantime, the contemporary array of reproductive choices (none of which is very satisfactory) has a major catch. The liberal idea of choice is a limited notion of children: it permits others, and government policy, to say that women must sacrifice their jobs and competitive advantage because a planned pregnancy is a woman's 'personal' choice. It is only possible to recover some of the economic 'damages' of a child if planning backfires, by suing for medical negligence (Horin 1996). Men can argue that women chose to have children (at that time rather than later), and can construe their 'role' as a minor one which relieves them of responsibility for all the work. The 'timing' does not suit the pursuit of their careers: planned pregnancies in a market society casts men as innocent, women guilty. Such reasoning accounts for the biological time-clock debate in contemporary times, a resort to a new biological 'disability' suffered by women (regardless of the fact that men suffer from sperm decline with age), unheard of when children were essential to the family unit. In a society where children are personal financial and career liabilities, the modern man can exercise his biological preference to wait.

Conclusion

The biological time-clock—an insignificant difference rendered significant—creates a new link to committing women to sole responsibility for the care and socialisation of children, now that the regulations which institutionalised women's modern feudal status are gone.

The family is a problem for liberal democracies, as we have seen. Governments are reluctant to regulate the market in order to ensure that employers do not shirk their responsibilities for present and future generations. Regulating the market by the family wage created a structure of male power and control in the public and private world alike, and enabled the state to refrain from any further intervention in family relations. Thus the family was privatised under some dubious assumptions, namely that men would fairly share their private ownership of a publicly regulated wage intended for the whole family, and that mothers and children are ideally isolated from the public realm in families claimed to be havens of altruism.

Today the family wage is gone. The continuation of society is increasingly construed as a private choice made by each woman. This augments the potential for men of all classes to evade caregiving. Moreover, the calculable gains that accrue to the market and state from reproduction, provision of human capital and support for people's capacity to contract out their labour disappear from view whenever having children is reduced to an individual's choice. The labour market will never accommodate, let alone welcome the future generation without a new institutional settlement. For although women's status is less ascribed, the way that parents divide their time between paid work and child-rearing, and arrange alternative care and education is a significant issue in explaining the tensions and confusions about family life. We will now turn to the various ways in which caregiving is hindered or helped by government policies.

9

The greatest welfare system ever devised?

Caregiving is a contentious policy issue as the twentieth century ends, as it was when governments turned to the family wage. Family life faces a harsh climate of intense economic competition, cutbacks in public services, and demands for higher and higher productivity. Unemployment has been a grim presence for twenty years. Far from bringing a bright 'post-industrial' future of cooperative work, income support and leisure, as some hoped, unemployment has degraded work and resulted in political isolation, poverty and insecurity for many around the world (Pixley 1993b). Unemployment will not be reduced until new national and international regulations are imposed on the market, and economic policy is subordinated to social policy. Meantime, women's increased employment and decreased child-bearing is occurring while different forms of public and private dependency are rising. Chronic unemployment means that women cannot depend on husbands for a potential economic protection that no longer exists (Beck 1992 p. 111). A long-term decline in both apprenticeships and teenage employment means that 'children' remain financially dependent on parents and state education well into 'adulthood'. 'Adult' status is now itself achieved at various ages; if consumers are adults at twelve years for airline companies, for the Australian Commonwealth Government some 'customers' are not adults until age 25. The ageing population raises the issue of caring in a new, often over-dramatised way, as though all people over 65 are helpless and completely dependent, which is far from the case.

Governments are taking a new look at the various models of family life, some in an implicit hope that caring can be rearranged without much state expenditure or major efforts by governments to improve the economic situation. Other nation-states are, however, doing a great deal more for families to support the work of caring, despite the detrimental influences of international markets.

Policies about caregiving—which idealised family?

Rich and poor families

In this climate, it is unsurprising that family policy is politically contested, with families themselves unsure about how best to demand support. Left-wing and right-wing party wrangles over which party is the more fundamentally 'anti-family' really depend on marginal electorate votes on the 'preferred' idealised family that is held up as the model. A marginal seat is where the notorious swinging voter, or uncertain, undefinable 'family' apparently resides. Political models range from the male domination of the bourgeois family wealthy enough to appear self-sufficient, the former male worker model with protected wages, to the more recent efforts to defend the rights and needs of women, children and teenagers in various ways and/or to support low-income households in harsh times.

All political parties used to assume that women were dependent subordinates upon whom everyone depended: thus in the Anglo-American countries in particular, services such as childcare and looking after the elderly were designated women's unpaid, private duties. Instead, political divisions occurred over the extent to which low-income families should receive government cash support at the more difficult stages of the life course, in particular, child-rearing and old age. This always neglected the extent to which wealthy people gained 'welfare' in the form of tax deductions and employment perks. Conflict over whether policy should be aimed at alleviating poverty (at least) among the poorer households or to providing support for all households of all socio-economic levels remains to this day. The alternatives are a residual system where 'vertical equity' is the aim and support is funded by taking from the top and giving to the bottom income levels, or a universal system in which 'horizontal equity' is the aim, and all households are entitled to support at particular life course stages. In Australia at present, politicians face a volatile electorate over the extent to which tax and occupational welfare systems should support middle- and upper-income households, and whether this might further weaken the residual, 'safety net' system of poverty alleviation and efforts to require employers to heed family needs (through the Industrial Commission).

Justice, male domination and families

Today such concerns about justice between rich and poor families are as relevant as ever. Yet female sole parents and their children have the greatest incidence (or risk) of poverty of any household type (Saunders 1994, p. 269). In this regard, it is curious to note that the modern recognition of children as financial liabilities coincided with the repeal of preference to fathers in English custody law late last century (Harrison 1991, p. 231). A more contemporary question, therefore, and just as important, also divides family policy. This question is about whether, inside each family, family relationships are 'beyond justice'.

Susan Moller Okin (1989) suggests that most political theorists idealise the family as being a place 'beyond justice'. Affection and a unity of interests are said to prevail so that standards of justice are irrelevant. Indeed, the intrusion of standards of justice—for each of the different members of families—is said to dangerously jeopardise the family ideals of intimacy, harmony and love: all the 'higher virtues'. In contrast, justice within the family involves recognising men and women, children, young adults and elderly of both sexes as 'discrete persons with their own particular aims and hopes, which may sometimes conflict' (Okin 1989, p. 32). Opponents call this justice 'political correctness'.

If families are beyond justice and united in interests, like lifeboats in a sea of self-interest, there is no need to inquire which members of families are most vulnerable to neglect and abuse or the mere threat of desertion, or the most likely to change their whole lives in order to manage family commitments. If love and intimacy prevails, it is tediously calculating to inquire about the numerous women and children facing moderate to severe poverty upon divorce (Okin 1989, pp. 32–3). In the idealised, sentimentalised vision of the benign family of welfare and intimacy, only 'strangers' are malign. Those financially dependent and secluded from the 'everyday' world are presumed to rely on the authority, loving care and protection of the 'provider'. Allan Bloom in *The Closing of the American Mind* of 1987 takes the traditional liberal view that women are by nature subordinate, men are selfish. Women must therefore submit so that men do not become violent. According to Bloom, the contemporary problem is that feminism has eroded the family: 'women are no longer willing to make unconditional and perpetual commitments on unequal terms' (cited Okin 1989, pp. 34–5). This, for Bloom, signals a closed mind to the detriment of able-bodied men.

What is caring?

So much for the needs of the frail and helpless. Many seem to prefer that women provide all the care (to the able-bodied as well) on unjust terms. Yet caregiving in a market society has been profitable for some—the experts. Caring is both public and private. Most modern welfare states have made two assumptions: that care should remain mostly private and that care is a public responsibility, with professionalisation from cradle to grave, or from early childhood education through to geriatric treatment. Public authorities have provided some substitute care, but many merely provide expert advice to private caregivers. As Arnlaug Leira points out about even the Scandinavian system, noted for generous caring services, public care confirms and affirms the private responsibilities of the primary carer—the mother, the elderly wife and the daughter. Every day, women juggle caring and employment through informal childcare, family and friendship networks, government agencies and reciprocal arrangements (Leira 1992, p. 28). Although caring-related state provision has increased as women joined the workforce, only a few countries have required the market and workplace to institutionalise their responsibilities to families as well.

Liberal democracies provide two kinds of entitlements more or less, to safeguard people against the chill winds of modern life. Employment-related entitlements safeguard people from being pure commodities on the labour market. Many Western governments came to accept that sickness, old age and lack of employment opportunities prevent people from selling their capacity to labour. The simple fact is that humans cannot survive as perpetual commodities, but require the means to 'decommodify' their persons when they are unable to be gainfully employed. Old age, sickness and unemployment benefits, pensions or insurance schemes were introduced throughout the West in the early twentieth century in order to ward off destitution and starvation. The extent of 'decommodification' so involved (Esping-Andersen 1990) varies between countries, and many countries provide very few entitlements to the intermittently or never employed. So nearly everywhere men have been the chief recipients.

In contrast, the caring-related entitlements of the welfare state are more recent and residual. These entitlements range from the trivial 'baby bonus', the allowances or 'endowments' for children, to paid maternity leave (in some countries) and pensions to those without breadwinners in order to support their family responsibilities. Variation across countries is equally marked, and is rarely comparable to the extent of a country's employment-related entitlements to 'decommodification'. The emphasis on the essential benefits of decommodification avoids, moreover, the fact that women were largely excluded from 'commodification' (Orloff 1996). It also implies that a situation of either decommodification or 'non-commodification' is pretty similar, yet sickness for example is rewarded by paid leave for the one and nothing, not even care replacement, for the other. Given the evidence of Chapter 4, that annual hours of unpaid domestic and caring work exceed that of paid labour, this is a lot of non-commodified labour to ignore (Pixley 1996).

In contrast to decommodification, caring entitlements remain residual, according to Leira, because of men's 'collective choice of non-participation in childcare' and a double standard about caring (1992, p. 175). Women are presumed biologically closer to caregiving where children are concerned, although caring for elderly parents is more ambiguous. Elderly people value their independence, capacity for reciprocity and a relation with their adult children best characterised as 'intimacy at a distance'. These beliefs are most prevalent among Anglo-Americans, whereas other cultural traditions support either greater or lesser responsibility for their elders (Elliot 1996, pp. 129–30).

The altruism of affection and love imbued in 'caring' avoids its two different meanings—caring for and caring about others. Although there are strong cultural objections to looking on childcare as labour, caring *for* a needy dependant is difficult, time-consuming work, whereas caring *about* someone involves affection and love (Dalley 1988). Furthermore, ways of caring for one's biological dependant, such as an infant, do not arise from instinctual messages. Rather, all the intricate practices of infant care must be learned (even the tediously reiterated 'naturalness' of breast-feeding), and these vary cross-culturally. Caring for a frail parent is not 'instinctual' either. In contrast, caring about and loving someone are not really linked to biology at all (Leira 1992, pp. 15–16). One can care about someone very deeply even if one only sees them at the beginning and end of the day. The double standard allows men to care about dependants while women are expected to care *about* the family through doing all caring *for* dependants. Able-bodied teenagers and men frequently manipulate this distinction to their advantage, especially when caring for people involves dull chores like garbage and dirty dishes.

Mother as carer

Social policy is currently caught between an uncaring market and a legacy of the family wage days, when caregiving was mother's labour of love requiring expert advice but little actual support or reciprocity. Many analysts, for example Sheila Shaver (1993) and Diane Sainsbury (1996), compare two broad models of policy provision for households, the male bread-winner and individual models, which assume either difference or sameness. The 'individual model' of sameness, which suggests that both mothers and fathers should be earners and carers, will be dealt with later. It is a recent innovation, and while, for example, Sweden and the United States both subscribe to elements of this model, the outcomes for each are virtually opposites (Sainsbury 1996). This is partly because Sweden's policies promote shared family roles and economic policies to foster high levels of employment, but the United States does neither.

The male breadwinner model still exists in some countries, however, very little remains of it in Australian policy (Shaver 1993). A 'pure' breadwinner model entails a familial ideology of marriage only, separate spheres and a strict division of labour: wife cares and husband earns. Difference prevails. Entitlements to any benefits, pensions or tax deductions all depend on whether the spouse is a Wife/Mother or a Husband, and the person who receives all payments is the head of the household—usually the Breadwinner but may be a Widow, bereft of her male breadwinner, rarely an unmarried mother. Taxation deductions and benefits are calculated on the household or family unit as a whole (joint income). Wage and employment policies are directed to men, and unpaid caring work is private. The whole household contributes to any insurance schemes, so in Europe and North America many old age, unemployment and sickness benefits require contributions from wages, whereas in Australia superannuation is recent and like other individual systems requires 'individual' contributions which of course are less for intermittent workers on lower pay (Sainsbury 1996, p. 42).

On the issue of taxation, Richard Titmuss' analysis of policy in the 1950s was exemplary in showing the differences between 'welfare' payments paid directly to very low income groups, and 'fiscal welfare' (such as tax deductions and rebates on joint income for dependants or even business luncheons) and 'occupational welfare' (such as company houses, private school fees, health schemes and superannuation). These are frequently far more valuable and receive none of the stigma of conventionally understood welfare (Titmuss 1963, pp. 34–55). In addition, men are the chief recipients of fiscal and occupational welfare, whereas women are the main recipients of 'welfare' and the stigma as well.

Different policies shape later changes, and in Australia state provisions for caring that initially developed, such as childcare services, were largely of cash rather than in kind. In contrast to the French system, for example, in the early twentieth century Australian childcare became professionalised in the kindergartens for the rich and charity-run nurseries for the 'fallen' mothers 'obliged' to work. Kindergartens expressly excluded meeting women's needs. Thus pre-school education for children until the 1970s was not a service for 'minding' children, because that only served mothers and might enable them to take employment (Brennan 1994, p. 8). Mother was expected to wait on the experts.

In the early twentieth century, some direct and indirect government payments provided a little income support for private 'caring labour', although most of it was directed to the male breadwinner. Thus, in Australia, apart from the £5 'baby bonus' to the mother to encourage breeding, the major payments for children until 1941 went to the breadwinner as a tax deduction, such as the Concessional Deduction for a dependent spouse and the child tax deduction. As Kewley notes, deductions are of most benefit to higher-income groups (with higher marginal tax rates) and have relatively little or no value to low-income groups (Kewley 1973, p. 210). Such 'fiscal welfare', widespread in other countries too, obscured the state benefits to wealthy families gained through the tax system.

In contrast, Child Endowment, introduced in 1941, was a direct payment to all mothers of 5 shillings per week, with its key aim being poverty alleviation during the war when wages were depressed, rather like the aims of child payments during the 1980s to 1990s with the Accord controlling higher wage demands. Many commentators argue that the consistent opposition by unions to the threat of their 'family' wage levels being undermined by government provision of Child Endowment to mothers, and the way Child Endowment was indeed used to restrain male wages, hardly suggest it was a 'reward' for motherhood. It was also residual (Shaver 1993, p. 6; Bryson 1992, p. 168; Cass 1983).

The national Widow's Pension, also introduced during World War II, was the first recognition of caring responsibility as a reason for state support to enable some mothers to remain 'non-commodified' or not obliged to work. At that time, the pension was claimed to be necessary because of mothers' essential 'national service' in child-rearing which, it was argued, could not be conducted properly if they were in paid employment. The state should therefore step in because widows, deserted or divorced wives had lost a man to 'maintain' them and their children. Those mothers who had neither a de facto nor de jure husband to lose, or were not of 'good character' did not receive the pension at all. With all the other new payments during that time, such as unemployment and sickness benefits (1945), the main assumption was that wives were dependent on husbands (Shaver 1993; Bradbury 1996, p. 8).

Policy ideas about the morally correct family of a male breadwinner and female dependant, united only via legal marriage, remained entrenched during the long period of Coalition governments (from 1949 to 1972). 'Helping those who wished to help themselves', government tax deductions for dependants, as well as for medical and life insurance, superannuation, private schools and home mortgages, gave the wealthier breadwinner a comfort unknown to pensioners (Elliott 1978, p. 33). Government policy's predilection for the morally ideal, male breadwinner family did not start to weaken until the Whitlam Government (1972–75). Poverty alongside full employment was 'discovered': the main 'disabilities' were 'old age, lack of a male breadwinner, a large number of dependent children, recent migration and prolonged illness' (Henderson et al. 1975, pp. 196–7). Given the assumptions of the male breadwinner model—that divorce is a 'fault', that recent arrival to Australia is a handicap since the 'wage earners' welfare state' only enabled housing and health provisions from accumulated wages, that only men should earn income and women have few options for independence—this discovery was not very surprising.

Thereupon, old age pensions were raised and caring payments for unmarried mothers began in 1973. Marital status and gender-specific distinctions (Mothers, Wives and Widows) were finally removed with the introduction of the umbrella term 'Sole Parent' Pension by 1989. Tax treatment of families changed by replacing child rebates and Wife deductions with Family Allowances paid to the 'primary carer' in 1977 and Dependent Spouse and Sole Parent Rebates instead. All these changes resulted in a greater focus on poverty alleviation at the lower end of the income scale rather than fiscal welfare for the more well-off male household head, and a gradual move away from gender-based notions of dependency. By the end of 1995, most family assistance was directed at those on lowest incomes as a gender-neutral safety net, with the main emphasis on encouraging adults of either sex into the labour market (Bradbury 1996, pp. 9–11). Why did Federal family policy change, in the space of 30 years, from upholding one 'ideal family' which primarily entailed an unpaid home-making wife, to this gender neutrality?

Gender-neutral family policy—the growth of the individual model

The individualised model, Sainsbury suggests, may end women's financial dependence on a husband, however, if women have no means to be financially *independent* (with childcare services and employment opportunities), individualisation can make the financial situation of women and children even worse (Sainsbury 1996 pp. 186–7). In the individual model, marriage is not obligatory for income support, and fathers and mothers are *assumed* to share both roles of earning and caring equally. Entitlements are based on and received by the individual deemed in need of support, as 'parent', unemployed or carer in various capacities. As Sainsbury points out, however, unless there is a fundamental aim to *reconstruct* gender roles, in labour market and employment programs for women, as much as public childcare and paternal and 'parental' leave, the individual model can be detrimental for women. 'Gender neutrality' offers little benefit to families in contrast with 'gender reconstruction', whereas even recognising differences between men and women, to compensate the economically disadvantaged sex, may bring greater equality for women and children than mere neutrality. Even so, such recognition of disadvantage, for example through a sole 'mother' pension, is usually insufficient for a woman to establish and maintain an autonomous household with her children above the poverty line (Orloff 1996). 'Gender reinforcement', such as a return to some form of family wage with separate spheres, is particularly detrimental if related to women's entitlements as wives, but sometimes less so if based on the principle of care ('mothering'). There are different mixes of these breadwinning and individual models across OECD countries (Sainsbury 1996, pp. 172–3), although the only individual model which reduces inequality aims for 'gender reconstruction' in both caring and earning.

So it is important to remember that individualisation developed just when high levels of unemployment, from 1975 on, resulted in a fiscal crisis, and also coincided with a so-called tax revolt since that time. This situation is common to many countries. Australia is one of the few Western countries with unlimited duration unemployment benefits for any resident unable to find employment with no other means of support (Jones 1996, p. 29). Payments are well below average wages (just over $8000 p.a.) but are not conditional on previous employment, unlike many other countries. Australia's total social security payments bill (including all pensions as well) was, in 1992–93, $41 billion or 35 per cent of all public sector outlays from all levels of government (AIH&W 1995, p. 9). Successive Federal Governments, unable and unwilling to restore full employment, have ever since been trying to reduce the numbers on unemployment benefits and to raise contributions for old age provision from employers and employees (compulsory workplace superannuation).

The Fraser Government initially tried encouraging women to stay at home in the late 1970s (by retaining the dependent spouse rebate) and keeping direct child-related payments low (Cass 1996, pp. 17–22). Such rebates enhance the husband's privileged position by pitting a wife's potential earnings against a deterioration in her husband's tax position (Sainsbury 1996, pp. 183–4). In the 1980s and 1990s, child-related payments rose considerably under the Labor Governments, while the efforts to reduce unemployment payment costs focused on encouraging unemployed and other recipients of pensions or allowances into the labour market no matter what sex. The 'active society' was a concept embraced across the Western world in the 1980s: promoted by OECD policies, the active society is set in distinction to the so-called 'passive' receipt of unemployment payments (Pixley 1994). That is, governments are prepared to provide some support against starvation only if every individual demonstrates that she or he is actively 'participating' in 'society' (looking for jobs, training and so forth). Australian unemployment allowances are no longer paid jointly to a couple since 1996, but individually, to encourage women into casual employment.

Also, family responsibilities of single parents are still acknowledged, in the Sole Parent Pension, however now only until the youngest child reaches sixteen years old. Withdrawal from the labour market for child-rearing is certainly treated with higher regard in Australia than it is in North America where single mothers are supported, at most until a child is twelve years old and in some cases (Alberta, Canada) only until an infant is six months old (Baker, in press). Thereafter single mothers (also the former category of 'Widows') must support themselves in the labour market and childcare market. This is the dark side of 'gender neutrality' given women's lower pay and limited job opportunities. Moreover, Australia, as elsewhere, has over a million and a half people trying to find around 40 000 jobs at any one time, but this has not deterred governments from hoping that people can find casual work. Many casual jobs are 'female' ones, and this has been a primary reason for the new gender neutrality (Pixley 1994). Conservatives, however, argue that their ideal family of bread-winner and dependent wife has been 'discriminated' against. Ignoring the influence of OECD 'active' and European Community 'reinsertion' policies, their view is that feminism has influenced previous Labor Governments' family policies to an 'anti-family' bias.

Neutrality or reconstructing gender roles?

What other major changes in family and social policy might support this view? Divorce became a 'no-fault' procedure after the 1975 Family Law Reform introduced by the Labor Government. The increase in divorce the following year settled soon after that. Contemporary marriage rates do not support the criticism that this reform has caused the 'death of the family' (Pinkney 1995). Some argue that the removal of a 'guilty' party for a divorce has advantaged more men than women in property settlements, however this is a contentious view (Okin 1989, pp. 161–7). Others suggest a public accusation of fault, with its inquisitorial procedures, may lead to unfairness and bitterness, it may be an obstacle to sensible post-divorce arrangements and to the non-custodial parents' willingness to support the children of the marriage (Harrison 1989, p. 48). Women, who are nearly always responsible for the children after divorce, certainly need fairer settlements than an 'equal' division that usually results in unequal outcomes. Although conservatives want government intervention to force unhappy couples to remain together, no-fault divorce, per se, is not the cause of the poverty faced by sole mothers and their children.

Another major family policy change was abortion reform. South Australia was the first state, in 1969, to follow the 1967 legislation in Britain (Siedlecky & Wyndham 1990, pp. 78–81). In addition, abortion is now available through Medicare. Conservatives are well-known opponents of abortion, whether free or not, with a few women promoting the idea that criminalising abortion may increase women's 'leverage' on the father, but this depends on socio-economic status, for there is little an unemployed or low-wage father could 'pay'.

The Child Support Scheme, begun in 1988, is a compulsory method of enforcing parental financial responsibilities in cases of divorce and separation, usually upon the absent father. The Federal Government uses the tax system to enforce 'non-custodial support' for sole parents, and support is based on the ability of the non-custodial parent to pay (Jones 1996, p. 28). While touted to reduce child poverty, these schemes are also used to reduce public outlays and to 'Get Those Deadbeat Dads', as the Canadian Government proclaimed (Baker, in press). Although the Australian scheme is fairer than those in North America, it has not been very popular among some men, who have attacked the scheme and the Family Court, sometimes with violence. For women trying to flee from violent partners, the scheme has not increased their safety or that of their children, nor has it done much to raise the living standards of these families, another dark side to gender neutrality. It has, however, reduced the stigma faced by many sole parents requiring a pension from the state. Conservatives support forcing individual men to pay, although it is not so consistent for liberals committed to a non-interventionist state (Tapper 1990).

Maternity and parental leave are recent innovations in Australia. In contrast to gender-neutral policies, these provisions are an essential element in promoting 'gender reconstruction' of shared family roles, earning and caring by mothers and fathers (Sainsbury 1996, p. 191). Baker's comparative study shows that France, Germany, the Netherlands and Sweden have long regarded maternity and parental leave as 'a maternal and child health issue, a form of employment equity for women, an inducement to reproduction, and a citizenship right for every employed woman'. In contrast, she suggests that English-speaking countries have generally regarded it as an irritating expense for employers, or a deterrent to hiring women (Baker 1995, p. 163). Countries differ in commitment and philosophy, and also in the rate at which previous earnings are replaced while on leave, from a low of 57 per cent in Canada to 100 per cent in the Netherlands and Germany (Baker 1995, p. 160).

In Australia since 1979, nearly 94 per cent of women have been covered by awards with maternity leave provisions. But leave is unpaid and requires twelve months' previous continuous service for eligibility. Women taking maternity leave are overwhelmingly employed in the public sector, and as a 1985 study showed, 69 per cent of women employed in private sector jobs who qualified for the leave did not take it, many being unaware of their entitlement. The Australian Council of Trade Unions (ACTU) and the Arbitration (now Industrial) Commission have played a major role in promoting child-related leave, a far cry from their previous insistence on keeping wives permanently at home. In 1990 parental leave became available to all men and women in the workforce, and in the Commonwealth public service there is a further provision of twelve weeks' maternity leave on full pay (Brennan 1994 pp. 155–6). In this respect, then, Australian policy has made a few halting steps to shared family roles.

At the time of writing, Australia's leave provisions are more flexible and generous than those of a country such as Britain but limited in comparison to most European countries. Thus Germany provides fourteen weeks of maternity leave at 100 per cent of previous earnings for all insured employees, and sickness funds for up to five days' leave a year for each sick child under eight years old (Baker 1995 pp. 169, 171). Where such leave is adequate, women's economic status has improved considerably as a consequence of maternity leave, given the heavy price in lifetime earnings and job security for women who must resign for every birth. Health and safety for mother and child at childbirth are also important gains. Parental leave is a recognition that the whole society needs a future generation. The fact that many employers and the older generation resist making more generous provisions is only a further illustration of the double standards about 'the family', especially in English-speaking countries.

Few men, however, have taken parental leave seriously even when it comes with full wage replacement (Baker 1995, p. 187). In Australia at least it has increased men's awareness of their child-rearing responsibilities and led to pressure for work-related childcare (Brennan 1994, p. 156). Baker suggests that women still do the bulk of child-rearing (and all the other domestic tasks) because leave legislation—even in enlightened countries such as Sweden—exists in a gender-segregated labour market with male 'care-free' employment patterns and employer pressures, especially in the private sector (Baker 1995, pp. 187–8). Others suggest that men simply choose not to care for their own children, whatever the inducements (Leira 1992), however in those Swedish familes where both parents hold similarly well-paid jobs, 40–50 per cent of the fathers take parental leave, compared with 25–30 per cent of men in general. In 1995 legislation in Sweden earmarked one month of the leave to the father, a 'daddy month' which cannot be transferred to the mother (Sainsbury 1996, pp. 191, 196).

Another vital element in gender reconstruction is public provision of childcare, and support for employed parents. In Australia, the Childcare Cash Rebate, introduced in 1994, is for work-related childcare expenses incurred when parents are employed, studying, training or looking for work. Under the Labor Government it was paid through Medicare, not the tax system. More importantly, the increase in Commonwealth-subsidised childcare places has resulted in meeting two-thirds of the demand by employed parents for childcare services for 0- to 4-year-olds. In addition, a National Accreditation System ensures that childcare is high quality. However, the principle of 'affordable, quality childcare' is only for employed parents on low to middle incomes, which has marginalised the childcare needs of families where neither parent is in the workforce. In comparison with 'the best-served nations', Finland, Sweden, Denmark and France, childcare provision is not exceptionally high, although Australian provision is extensive in comparison with the United States and Britain (Brennan 1994, pp. 206–7, 210).

The individualised model under attack

In general, the rise in married women's employment has, by definition, undermined the financially dependent home-maker conception of the family entrenched for so long in family policy. Along with abortion and so-called 'easy divorce', this is probably the most contentious issue in the political debates over the ideal family. Yet employed mothers are relatively easy (and overworked) targets of attack, compared to employer discrimination about family life and men's resistance to taking responsibility for their own domestic chores, let alone for their children. It is possible that women increase their leverage within marriage by having access to their 'own' earned money, for they may be able to impose domestic obligations on men. However, the fact that women remain the major caregivers, while also being breadwinners, is not lost on women. So a major tension in families, let alone family policy, is how to balance the constraints and so-called choices between market and non-market work.

Recent arguments suggest that upper- and middle-class couples are the most advantaged from their dual-earning status, on the grounds that most low-income households are one-earner or non-earning units (Jamrozik & Sweeney 1996). This idea is supported by British sociologist Catherine Hakim, who suggests that 'career women' are quite different from the majority of women who 'prefer' part-time jobs at most, which do not detract from a lifetime of home-making and caring (Hakim 1995; Ginn et al. 1996). Such suggestions are immensely popular among conservative politicians.

During the 1980s and 1990s, the Australian Liberal–National Party Coalition constantly criticised Labor Government policies promoting gender neutrality as well as the more reconstructive childcare and leave provisions for employed mothers and fathers. The Coalition claims these measures discriminate against mothers who stay at home. Policy options are frequently posed as 'which family' should be supported—the 'woman who stays home' family or the two-earner family. In political rhetoric, both sides claim the other is 'anti-family'.

Promoters of traditional family policy tend to favour a home-makers' allowance, or at least an emphasis on tax rebates for dependent spouses and reprivatisation of childcare (Bradbury 1996; Pinkney 1995; Brennan 1994, pp. 212–13). The Coalition claims that a 'comprehensive' family package must focus on 'the stable family'.

The debate is fundamentally a contrast between an egalitarian ideal which requires reconstruction to foster shared family roles, and those who want to reinforce gender divisions, especially by reducing the incentives for married women to enter the labour force. Gender reinforcement gains popularity, however, for many are aware of the problems inherent in gender-neutral reforms, even more so in a situation of long-term recession, women's labour market disadvantage and revenue reductions. Neutrality does little to modify outcomes for the family and is often detrimental to women (for example, in lack of superannuation or the phasing out of Widow's Pensions), particularly when its basis is in government cut-backs, rather than support for family members in their own right. Neutrality does not lead to egalitarian outcomes when women's existing disadvantages, such as low pay, remain, and thus the recognition of disadvantage, which may reinforce gender divisions, often provides a more financially beneficial outcome than neutrality.

Many people are therefore confused about the gains and losses of two-earner families or rather, 'working mothers', and the separate problem of dependent wives. Confusion lends support to conservative calls to reinstate the old breadwinner model, a popular option too with certain types of men. So, let us consider whether two-earner households are only at the 'privileged' high income level, in comparison with a declining male breadwinner middle class, the so-called 'battlers'. A number of criticisms have been made of these views. First, the fact that many married women take paid employment has been shown by Peter Saunders to have reduced the number of families who live in poverty. Between 1981–82 and 1989–90, there has been a marked upwards redistribution of male income, only to the very top decile, but if all married women had earned no income at all, there would have been even greater income inequality. That is, if fewer women had jobs there would have been greater income reductions in the middle to lower deciles of gross income, and a higher increase at the top decile (Saunders 1993, pp. 30–2).

Inequality between families has, therefore, been reduced through married women's earning. The increased inequality is instead due to declining wages and soaring top (male) salaries, which is exacerbated by deregulation of the labour market, increased costs in housing and in parental responsibility for teenagers and adult 'children'. Over a longer time also, the declining number of secure jobs and growth of casual and sweated trade jobs, as well as the lack of employment opportunities for so many women and men, are further dividing rich and poor families.

Second, the return to the long-term decline in fertility since the post-war baby boom means that there are less children over a shorter time in need of physical care. Also, women (and men) are living longer. Perhaps feminist influence has fostered women's move into the workplace, but the issue is about women's needs for more public sources of fulfilment and for an independent income. If the time devoted to children occupies a smaller portion of a woman's life, women may not find home-making for an able-bodied man very rewarding. An analysis of the 1988 National Social Science attitude survey showed that more than 80 per cent of both men and women think that married women should be employed both before and after child-rearing. The problem remains how to ensure adequate support during the intensive child-rearing years, while also ensuring that labour market disadvantage does not result in later poverty for 'unemployable' dependent wives or widows.

A third important factor is the ethnic diversity in Australian families' employment patterns, as elsewhere. Traditional Aboriginal child-rearing practices, where one woman is usually responsible for a number of her relatives' children on a daily basis (Laurie & McGrath 1985), may well be a reason for the relatively high proportion of Aboriginal women in modern leadership positions. Among immigrants, as Bruce Bradbury shows, there are substantial variations in the labour market behaviour of different birthplace groups of mothers. Looking at married mothers with at least one child under 15 in the 1986 Census, only 27 per cent of Lebanese-born women were working or looking for work (but mostly full time), whereas the Australian average was 49 per cent (but more than half of that was part-time work). Comparing the similar rates for Australian-born, Italian-born and Greek-born, there was a higher per cent of Greek-born mothers in part-time than full-time work than the other two groups. In contrast, among mothers born in Vietnam, 70 per cent were in the labour market and most of them were in full-time employment. New Zealand- and English-born mothers had a higher workforce participation than the Australian average (Bradbury 1996, pp. 17–18). The numbers of sole parents in Australia are not large, as we saw in Chapter 1, and although 40 per cent of sole parents in Australia are employed (compared to 75 per cent in Canada, for example: Baker, in press), governments want to move more into the labour market. In contrast, married mothers receive more mixed messages. This double standard is partly a consequence of the recession, partly a revival of conservative morality in a contradictory liaison with economic liberalism.

Reinventing the breadwinner family model?

In these times of high unemployment and budget cuts, the idea of reinventing a male breadwinning traditional family monolith, for which a comprehensive 'family policy' could be devised, has no meaning in contemporary Australia (Pinkney 1995, p. 24; Bradbury 1996, p. 17). Systematic variations in the life course and of class and ethnicity were neglected in the past when the traditional family seemed so predominant. What is the likely outcome of reinforcing gender divisions today?

Looking at Table 9.1 which shows the 1995 provision of caring and dependency-related payments in the Australian social security and tax system, it is clear that the Hawke and Keating Governments have favoured direct, means tested payments for a variety of family situations, which have the main aim of alleviating poverty among the poorest families in Australia. In 1996 the new Howard Government intends to cut subsidies to community childcare and, in order to 'encourage' parental support, restrict allowances for unemployed teenagers (between sixteen and twenty years of age) and to students who now do not attain 'independence' until age 25. In return for major cuts to nearly every program offering support to

Table 9.1 Caring and dependency-related payments in the Australian social security and tax systems, 1995

	Eligibility	Maximum rate[a]	Income unit	Income period	Income threshold[a]
Dependent spouse payments					
Dependent Spouse Tax Rebate	Taxpayer for a dependent spouse without children	$1211 p.a.	Personal (spouse)	Financial year	$282 p.a.[b]
Partner Allowance	Partners of allowees and pensioners without children, over 40 and with no recent labour market experience	$136 p.w.	Mixed	Fortnight	$236 (spouse) $30 (allowee) p.w.
Wife Pension	No new grants from July 1995. Existing wife pensioners continue to be eligible.	$136 p.w.	Family	Estimated annual	$78 comb p.w.
Caring-related payments					
Sole Parent Tax Rebate	Sole parent caring for at least one dependent child	$1137 p.a.	Personal (dependent)	Financial year	–
Sole Parent Pension	Sole parent caring for at least one dependent child	$163.05 p.w.	Personal	Estimated annual	$57 p.w.
Parenting Allowance	Married (or de facto) primary carer of children under 16	$136 p.w.	Mixed	Estimated annual	$236 (partner); $30 (allowee) p.w.
Basic Parenting Allowance	Married (or de facto) primary carer of children under 16	$30.60 p.w.	Personal (carer)	Estimated annual	–
Carer Pension	Person providing constant personal care to a 'severely handicapped' pensioner/beneficiary	$136 p.w.	Family	Estimated annual	$78 comb p.w. (10 hr limit educ/emp)
Domiciliary Nursing Care Benefit	Principal carer of a person with a severe disability	$27.10 p.w.	Personal (client)	–	–
Child-related payments					
Basic Family Payment	Parent/guardian having care and control of child under 16	$10.85 p.w.	Family	Financial year	$61,020 p.a.

Table 9.1 *continued*

	Eligibility	Maximum rate[a]	Income unit	Income period	Income threshold[a]
Additional Family Payment	Parent/guardian receiving BFP	$33.60 (child <13) $47.05 (13+) p.w.	Family	Financial year	$21,700 p.a.
Child Disability Allowance	Parent or guardian providing daily/substantial care and attention for a dependent child with a disability	$34.75 p.w.	–	–	–
Childcare Cash Rebate	Parent of child under 13 in formal or informal childcare	$28.80 ($1502 p.a.)	–	–	–
Childcare Assistance	Child under 12 in childcare centre registered with the Children Services Program in HSH	$96 p.w.	Family	Estimated annual	$485 p.w.
	Child in before and after school care	a) 69c p.h. b) 37c p.h.	Family	As for AFP	Eligible AFP a) full rate b) part rate

Notes: a) Rates and thresholds as at July 1995. Tax rebates and thresholds for 1994/95 tax year.
  b) Refers to income threshold of dependent ('non-earning') spouse.
Source: Bradbury 1996, p. 13

people through the life course, the Coalition is providing 'incentives' to mothers to stay at home full time. In raising the tax-free threshold to $2500 for single-income families, a family with one child under five remains eligible if it earns up to $65 000, and with three children if it earns up to $71 000. Full-time, 'non-working' or 'primary caring spouses' can receive up to $4535 a year in unearned income from shares, property and family trusts without removing the taxpayer's eligibility for the $2500 rebate, whereas primary carers who work part time for any earned income at all will not qualify. The 'reward' for staying at home is roughly an extra $9.60 a week (if one child), and about 590 000 households will gain either slightly more or less of this far from princely sum (*Sydney Morning Herald* 19 February, 12 August 1996).

Social policy is thus moving away from poverty alleviation and some of the support for mothers as earners. Does this mean that it will provide a so-called 'choice' between market and non-market work, as is claimed? The Howard Government's support for home-makers through the tax system is not going to make anyone on a full salary suddenly give it up and run home for the temptation of $9 a week, which in most cases will be controlled by the breadwinner. The Coalition Government's Family Package, generally, is not inspired by individual citizen rights but by the ideals of women's 'choice', parents' rights over children and marriage counselling—a common theme in the conservative literature. The 'stable family' is supposed to be 'the greatest welfare system devised by any nation', according to John Howard at the 1996 election (*Sydney Morning Herald* 19 February 1996). In the Family Tax Initiative, pressure on part-time workers to cease employment and undertake all 'primary' care could intensify where the spouse (usually the father) can see personal tax advantages in a higher threshold, the new opportunity for income splitting in the unearned income component, and the implied opportunity to evade caring work altogether.

In contrast, a far more adequate income support for parent–carers, such as the proposal from the Australian Family Association for a 'Homemaker's Allowance' (Bradbury 1996), and various feminist arguments about valuing women's difference, such as Carole Pateman's idea for a basic income (1988a), make a different defence. Women would thereby have the autonomy of their own income and their citizen status would be enhanced through financial recognition of their participation in the society through child-rearing. We are here comparing the Coalition's proposal to reinforce gender divisions via paying the husband, with one that recognises gender and income inequalities by paying women, a revaluation of difference.

Both proposals assume that children are best raised in the isolated home by one person who is thus 'rewarded' for providing the 'public goods' aspect of children. Whether children have individual rights and, as future citizens may have wider needs, is not encompassed in these assumptions. Leaving aside this difficulty, an initial question is whether couple families at most income levels should receive specific support to give carers a 'choice' not to enter the labour market, either with the home-makers' allowances or by increasing the dependent spouse rebate (Bradbury 1996, pp. 32–3). A commonly held argument is that two-earner families have tax advantages over single-earner families, because they have two tax thresholds. Bruce Bradbury and Elizabeth Savage both argue, however, that an incentive or choice to stay out of the labour market, for couple households on lower income levels, turns into a constraint against taking paid work. That is, it imposes a work disincentive which tends to keep low-income households in greater poverty. Savage suggests it is important not to confuse women's employment status with the value of child-rearing activities (Savage 1994), as will be explained below.

A home-makers' allowance or rebate affects most married women because women earn less than men. Only women with highly marketable skills can or could earn enough to be uninfluenced by work disincentives and the childcare related costs of employment. If rebates or parenting allowances for caring are paid only to non-employed carers (as is their point), two households with the same joint income will be treated unfairly. This is because for each single-earner household with the same income as a two-earner household (say $40 000), only the single-earner household gains the rebate, as well as the unpaid home-produced goods and caring services. The two-earner household of the same total income gains no rebate, nor any recognition of the costs and value of the caring work necessitated by children, that must be done at night and weekends for those in paid work who thus forfeit leisure as well (Savage 1994). By ignoring the domestic caring work of employed parents, such allowances and rebates ironically reinforce the traditional perception that, because household caring work is unpaid and untaxed, it is of no economic value.

Means tested payments for caring work based on the whole family income thus say nothing to the two-earner family who stand to lose up to half the $40 000 joint income if one spouse stays home. Savage suggests caring work payments should be unrelated to employment status. If the means test was on the higher-income earner (usually a male), this would show the standard of living more accurately, put some value on the unpaid work, and not penalise women who do take paid work with severe effective marginal tax rates and limits to choice of the extent of paid and unpaid work they do. The case for a 'carer's wage' that is conditional on non-employment, ultimately rests on an assumption that the 'choice' of employment, over staying at home to care for children, is socially undesirable (Bradbury 1996, p. 34). In contrast, by testing the higher-income earner alone, a caring allowance or rebate does not penalise lower-income men *and* women, and as Savage says, 'it recognises the contribution of households rearing children, not the way they choose to do it' (1994, p. 4).

Neverthless, a means test does not address the social context for making choices and the consequences of full-time mothering, for it still leaves many women vulnerable in later years. Many women give priority to their husbands' careers, despite their personal ambitions, because of labour market discrimination and women's low pay (Okin 1989, pp. 149–55). Thus why should women of whatever socio-economic background be denied their own source of income, face severe poverty on divorce, and move to old age without the benefit of occupational superannuation, even though they have provided the 'public goods' aspect of children? In other words, women should not be submerged in the family, but treated as citizens in their own right.

If it is agreed that carers should have their own independent source of income, a burning issue is how to finance it. Given limited government revenue (and soaring male salaries), fairness suggests that low-income households should receive the major support, for the sake of the children and their parents. In fairness, the highest rates of child payments should be directed to them, regardless of adult employment status. Accordingly, perhaps the higher-income male salary earner whose career benefits most from the unpaid work of his spouse could be required to share his income more directly, rather as the Child Support Agency does for families that have separated (Bradbury 1996, pp. 35–6). Susan Moller Okin similarly suggests that for those who remain in traditional arrangements, the husband should pay half his income (rather than 'share' it when it suits him), not for 'services rendered' but simply because since both of them work, 'there is no reason why only one of them should get paid' (Okin 1989, p. 181). Many might argue that men would not like to split their salary and arrange equal superannuation formally at the beginning of a traditional breadwinner family partnership—if so it would only point to the present injustice of such a vulnerable relation for exclusive homemakers, before it began!

Women and children as citizens?

This leads to the critical question of the extent to which policy can effectively support the rights of individual members of households—women, children, disabled and older people—as well as men. Institutional arrangements to provide different needs for care would need to be funded by a progressive tax system, that is, one that taxes higher incomes at a progressively higher rate and (with Australia's total tax rate only just higher than that of Turkey, of all OECD countries) higher than at present (AIHW 1995, p. 34). Yet, individual rights conflict, so when 'rights' are emphasised, government efforts to increase the tax revenue will be resisted by those able-bodied and relatively unencumbered individuals claiming the right to compete on the market. With limited resources, governments often recast the rights of less vocal or less 'influential' family members, such as teenagers, sole parents and students, as 'selfish' or opposed to the family. One of the least effective solutions to care arrangements, where contemporary trends in Australia are heading, is the cutback to public services for families and the expensive, but because so thinly spread, trivial rebate increase for home-making in the name of returning 'choice' to families. Thus the market becomes the only source of support for more and more families.

So the ideals of women's rights, children's rights and the rights of the elderly are far from secure, but if governments fail to support them, will our normative expectations of an egalitarian family be further removed from experience? To take one example, the individual right to bodily integrity. It is highly unlikely that even conservative governments would try to remove laws that prohibit child abuse. But if there are no preventative measures, dependable childcare, social support services and, failing these, effective child protection agencies, these laws are irrelevant.

This highlights an inherent drawback in the model of individual rights for all family members: the neglect of the social context of rights in economic liberalism. Individual rights are concerned with free choices, contracts and utilitarian calculations, where the family is lost to the model of the rational actor, the contracting entity with no obligations to others. The market and the conditions giving rise to the choice remain untouched.

Similar problems emerge in individualised family policies: the individual right to superannuation is dependent on the length and income level of workforce participation. It spells poverty for those women who have been full-time 'mothers' in their past. In this case a combination of individual entitlements, but with the whole family income as the unit of contributions and benefits, provides a better financial outcome for women, for it recognises the labour market disadvantages of women; that is, even the breadwinner model can sometimes be applied fairly (Sainsbury 1996, pp. 190–5).

Everyone is left confused as to the best future for the family. The individual right for women to compete in an unregulated labour market with men, rules out responsibilities outside the market, and either rules out the creation or continuation of family life or reinforces male control over it. The potential to increase atomisation under a contractual model, where intimate bonds become more fragile and liable to bleak calculations of personal utility, give rise to nostalgia for the old breadwinner model—the answer to everyone's dreams for welfare and mutual affection. But the old household head model has all its previous, discretionary potential to act detrimentally against women's and children's rights. In the process of denying justice, the potential for love and intimacy on equal and mutual grounds is also lost. This means that individual rights are a necessary but not a sufficient condition of the kind of family support that could ensure everyone's wellbeing.

Can the state make a difference?

If neither the breadwinner nor the pure individualising model, what then? Many families are weighed down by high expectations from governments—suspiciously far too high in relation to the extent to which families can be further burdened with tasks formerly done by the state. Maybe it is time to stop blaming the family for every ill in society while spuriously praising it as the nation's greatest invention. Perhaps the solutions are to be found in the labour market. Maybe we should turn a beady eye on government's responsibility to families—to reshape that market and to provide public services to replace the market.

In Australia, expenditure on welfare services rose by 72 per cent between 1987 and 1995, yet it still accounted for only 2.7 per cent of total public sector outlays in 1992–93. (As a per cent of GDP, the United States' level of expenditure was, by then, just below Australia's.) This outlay came from all levels of government and includes housing, children's services and child welfare services, services for frail older people and services for people with disabilities. These services cover a substantial range of human needs and they replace or add to the personal care provided by 'the family' and by private charity. The rise in outlay was mainly due to expansion in the number of childcare places and in aged and disability welfare. Although the total outlays from the public sector on welfare services came to $4.4 billion, it has been estimated that if the time spent by individuals providing care for free were costed, as well as private sector expenditure, the total value of welfare services in 1992–93 would come to $22.5 billion. This estimate does not include the time taken in caring for one's own children, except when they are sick or disabled (AIHW 1995, pp. 3–19, 32–6), which would significantly increase the evaluation of unpaid care, as we have shown in Chapter 4.

Governments, it seems, even when making efforts to increase caring services, as the Labor Government did, hardly begin to share in the vast contribution to welfare made by families. Turning a blind eye on all this, the Coalition Government in 1996 started dismantling welfare services and increasing the cares of families. According to the Lyons Forum, a body funded by the Liberal Party, the main social contribution of 'intact families' is their apparent lack of reliance on public resources (their 'negative contribution'). But even 'intact families' apparently offer few benefits to society. Their 'positive contributions' only 'include raising children to taxpayer status, contributing to the community economy, and building houses' (Lyons Forum 1995, p. 10). For all the praise and 'recognition' of this great institution by neo-liberals, the implicit ideal is fundamentally anti-family, and the practice of neo-liberal governments everywhere demonstrates this amply.

Quite opposite to this is a thoroughly interdependent family ideal which has emerged over the past twenty years. At one level this promotes the interdependency of men and women in sharing housework and child-rearing equally along with the earning. But, as we have shown, this ideal of reconstructing the gender divisions of home and market is far from being commonly practised. As Sainsbury argues, Sweden is closest to promoting shared family roles, even though men are still fairly reluctant participants (1996, pp. 191–2). Far from neglecting children, however, Sweden has dependable public childcare and in all of Scandinavia everyone is committed to children having the same rights against violence as adults—a slap is a physical assault at any age. Swedish women's 'rights' as earners are fostered by generous provision of childcare and an active labour market policy. This means they gain access to occupational benefits as earners, while also being entitled to benefits related to care, with the assumption that an employed mother is the norm. Leave provisions for both parents' caring responsibilities are the other essential element in requiring the labour market to respond to the institution of the family (Sainsbury 1996, p. 192).

In the English-speaking countries, in contrast, the cares of family life stem partly from lack of government expenditure. In the case of care-related provision, public services are always preferable to employer-provided services, where care is subordinated to employers' needs, *or* to profit-making services, where quality is sacrificed to profit. Yet it is clear that the overburdened family is also a result of the reluctance by English-speaking nation-states to regulate the labour market. So if Sweden is exemplary in this respect, the concept of 'time sovereignty' from Germany, where workers can structure their work day around their caring responsibilities, is another regulation to benefit family life. In addition, mobility provisions for spouses to gain jobs if one partner moves, and equal remuneration for men and women, are just as important for supporting a 'stable', even an intact family model. Perhaps most essential of all is a major reduction of the working day—instead of the current 50- to 70-hour week 'enjoyed' by those in employment—so that families can enjoy time together.

This, along with public provision of services, both creates more employment and reduces the cares and burdens of family life.

The point of reconstruction of gender divisions is not so that women become like men, but so that men and women may live decent lives together. In order for women to act in the public world and to enjoy mothering as well, they cannot be confined by a family policy of double standards. Thus some countries' policies have supported new gender relations, particularly sharing the roles of caring. Yet children and young adults also have their own needs; furthermore, the nation-state and the labour market need these new social beings. Either the future adults of the world are blamed for having 'nothing to do', with all the pathologies that entails, or they are welcomed into adulthood as future citizens responsible for acting in public life, and with creative, cooperative skills to contribute to economic life. We reap what we sow. From childcare as education through to job opportunities, the future generation often finds rejection. But why not give the young hope? Among all the arenas of social life that constrain young people's capacities for beginning the social world anew, in families as in public life, employment is critical. Thus it is hardly unreasonable to expect employers to devote time to training new entrants in the labour market, and to pay for public education and training perhaps through a training levy. This, of course, depends on the capacity and honesty of governments and vigorous public debates.

So, although the gender reconstruction model shows the pathway towards justice between couples with interdependent family responsibilites, perhaps a more institutional approach might lead to social and economic policies that incorporate our interdependencies at the societal level. That is, the family is not just a micro-level aggregation of people (as according to economic liberalism). As an institution, the family is also a small firm or bureaucracy, or rather a 'meso-level institution' that interacts with other such institutions in the state and the market. And at this level, the bureaucracy and the firm depend on families. Despite the conventional view, none are discrete institutions trying to survive according to their own logic. The lone family is the basis for the continuation of social life, yet it is uncared for and unable to shape other institutions through the democratic process. The market needs families, in a quite fundamental sense, for all its activities, yet it assumes single adults and externalises all the costs onto families while keeping all the gains. Governments do need new taxpayers, and preferably future 'citizens', yet they rarely intervene to control the market. Instead, many contemporary governments cannot decide how best to 'control' the family, at the expense of some—women and children—and by neglecting them all for the sake of a free market.

The double life of the family

For all our aspirations for dependable loving family relations, few people achieve this state of affairs. Yet does this mean that people simply abandon their belief that babies should face a happy childhood, loved and wanted, and that some warmth and affection could carry on throughout our lives?

This book does not suggest that modern expectations of equality, fairness, mutual respect and also 'love' in family relations are 'too high'. Rather, our aim has been to understand the processes that lead to this disappointment and to begin to identify the points at which they might be altered. Our 'personal life' has been the product of historical changes which created this social space. In this sense it is not independent or autonomous from wider social institutions. The very self-understanding of participants in family relations is drawn from the experience of markets and liberal political arrangements. This has prevented the fact of domestic labour *as labour* from being acknowledged for far too long. So, the demand for equality in this sphere, now that it has arisen, must be taken seriously. Significant parts of people's lives are invisible to them. Too often it has been assumed that the problems of our personal family life must be solved individually and privately through interpersonal negotiation. This notion too is, as we have argued, one of the illusions of the myth of the nuclear family. Such a belief has been the cause of much frustration and self-blame. It has also inhibited the search for solutions through reforming the labour market and the state.

The gap between our normative expectations of family life and our disappointing experience of it can also be reduced by raising the quality of our experiences. This is not as difficult as it may at first seem. Some countries have devised policies to ensure that key institutions take their responsibility towards families seriously. However, whenever the market and the state externalise the costs of a stable social world onto families, family life suffers. Babies cannot make exchanges. Family life cannot be built on the rationality of the market or there will be no market in a generation. Neither can the family become a reified actor subsuming the needs and interests of its various members, especially if in practice this amounts to the subordination of the family to the will of the household head. Individuals in families occupy different positions and therefore have discrete and individual needs. While the rhetoric of retrenching the welfare state preaches noisily about how families are best at providing welfare, in practice these policies make it more difficult to achieve our ideal of family life. Only significant spending in recognition and support of the diverse needs of individual family members can bring us closer to the kind of intimacy we crave. No intimacy without equality, no equality without a fairer organisation of economic life and policies that promote the independence of women and welcome children into a secure yet happy family *and* social life. Greater transparency in these relations reduces the necessity for the family to lead a double life.

Notes

Chapter 1

1. According to *Collins English Dictionary*, when used in the sociological sense, a norm is 'an established standard of behaviour shared by members of a social group to which each member is expected to conform'. A discussion of Luhmann's concept of 'normative expectations' occurs later in this chapter.
2. After November 1994 the annual publication *Labour Force Status and Other Characteristics of Families Australia* was discontinued. Data from this publication represents the most recent published estimates available at the time of writing.
3. According to the Australian Bureau of Statistics a 'couple family' is a family 'in which there are two married persons and these persons are husband and wife'. 'Persons are' further 'classified as married (husband and wife) if they are reported as being married (including de facto) and their spouse was a usual resident of the household at the time of the survey' (ABS 1994a, pp. 50–1). In 1991, the time of the last census, 8.2 per cent of couple families were de facto relationships.
4. By the year 2000 the proportion of Australian women not married by the time they reach 35 years of age is expected to exceed 20 per cent, the highest level in Australian history.
5. If a population is to replace itself in the long term, without immigration from overseas, it is necessary that the total fertility rate should be higher than 2.115 (Hugo 1992, p. 8).

6. Although Aboriginal and Torres Strait Islander people are too small a proportion to influence aggregate life expectancy of the Australian population as a whole, regrettably, life expectancy among Aboriginal and Torres Strait Islander people is considerably lower than for the rest of the population.

7. It has been common to attribute the fall in size of the average Australian family to the widespread adoption of the contraceptive pill in the 1960s, but it is the continuation of a trend which began in the late nineteenth century (Carmichael 1988). It is estimated that Australian women of child-bearing age during the 1850s averaged at least seven live births (Gilding 1991, p. 65). The average number of children borne by married women aged between 45 and 49 fell from more than six in 1901 to three in 1942, reached its nadir in the 1970s, and in the 1986 census had recovered slightly to be less than three (Gilding 1991, p. 76; Hugo 1992, p. 58). Painstaking historical research has shown that late marriage has been used to keep fertility levels well below the maximum since (at least) the seventeenth century, and postponing marriage was a typical response to economic recession (Anderson 1979, pp. 51–2). The current tendency to marry later, which became evident in the 1970s, conforms with this general trend (Carmichael 1988). Over the last two decades Australian women have, in contrast to their own mothers, delayed having children until middle and later child-bearing years. Women delaying child-bearing are not a random cross-section of the population but are disproportionately 'drawn from more highly educated, dual income, higher status, professional groups' (Hugo 1992, p. 23). This suggests that a woman's career influences the timing of births. According to McDonald, 'increased childlessness and the delay of the first birth . . . are not simply products of economic recession' and are 'unlikely to be reversed' (1989, p. 102).

8. The most spectacular growth, due chiefly to ageing and late marriage, is among lone adult households, which increased 56 per cent between 1976 and 1986, compared with an increase of 8 per cent for married couples with dependent children over the same period (Hugo 1992, p. 29). Household formation has continued to 'outstrip population growth' so that 'households became smaller' (Gilding 1991, pp. 127–8). Projections show that lone adult households will become the dominant household next century (Ironmonger & Lloyd 1990). Greater life expectancy for both women and men, and falling family size and the later timing of births, have also resulted in steadily increasing numbers of couple households without dependent children.

272 THE DOUBLE LIFE OF THE FAMILY

Chapter 2

1. We have deliberately chosen the word Xmas in preference to 'Christmas' because we believe this spelling will remind the reader that we are here speaking about a ritual which is secularised, part of the working calendar in Australia. Xmas Day is a public holiday for all, regardless of their personal religious orientation. This calendar date applies to work, school, shopping hours, transport, news services etc. In this sense it is a secular event which all Australians, Christian or otherwise, are obliged to endure.

2. The text of Keating's speech is provided in *Just Policy*, No. 5, February 1996, p. 12. Both authors also heard the speech, with its aside about Mars.

3. Stephen J. Gould has pointed out that evolutionary theorists distinguish between analogy and homology. Birds and insects both have wings (analogy) but morphologically, birds' wings and human arms are homologous, and could be descended from a common ancestry, while the structure of insects' wings is entirely different and is derived from different ancestry (Gould 1977, p. 254)

4. This picture of a semi-naked man and baby is part of a genre of posters which have as their subject semi-naked male models handling infants. The most popular is called *La Infant* (publisher, Athena UK, Harlow). When the poster came out in 1992 in Australia it sold approximately 80–100 copies a month. It is selling (in 1996) about 30–40 per month, which the distributor (Palmer Trading, Melbourne) states still indicates a popular poster in reasonable demand. The larger sized posters ($15 retail) sell the best.

5. A study of taxable income by postcode found that the average income of residents of the North Sydney electorate was among the top 20 per cent of all incomes and had risen 50 per cent faster than the average for other regions during the period of the ten years of Labor Government 1983–93 (personal communication, Phil Raskall and Robert Urquhart).

6. The debate about whether audiences are manipulated by the culture industry is one that we do not have the space to enter into here.

7. The authors would like to thank students of Michael Bittman's course Investigating the Modern Family, for allowing us to draw on their transcripts and semiotic analyses of various segments of *The Simpsons* during 1991.

8. At the time when the book was in production, the ABS (1996c) released results of a survey of 6300 women in Australia, *Women's Safety, Australia*, Cat. no. 4128.0.

Chapter 3

1. In societies based on the patrimonial household, the economic objective is to maximise the wealth of the household and the allocation of resources and duties is based on the relation to the male head of the household, namely the patriarch (Weber 1968, p. 1010).
2. The anthropologist Robert Lowie points out that in most human societies:

    practical points of view are foremost in inaugurating and maintaining the conjugal state. They eclipse romance not only amongst aborigines, but virtually everywhere except in the small circles of Western society. Romance need not be absent, but it is held inessential for that serious part of life which is marriage . . . Individual attraction, we repeat, is not the basic factor; our own immediate ancestors and virtually every other society in human history would have rejected contemporary Western conceptions as absurd and vicious in principle. (quoted in Macfarlane 1987, p. 124)

3. Binding the infant's limbs close to the body by winding them tightly in a cloth bandage.
4. Stone's views that parents had little emotional attachment to their children and neglected them are disputed by Linda Pollock (1983). Pollock's study of diaries and autobiographies from 1500 to 1900 in Europe and America suggests parental attachment and concern were possibly widespread. There is an obvious objection to theories based on the thought of the literary classes during this period as they can hardly be considered representative of the whole population. Nevertheless, Pollock is not questioning a change in the significance of children, nor that wet nurses were commonly used then, she only queries the interpretation of 'neglect'.
5. While the inspiration for many of Anthony Giddens' ideas about the emergence of a 'pure relationship' between truly independent partners are drawn from the work of the Becks (Beck & Beck-Gernsheim 1995), he neglects their emphasis on the contradiction between these expectations of relationships and the vestigially feudal relationships of the household in which they take place. We argue for a position similar to that of the Becks.

Chapter 4

1. Chris Beasley's *Sexual Economyths* (1994) is a recent argument about domestic work as the repressed underside of the economy.
2. Ironmonger's GMP is somewhat less than GDP because he moves the imputed rental value of owner-occupied housing across to GHP as the part of the capital contribution to value added in the household.
3. Although they are not strictly household productive activities, a group of 'voluntary work and community participation' activities—helping sick adults or adults with a disability, helping able adults, voluntary work, religious activities, civic responsibilities and other participation, and the travel associated with these activities—might also be considered unpaid work. This approach is taken in the preparation of extended (also called 'satellite') national accounts by the Australian Bureau of Statistics (1990). The unpaid assistance provided by relatives and others in family and small businesses is grouped with (paid) labour force activities.
4. We have followed the ABS practice of treating married and de facto couples as equivalent. See note 3 Chapter 1.
5. Anti-discrimination legislation, e.g. in New South Wales in 1977.
6. Affirmative action (Federal Act, 1984) and equal employment opportunity legislation, particularly the *Human Rights and Equal Opportunity Commission Act 1986* (Cwlth).
7. See, for instance, *Sharing the Load* campaign, Office of the Status of Women, 1992
8. The life course stages that are detailed here are (1) a 'son or daughter' living at home with their parents (2) 'sharing' accommodation with non-related others (3) 'living alone but under age of retirement' (4) married/de facto without ever having had children (5) married/de facto with youngest child under two years of age (6) married/de facto with youngest child under school age (7) married/de facto with youngest between five and nine years of age (8) married/de facto with youngest child between ten and fourteen years of age (9) married/de facto with a child of fifteen or more years of age currently living at home (10) sole parent with youngest child under fifteen years (11) sole parent with youngest child fifteen or over (12) 'empty nest couple' (below retirement age) (13) childless couple above retirement age (14) above retirement age and living alone (15) non-nuclear family households and (16) visitors and others.

Chapter 5

1. The research on which this chapter is based was made possible by an Australian Bureau of Statistics Research Fellowship. The authors would also like to acknowledge the assistance and support provided by the Households Research Unit, Department of Economics, University of Melbourne. A more detailed analysis of this material is presented in Bittman 1995.

2. Research into how a belief in the value of sharing housework, child care and shopping equally can be combined with a failure to do so in practice—a situation called 'pseudomutuality'—can be found in Chapter 6.

3. Time use information comes from detailed diaries in which the respondents record all their daily activities. When processed these diaries tell us how much daily time Australian women and men devote to housework, childcare, shopping and all other activities. The final 1992 sample contained 13 937 diary days of respondents 15 years of age and over, collected at four separate times of the year with the aim of representing seasonal variation (ABS 1993c).

4. Michael Bittman, in conjunction with Duncan Ironmonger and Sue Donath of the Households Research Unit, University of Melbourne, developed the method of standardisation. For more detail about this procedure see Bittman 1995.

Chapter 6

1. This chapter draws heavily on Bittman and Lovejoy 1993. Methodological details are presented in detail in this article. The authors are greatly indebted to Elsie Holmstrom (1985) who first suggested this idea of the disjunction between the conclusion drawn from attitude studies and time use data. Her paper has not received the attention it warranted. The data reported here was collected with the enthusiastic collaboration of students of the Investigating the Modern Family elective, University of New South Wales. Without the eager cooperation of these students this project would not have been possible. The authors wish to acknowledge the contributions of the following students: Adrienne Broe, Heather Coney, Zoyrese Conoplia, Joyce Dias, Thoa Dinh, Peter Donnelly, Kylie Dykes, Danielle Fitzgerald, Cassandra Gauld, Margaret Gibbons, Janelle Hart, Caroline Haski, Edward Johnston, David Karofsky, Shelley Lindsey, Kevin Lo, Susan Lyons, Judy McCormick, Mandy Mayer, Julienne Mostyn, Andrew Peteru, Leah Quinn, Vicky Sharpe, Tim Shumack, Lepa Sucur, Jennifer Thrush. The program for analysing this data was developed by Frances

Lovejoy. The authors wish to express their gratitude to these students and to Frances Lovejoy.

2. Characteristics of the sample obtained, from people living in the Sydney region, are set out in Appendix A of Bittman and Lovejoy 1993.

3. Care was taken to ensure that questionnaire items were comparable with previously published data so that results could be interpreted within the framework of firmly established findings from large-scale studies.

4. Differences between women's and men's mean scores are statistically significant, especially when women are compared to their partners (p < .0005 for both the six- and the seven-item scale, using a paired t-test). Baxter, Gibson and Lynch-Blosse found a similar mean Sex Role Attitude Score for women (10.99 compared with our finding of 10.23) but a more traditional attitude among men (14.03 compared with 11.57 among our sample) (personal communication 24/12/91).

5. The Class Structure of Australia Project, conducted by Baxter, Chat, Western and Western in 1993 found that 93 per cent of men and 97 per cent of women across the nation agreed with this statement (personal communication and Baxter & Western 1996).

6. Younger groups are significantly more 'egalitarian'. Chi square p < .003 with 4 df, and p < .0003 for the expanded scale (see also Baxter et al. 1990, pp. 58–9).

7. Following the procedure set out by Oakley (1974b, p. 210), in the semi-structured interview, the interviewer guided respondents through an account of a 'normal day' and the variations to this on 'weekends', before asking them to estimate the time spent in indoor and outdoor housework, childcare and shopping.

8. p < .0005, paired t-test.

9. p < .0005, paired t-test.

10. p < .05, paired t-test.

11. From 16.5 hours in the Time Use Survey to about 11.6 hours per week based on respondents' own estimates.

12. The 1995 Housework Expectations Survey was conducted by telephone interview, using the *1994 Sydney Telephone Directory* as a sampling frame. This provided a sample of 220 persons (fairly representative of Sydney's population). Our thanks to the students who conducted these interviews: Gabrielle Alley, Timothy Anderson, Lorana Bartels, Kylie Bastian, Danielle Beck, Emma Bellamy, Berlinda Choy, Simonne Davis, Suzanne Dawson, Elizabeth Deagan, Suzanne Donnellan, Charisse Duval, Lucinda Ferguson, Linda Gregory, Jacinta Harkin, Kim Hennessy, Carrie Hill, Andrew Howes, Barbara Hui, Skye Inman, Cherie Jenkins,

Yvonne Johnsun, Amanda Kerr, Adriana Kingston, Simone Kippax, Adina Krausz, Georgia Krongold, Jedda Lemmon, Russell Lewin, Lieu Van Thanh, Jodie Little, Sonia Mourad, Michelle Onley, Miranda Petkovic, Danielle Quy, Belinda Roden, Jessica Romeo, Jacqueline Rosen, Michelle Ryan, Katherine Shea, Ann Sweeney, Bilyana Trposka, Sonia Wechsler, Marlene Wilk.

13. Of course some women do own delicate lingerie, but most women's underwear and stockings or pantyhose are 'these days' machine washable (provided 'care' is taken!). By contrast, both men and women wear woollen sweaters, even linen shirts and trousers, and non-colourfast T-shirts are very popular with children, but there again, one can hardly talk about whether people may or may not have developed 'folk skills'—on virtually every garment that is purchased 'these days' is a label with precise washing instructions as above. It raises the question of whether all these men may have overlooked reading, or not have had to read the labels on their own clothes. It also puts in doubt Gershuny's suggestion about the long time it may take for men to become proficient at household tasks, in that one's ability to read washing instructions can hardly be construed as a case of 'lagged adaptation'.

14. Since difference is the opposite of sameness, and inequality the opposite of equality, inequality often becomes invisible in comparisons of sameness and difference.

Chapter 7

1. As Becker puts it, 'the commodity output maximised by all households is not to be identified with national output . . . but includes conversation, the quantity and quality of children', 'the quality of meals', 'prestige, recreation, companionship, love and health status' (Becker 1974, pp. 310, 301).

2. Becker proposes that women's greater domestic skills here are innate, due to biology ('differences in intelligence, education, health, strength, height, personality, religion and other traits') (Becker 1974, pp. 314–15).

3. Becker proposes that a partner's incentive to shirk duties or to take more household 'output' is weaker if that person (M) 'cares' about the partner (F) because 'a reduction in F's consumption also lowers M's utility' (Becker 1974, pp. 329–30).

4. As England and Kilbourne note, there have been a number of sociological theories which *assume* that greater earning power translates into greater marital power, notably the work of Blood

and Wolfe, Scanzoni and Chafetz (England & Kilbourne 1990, pp. 164–6).

5. A major drawback of the exit option is that children become increasingly disconnected from male earnings and subject to poverty (England & Kilbourne 1990, p. 183).

6. This is monopsonistic competition, with a single buyer, such as the Australian Defence Forces which is the only employer to hire soldiers in Australia. A few buyers can set all working conditions and deny job opportunities (Mumford 1989, p. 84).

References

Allen, J. 1982 'Octavius Beale Reconsidered' *What Rough Beast?* eds Sydney Labour History Group, Allen & Unwin, Sydney

Anderson, M. 1979 'The Relevance of Family History' *The Sociology of the Family: New Directions for Britain* eds C. Harris et al., Sociological Review Monograph 28, University of Keele, Keele

Aries, P. 1973 *Centuries of Childhood* Penguin, Harmondsworth

Australian Bureau of Statistics (ABS) 1990 *Measuring Unpaid Household Work: Issues and Experimental Estimates* Cat. no. 5236.0, ABS, Canberra

——1991 *Divorces, Australia* Cat. no. 3307.0, ABS, Canberra

——1993a *Australian Families: Selected Findings from the Survey of Families in Australia 1992,* Cat. no. 4418.0, ABS, Canberra

——1993c *Time Use Survey Australia: User's Guide* Cat. no. 4150.0, ABS, Canberra

——1994a *Labour Force Status and Other Characteristics of Families Australia* Cat. no. 6224.0, ABS, Canberra

——1994b *Unpaid Work and the Australian Economy 1992* Cat. no. 5240.0, ABS, Canberra.

——1994c *How Australians Use Their Time* Cat. no. 4153.0, ABS, Canberra.

——1994d *Australian Social Trends* Cat. no. 4102.0, ABS, Canberra

——1994e *Births, Australia* Cat. no. 6206.0, ABS, Canberra, March

——1994f *Child Care Australia* Cat. no. 4402.0 ABS, Canberra

——1995a *Average Weekly Earnings, States and Australia* Cat. no. 6302.0, ABS, Canberra, November

——1995b *Employee Earnings and Hours, Australia* Cat. no. 6305.0 (preliminary), ABS, Canberra, May

——1996a *Estimated Resident Population by Sex and Age; States and Territories of Australia June 1994 and Preliminary June 1995,* Cat. no. 3201.0, ABS, Canberra

——1996b *Labour Force, Australia* Cat. no. 6203.0, ABS, Canberra, January

——1996c *Women's Safety, Australia* Cat. no. 4128.0, ABS, Canberra

Australian Institute of Family Studies (AIFS) 1995a 'Cost of Children in Australia' *Family Matters* no. 41, Winter

——1995b *Work and Family* no. 10, December

Australian Institute of Health and Welfare (AIHW) 1995 *Australia's Welfare 1995: Services and Assistance* AGPS, Canberra

Bachrach, P. & Baratz, M.S. 1962 'The Two Faces of Power' *American Political Science Review* 56, pp. 947–52

——1963 'Decisions and Nondecisions: An Analytical Framework' *American Political Science Review* 57, pp. 641–51

Baker, Maureen 1995 *Canadian Family Policies: Cross-National Comparisons* University of Toronto Press, Toronto

——in press 'Social Assistance and the Employability of Mothers: Two Models from Cross-National Research' *Canadian Journal of Sociology*

Baldock, C.V. & Cass, B., eds 1983 *Women, Social Welfare and the State* Allen & Unwin, Sydney

Barrett, M. & McIntosh, M. 1980 'The "Family Wage": Some Problems for Socialists and Feminists' *Capital and Class* no. 11, Summer, pp. 51–72

——1982 *The Anti-Social Family* Verso, London

Barron, R.D. & Norris, G.M. 1976 'Sexual Divisions and the Dual Labour Market' *Dependence and Exploitation in Work and Marriage* eds D.L. Barker & S. Allen, Longman, London

Barthes, R. 1973 *Mythologies* Paladin, Frogmore, St Albans, Herts

Bateson, G. 1973 *Steps to an Ecology of Mind* Paladin, Frogmore, St Albans, Herts

Baudrillard, J. 1983 *In the Shadow of the Silent Majorities* Semiotext(e), New York

Baxter, J. 1993 *Work at Home: The Domestic Division of Labour* University of Queensland Press, St Lucia

Baxter, J., Gibson, D. & Lynch-Blosse, M. 1990 *Double Take: The Links Between Paid and Unpaid Work* AGPS, Canberra

Baxter, J. & Western, M. 1996 'Satisfaction with Housework: Explaining the Paradox', presented at the Fifth Australian Family Research Conference, Brisbane, 27–29 November

Beasley, C. 1994 *Sexual Economyths* Allen & Unwin, Sydney

Beck, U. 1992 *The Risk Society: Towards a New Modernity* Sage, London

Beck, U. & Beck-Gernsheim, E. 1995 *The Normal Chaos of Love* Polity Press, Cambridge

Becker, Gary 1974 'A Theory of Marriage' *Economics of the Family* ed. T.W. Schultz, University of Chicago Press, Chicago

——1981 *A Treatise on the Family* Cambridge University Press, Cambridge

Beechey, Veronica & Perkins, Tessa 1987 *A Matter of Hours: Women, Part-time Work and the Labour Market* Polity Press, Cambridge

Beggs, J.J. & Chapman, B.J. 1988 'The Foregone Earnings from Child-Rearing in Australia' commissioned by the AIFS, Centre for Economic Policy Research, *Discussion Paper* no. 190

Benenson, H. 1991 'The "Family Wage" and Working Women's Consciousness in Britain, 1889–1914' *Politics and Society* vol. 19, no. 1, pp. 71–108

Ben-Porath, Yoram 1974 'Economic Analysis of Fertility in Israel' *Economics of the Family* ed. T.W. Schultz, University of Chicago Press, Chicago

——1982 'Economics and the Family—Match or Mismatch? A Review of Becker's "A Treatise on the Family"' *Journal of Economic Literature* vol. 20, pp. 53–63

Berg, A-J. 1994 'The Smart House' *Bringing Technology Home* eds C. Cockburn & R. Furst-Dilic, Open University Press, Buckingham

Berg, M. 1988 'Women's Work, Mechanisation and Early Industrialisation' *On Work* ed. R.E. Pahl, Blackwell, Oxford

Berk, S.F. 1985 *The Gender Factory: The Apportionment of Work in American Households* Plenum Press, New York

Berk, S.F. & Shih, A. 1980 'Contributions to Household Labour: Comparing Wives' and Husbands' Reports' *Women and Household Labour* ed. S.F. Berk, Sage, Beverly Hills, pp. 191–227

Bernard, J. 1976 *The Future of Marriage* Penguin, Harmondsworth

Bittman, M. 1990 'Division of Labour in the Household' Research Discussion Paper no. 11, Centre for Applied Research on the Future, University of Melbourne, Parkville

——1991 *Juggling Time: How Australian Families Use Time* Office of the Status of Women, Department of the Prime Minister & Cabinet, Canberra

——1992 *Juggling Time: How Australian Families Use Time* AGPS, Canberra.

——1995 'Recent Changes in Unpaid Work' Occasional Paper, Cat. no. 4154.0, ABS, Canberra.

Bittman, M. & Lovejoy, F. 1993 'Domestic Power: Negotiating an Unequal Division of Labour within a Framework of Equality' *Australian and New Zealand Journal of Sociology* vol. 29, pp. 302–21

Bittman, M. & Mathur, S. 1994 'Can You Buy Your Way Out of Housework?' paper presented to the XIIIth World Congress of Sociology, 18–23 July, Bielefeld, Germany

Bittman, M. & Pixley, J. 1995 'Great Expectations: Hyperconformity and Gender Difference in Housework "Standards"' unpublished paper presented at the Australian Sociological Association Conference, University of Newcastle, 5–6 December

Blank, R.M. 1993 'What Should Mainstream Economists Learn from Feminist Theory?' *Beyond Economic Man: Feminist Theory and Economics* eds M.A. Ferber & J.A. Nelson, University of Chicago Press, Chicago

Bluestone, B. & Ghilarducci, T. 1996, 'Rewarding Work: Feasible Anti-poverty Policy' *The American Prospect* no. 26, May–June, pp. 40–6

Boyers, R. 1971 *Laing and Anti-Psychiatry* Harper & Row, New York

Bracher, M. & Santow, G. 1988 'Changing Family Composition from Australian Life History Data' Working Paper no. 6, Australian Family Project, Research School of Social Sciences, Australian National University, Canberra

Bradbury, B. 1996 'Income Support for Parents and Other Carers' *SPRC Reports and Proceedings* no. 127, Social Policy Research Centre, University of New South Wales

Brannen, J. & Moss, P. 1987 'Dual Earner Households: Women's Financial Contributions After Birth of the First Child' *Give and Take in Families: Studies in Resource Distribution* eds J. Brannen & G. Wilson, Allen & Unwin, London

Brennan, D. 1994 *The Politics of Australian Child Care* Cambridge University Press, Melbourne

Brown, D. et al. 1990 *Criminal Laws* The Federation Press, Sydney

Bruland, T. 1985 'Industrial Conflict as a Source of Technical Innovation: The Development of the Automatic Spinning Mule' *The Social*

Shaping of Technology eds D. MacKenzie & J. Wajcman, Open University Press, Milton Keynes

Bryson, L. 1992 *Welfare and the State* Macmillan, London

Bureau of Immigration and Population Research 1994 *Immigrant Families: A Statistical Profile* AGPS, Canberra

Burns, A. 1983 'Population Structure and the Family' *The Family in the Modern World: Australian Perspectives* eds A. Burns, G. Bottomley & P. Jools, Allen & Unwin, Sydney

Caporaso, J.A. & Levine, D.P. 1992 *Theories of Political Economy* Cambridge University Press, Cambridge

Carmichael, G. 1988 'With This Ring: First Marriage Patterns, Trends and Prospects in Australia' Australian Family Formation Project, Monograph no. 11, Department of Demography, Australian National University and The Australian Institute of Family Studies, Canberra

Cass, B. 1983 'Population Policies and Family Policies' *Women, Social Welfare and the State in Australia* eds C.V. Baldock & B. Cass, George Allen & Unwin, Sydney

——1996 'A Family Policy 1983–1995' *Just Policy* no. 6, pp. 16–25

Castles F.G. 1985 *The Working Class and Welfare* Allen & Unwin, Wellington

——1994 'The Wage Earners; Welfare State Revisited' *Australian Journal of Social Issues* no. 29, pp. 120–45

Castles, F.G & Seddon, E. 1988 'Towards an Organisational Model of Marital Instability' *Australian Journal of Social Issues* vol. 23, no. 2, pp. 113–27

Chadeau, A. 1992 'What Is Households' Non-Market Production Worth?' *OECD Economic Studies* 18, pp. 86–103

Chodorow, N. & and Contratto, S. 1982 'The Fantasy of the Perfect Mother' *Rethinking the Family* eds B. Thorne & M. Yalom, Longman, New York

Clawson, D. 1980 *Bureaucracy and the Labour Process* Monthly Review Press, New York

Cockburn, C. 1985 'The Material of Male Power' *The Social Shaping of Technology* eds D. MacKenzie & J. Wajcman, Open University Press, Milton Keynes

Collinson, D.L., Knights, D. & Collinson, M. 1990 *Managing to Discriminate* Routledge, London

Commonwealth Arbitration Reports 1907–1908 'Excise Tariff 1906—Application for Declaration that Wages are Fair and Reasonable' vol. II *Ex Parte* H.V. McVay, Government of the Commonwealth of Australia, Melbourne

Connell, R.W. 1987 *Gender and Power: Society, the Person and Sexual Politics* Allen & Unwin, Sydney

——1995 *Masculinities* Allen & Unwin, Sydney

Copi, I.M. 1971 *The Theory of Logical Types* Routledge and Kegan Paul, London

Cowan, R.S. 1979 'From Virginia Dare to Virginia Slims: Women and Technology in American Life' *Technology and Culture* 20, pp. 51–63.

——1983 *More Work for Mother: The Ironies of Household Technology from the Open Hearth to the Microwave* Basic Books, New York

——1985 'The Industrial Revolution in the Home' *The Social Shaping of Technology* eds D. MacKenzie & J. Wajcman, Open University Press, Milton Keynes, pp. 181–201.

Cox, Eva 1995 *A Truly Civil Society* ABC Books, Sydney

Curthoys, A. 1986 'The Sexual Division of Labour: Theoretical Arguments' *Australian Women: New Feminist Perspectives* eds N. Grieve & A. Burns, Oxford University Press, Melbourne

Dalley, G. 1988 *Ideologies of Caring: Rethinking Community and Collectivism* Macmillan, London

Daly, Herman E. & Cobb, John B. 1989 *For the Common Good: Redirecting the Economy toward Community, the Environment and a Sustainable Future* Beacon Press, Boston

Davidoff, L. 1976 'The Rationalisation of Housework' *Dependence and Exploitation in Work and Marriage* eds D. Leonard Barker & Sheila Allen, Longman, London

Davidoff, L. & Hall, C. 1987 *Family Fortunes: Men and Women of the English Middle Class 1780–1850* Hutchinson, London

De Mause, Lloyd, ed. 1976 *The History of Childhood* Souvenir Press, London

De Tray, D.N. 1974 'Child Quality and the Demand for Children' *Economics of the Family* ed. T.W. Schultz, University of Chicago Press, Chicago

Dempsey, K. 1992 *A Man's Town: Inequality between Women and Men in Rural Australia* Oxford University Press, Melbourne

Di Stefano, Christine 1991 *Configurations of Masculinity: A Feminist Perspective on Modern Political Theory* Cornell University Press, Ithaca

Dobb, Maurice 1963 *Studies in the Development of Capitalism* International Publishers, New York

Donath, Susan 1994 'Neither Seen Nor Heard: Children in Economic Theory—A Feminist Analysis' unpublished MA Thesis, Department of Women's Studies, University of Melbourne

Douglas, Mary 1970 *Purity and Danger* Pelican Books, Harmondsworth

Durkheim, E. 1993 [1893] *The Division of Labor in Society* The Free Press, New York

——1938 [1894] *The Rules of Sociological Method* The Free Press, New York

——1952 [1897] *Suicide* Routledge & Kegan Paul, London

Easteal, Patricia W. 1993 *Killing the Beloved: Homicide between Adult Sexual Intimates* Australian Institute of Criminology, Canberra

Edgar, D. 1992 'Sharing the Caring' *Family Matters: AIFS Newsletter* no. 31, pp. 40–55

——1993 'Parents at the Core of Family Life' *Family Matters: AIFS Newsletter* no. 36, December, pp. 2–3

Edwards, M. 1984 *The Income Unit in the Australian Tax and Social Security System* Australian Institute of Family Studies, Melbourne

Edwards, S.M. 1989 *Policing 'Domestic' Violence* Sage, London

Ehrenreich, B. & English, D. 1979 *For Her Own Good: 150 Years of the Experts' Advice to Women* Pluto Press, London

Einhorn, Barbara 1993 *Cinderella Goes to Market: Citizenship, Gender and Women's Movements in East Central Europe* Verso, London

Eisenstein, Z. 1981 *The Radical Future of Liberal Feminism* Northeastern University Press, Boston

Electricity Services Victoria & Gas and Fuel Corporation of Victoria (ESV & GFCV) 1987 *Energy Use in Victorian Homes: Results of an Energy Survey of Households in Victoria* ESV & GFCV, Melbourne

Elliot, Faith Robertson 1996 *Gender, Family and Society* Macmillan, London

Elliott, G. 1978 'Two Steps Forward, Two Steps Back: An Australian Welfare State?' *Perspectives in Australian Social Policy* ed. A. Graycar, Macmillan, Melbourne

Elson, Diane 1994 'Micro, Meso, Macro: Gender and Economic Analysis in the Context of Policy Reform' *The Strategic Silence: Gender and Economic Policy* ed. Isabella Bakker, Zed Books, London

England, P. & Farkas, G. 1986 *Households, Employment and Gender* Aldine, New York

England, P. & Kilbourne, B.S. 1990 'Markets, Marriages and Other Mates' *Beyond the Marketplace: Rethinking Economy and Society* eds R. Friedland & A.F. Robertson, de Gruyter, New York

Esping-Andersen, G. 1990 *The Three Worlds of Welfare Capitalism* Polity Press, Cambridge

Eyer, Diane 1992 *Mother–Infant Bonding: A Scientific Fiction* Yale University Press, New Haven

Family Violence Professional Education Taskforce (FVPET) 1991 *Family Violence: Everybody's Business, Somebody's Life* The Federation Press, Sydney

Faulkner, W. & Arnold, E., eds 1985 *Smothered by Invention: Technology in Women's Lives* Pluto, London

Festinger, L., Riecken, H.W. & Schachter, S. 1964 *When Prophecy Fails* Harper & Row, New York

Feuer, Jane 1987 'Genre Study and Television' *Channels of Discourse: Television and Contemporary Criticism* ed. R. C. Allen, University of North Carolina Press, Chapel Hill

Fiske, John, Hodge, Bob & Turner, Graeme 1987 *Myths of Oz: Reading Australian Popular Culture* Allen & Unwin, Sydney

Flandrin, Jean-Louis 1979 *Families in Former Times: Kinship, Household and Sexuality* Cambridge University Press, Cambridge

Freud, S. 1976 [1905] *Jokes and Their Relation to the Unconscious* Penguin, Harmondsworth

Gershuny, J. & Brice, J. 1994 'Looking Backwards: Family and Work 1900 to 1992' *Changing Households: The British Household Panel Survey 1990–1992* N. Buck, J. Gershuny, D. Rose & J. Scott, ESRC Research Centre on Micro-Social Change, Colchester

Gershuny, J., Godwin, M. & Jones, S. 1994 'The Domestic Labour Revolution: A Process of Lagged Adaptation?' *The Social and Political Economy of the Household* eds M. Andersen, F. Bechhofer & J. Gershuny, Oxford University Press, Oxford

Gershuny, J. & Robinson, J.P. 1988 'Historical Changes in the Household Division of Labour' *Demography* 25, pp. 537–52

Giddens, A. 1991 *Modernity and Self-Identity: Self and Society in the Late Modern Age* Polity, Cambridge

——1992 *The Transformation of Intimacy: Sexuality, Love and Eroticism in Modern Societies* Polity, Cambridge

Gilding, M. 1991 *The Making and Breaking of the Australian Family* Allen & Unwin, Sydney

Gill, F. 1988 'Social Justice and the Low-Paid Worker' *Working Papers in Economics* no. 115, Department of Economics, University of Sydney

Ginn, J. et al. 1996 'Feminist Fallacies: A Reply to Hakim' *British Journal of Sociology* vol. 47, no. 1, pp. 167–77

Goffman, E. 1959 *The Presentation of Self in Everyday Life* Doubleday, New York

Glover, R. 1995 'Clean Bowled' *Sydney Morning Herald* 2 December

Goldschmidt-Clermont, L. 1991 *Economic Management of Non-Market Household Production: Relating Purposes and Valuation Methodologies* World Employment Programme Research Working Paper no. 174, International Labour Organization, Geneva

Goldstein, J. 1972 *The Psychology of Humour* Academic Press, New York

Goodnow, J. & Bowes, J. 1994 *Men, Women and Household Work* Oxford University Press, Melbourne

Gordon, L. 1982 'Why Nineteenth-Century Feminists Did Not Support "Birth Control" and Twentieth-Century Feminists Do' *Rethinking the Family* eds B. Thorne & Yalom M. Longman, New York

Gould, S.J. 1977 *Ever Since Darwin: Reflections in Natural History* W.W. Norton, New York

Gronau, R. 1977 'Leisure, Home Production and Work—The Theory of the Allocation of Time Revisited' *Journal of Political Economy* 85, pp. 1099–123

Habermas, J. 1970 'On Systematically Distorted Communication' *Inquiry* vol. 13, pp. 205–18

Hakim, C. 1995 'Five Feminist Myths about Women's Employment' *British Journal of Sociology* vol. 46, no. 3, pp. 429–55

Harris, C.C. 1983 *The Family and Industrial Society* Allen & Unwin, London

Harrison, Margaret 1989 'Who's to Blame?' *Family Matters: AIFS Newsletter* no. 24, August, pp. 46–9

——1991 'The Legal and Social Status of Children' in *Issues Facing Australian Families* eds R. Batten, W. Weeks & J. Wilson, Longman Cheshire, Melbourne

Hartmann, H. 1979 'Capitalism, Patriarchy and Job Segregation by Sex' *Capitalist Patriarchy and the Case for Socialist Feminism* ed Z. Eisenstein Monthly Review Press, New York

Harvey, A. & Niemi, I. 1994 'An International Standard Activity Classification (ISAC): Toward a Framework, Relevant Issues' *Fifteenth Reunion of the International Association for Time Use Research, Amsterdam, June 15–18, 1993*, eds N. Kalfs & A. Harvey, Netherlands Institute for Social and Market Research, Amsterdam

Henderson, R.F. et al. 1975 *People in Poverty: A Melbourne Survey* Cheshire, Melbourne

Hill, T.P. 1979 'Do-It-Yourself and GDP' *The Review of Income and Wealth* no. 1, March

Hirsch, S.R. & Leff, J.P. 1975 *Abnormalities in Parents of Schizophrenics: A Review of the Literature and an Investigation of Communication Defects and Deviances* Oxford University Press, London

Hirschman, A.O. 1970 *Exit, Voice and Loyalty* Harvard University Press, Cambridge, Mass.

Hochschild, A. 1989 *The Second Shift* Avon Books, New York

Holmstrom, E. 1985 'Women's Time and Men's Time, What We Say and What We Do' paper presented to Australian & New Zealand Association for Advancement of Science ANZAAS Festival of Science, Monash University, 26–30 August

Hopkins, Andrew & McGregor, Heather 1991 *Working for Change: The Movement Against Domestic Violence* Allen & Unwin, Sydney

Horin, A. 1996 'When a Birth is Far from a Blessing' *Sydney Morning Herald*, 28 September

Hoy, S. 1995 *Chasing Dirt* Oxford University Press, New York

Hugo, G. 1992 'Australia's Contemporary and Future Fertility and Mortality: Trends, Differentials and Implications' *Population Issues and Australia's Future: Environment, Economy and Society* National Population Council, AGPS, Canberra

Humphries, J. 1977 'Class Struggle and the Persistence of the Working-Class Family' *Cambridge Journal of Economics* 1, pp. 241–58

——1988 'Protective Legislation, the Capitalist State and Working-Class Men: The Case of the 1842 Mines Regulation Act' *On Work* ed. R.E. Pahl, Blackwell, Oxford

Huxley, Aldous 1976 [1962] *Island* Panther, St Albans, Herts

Ironmonger, D.S. 1994a 'National Time Accounts for the Household Economy' *Fifteenth Reunion of the International Association for Time Use Research* eds N. Kalfs & A.S. Harvey, 1993, Netherlands Institute for Social & Market Research, Amsterdam, June 15–18, pp. 55–67

——1994b 'The Value of Care and Nurture Provided by Unpaid Household Work' *Family Matters: AIFS Newsletter* vol. 37, pp. 46–51

——1994c 'Why Measure and Value Unpaid Work?' *International Conference on the Measurement and Valuation of Unpaid Work: Proceedings* Statistics Canada, Cat. no. 89–532E, Ottawa, pp. 34–41

Ironmonger, D.S. & Lloyd, C.W. 1990 *Household Populations and Projections of Households* Households Research Unit, Economics Department, University of Melbourne

Jacobs, Jerry A. 1989 *Revolving Doors: Sex Segregation and Women's Careers* Stanford University Press, Stanford

Jaggar, A.M. 1990 'Sexual Difference and Sexual Equality' *Theoretical Perspectives on Sexual Difference* ed D.L. Rhode, Yale University Press, New Haven

Jallinoja, R. 1989 'Women Between the Family and Employment' *Changing Patterns of European Family Life: A Comparative Analysis of 14 European Countries* eds K. Boh, M. Bak, C. Clason, M. Pankratova, J. Qvortrup, G.B. Sgritta & K. Waerness, Routledge, London

James, M. 1979 'Double Standards in Divorce' *In Pursuit of Justice: Australian Women and the Law 1788–1979* eds J. Mackinolty & H. Radi, Hale & Iremonger, Sydney

James, Michael ed. 1989 *The Welfare State* Centre for Independent Studies, Sydney

Jamrozik, A. 1994 'From Harvester to De-regulation' *Australian Journal of Social Issues* vol. 29, no. 2, pp. 162–70

Jamrozik, A. & Sweeney, T. 1996 *Children and Society* Macmillan, Melbourne

Jenson, J. 1990 'Representations of Gender: Policies to "Protect" Women Workers and Infants in France and the United States' *Women, the State and Welfare* ed L. Gordon, University of Wisconsin Press, Madison

Joint Select Committee on the Family Law Act 1980 *Family Law in Australia: A Report of the Joint Select Committee on the Family Law Act* vol. 2, AGPS, Canberra

Jones, M.A. 1980 *The Australian Welfare State* George Allen & Unwin, Sydney

——1996 *The Australian Welfare State* Fourth Edition, Allen & Unwin, Sydney

Junor, A. et al. 1993 *Service Productivity: Part-time Women Workers and the Finance Sector Workplace* Equal Pay Research Series no. 5, Department of Industrial Relations, Canberra

Kamerman, S.B. & Kahn, A.J., eds 1978 *Family Policy: Government and Families in Fourteen Countries* Columbia University Press, New York

Kaplan, G. 1996 *The Meagre Harvest: The Australian Women's Movement 1950s–1990s* Allen & Unwin, Sydney

Keating, The Hon. P. J. 1995 'The Labor Government and Social Policy: 1983–1995' *Just Policy* no. 5, pp. 3–8

Kewley, T.H. 1973 *Social Security in Australia 1900–72* Sydney University Press, Sydney

Khoo, S. & McDonald, P. 1988 'Ex-nuptial Births and Unmarried Cohabitation in Australia' *Journal of the Australian Population Association* 5, pp. 164–77

Killingsworth, M.R. & Heckman, J.J. 1986 'Female Labour Supply: A Survey' *Handbook of Labour Economics vol. 1* eds O. Ashenfelter & R. Layard, North Holland, Amsterdam

Korzybski, A. 1941 *Science and Sanity* Science Press, New York

Laslett, P. 1965 *The World We Have Lost* Methuen, London

Laurie, A. & McGrath, A. 1985 'I Was a Drover Once Myself' *Fighters and Singers: the Lives of Some Aboriginal Women* eds I. White et al., George Allen & Unwin, Sydney

Laurie, H. & Rose, D. 1994 'Divisions and Allocations Within Households' *Changing Households: British Household Panel Survey 1990–1992* eds N. Buck, J. Gershuny, D. Rose & J. Scott, Economic & Social Research Centre on Micro-social Change, University of Essex

Leach, Penelope 1994 *Children First: What Our Society Must Do—and is Not Doing—for Our Children Today* Alfred Knopf, New York

Leira, Arnlaug 1992 *Welfare States and Working Mothers: The Scandinavian Experience* Cambridge University Press, Cambridge

Lewis, J.M., Nicholas, L. & Smith, B. 1987 *Study of Home Energy Conservation vol. III* Department of Industry, Technology and Resources, Melbourne

Linton, R. 1936 *The Study of Man* Appleton-Century-Crofts, New York

Longtain, M. 1979 *Family Violence: The Well-Kept Secret* Beverly Hills, The University of Texas, Texas

Luhmann, Niklas 1979 *Trust and Power* John Wiley & Sons, Chichester

Lukes, S. 1974 *Power: A Radical View* Macmillan, London

Lyons Forum 1995 'Empowering Australian Families' Lyons Forum National Inquiry: Families and the Economy, Parliament House, Canberra

McDonald, P. 1989 'Can the Family Survive?' *Four Dimensional Social Space* eds T. Jagtenberg & P. D'Alton, Harper & Row, Sydney

——1990 'The 1980s: Social and Economic Change Affecting Families' *Family Matters: AIFS Newsletter*, no. 26, pp. 13–18.

——1995 *Families in Australia: A Socio-Demographic Perspective* AIFS, Melbourne

McDonald, P. , ed. 1986 *Settling Up: Property and Income Distribution on Divorce in Australia* AIFS, Prentice-Hall, Sydney

Macfarlane, Alan 1987 *The Culture of Capitalism* Basil Blackwell, Oxford

Mackay, H. 1993 *Reinventing Australia: The Mind and Mood of Australia in the 90s* Angus & Robertson, Sydney

MacKenzie, D. & Wajcman, J., eds 1985 *The Social Shaping of Technology* Open University Press, Milton Keynes

Macpherson, C.B. 1962 *The Political Theory of Possessive Individualism* Oxford University Press, Oxford

Madge, J. 1967 *The Tools of Social Science* Longmans, London

Malinowski, Bronislaw 1962 'Myth as a Dramatic Development of Dogma' *Sex, Culture and Myth* Rupert Hart-Davis, London

Mandel, E. 1968 *Marxist Economic Theory* Merlin, London

Marglin, S. 1982 'What Do the Bosses Do? The Origins and Functions of Hierarchy in Capitalist Production' *Classes, Power and Conflict* eds A. Giddens & D. Held, Macmillan, London

Marshall, Helen 1993 *Not Having Children* Oxford University Press, Melbourne

Marx, Karl 1973 [1936] *Grundrisse* Penguin, Harmondsworth

——1975 [1843–4] *Early Writings* Vintage, New York

——1954 [1863] *Capital Volume I* Progress, Moscow

Melendy, M.R. 1914 *Sex Life: The Pathway to Mental and Physical Perfection—The Twentieth Century Book of Sexual Knowlege* The Porter Company, Wellington

Millar, J. 1996 'Defining Family Obligations in Europe' paper presented at Social Policy Research Centre, Seminar Series, University of New South Wales

Mincer, J. & Polachek, S. 1974 'Family Investments in Human Capital: Earnings of Women' *Economics of the Family* ed. T.W. Schultz, University of Chicago Press, Chicago

Mol, H. 1989 'The Faith of Australians' *Four Dimensional Social Space* eds T. Jagtenberg & P. D'Alton, Harper & Row, Sydney

Morgan, D.H.J. 1975 *Social Theory and the Family* Routledge & Kegan Paul, London

Morris, D. 1968 *The Naked Ape* Corgi, London

Morris, Lydia 1990 *The Workings of Households* Polity Press, Cambridge

Mugford, Jane, Mugford, Stephen & Eastel, Patricia 1989 'Social Justice, Public Perceptions and Spouse Assault in Australia' *Social Justice* vol. 16, no. 3, pp. 103–23

Mumford, K. 1989 *Women Working: Economics and Reality* Allen & Unwin, Sydney

Myrdal, A. & Klein, V. 1968 *Women's Two Roles: Home and Work* Routledge & Kegan Paul, London

National Population Inquiry 1975 *Population and Australia: A Demographic Analysis* AGPS, Canberra

National Women's Consultative Council 1990 *Pay Equity for Women in Australia* National Labour Research Centre, AGPS, Canberra

Niemi, I. 1988 'Main Trends in Time Use from the 1920s to the 1980s' paper presented to the Meeting of International Research on Time Budgets and Social Activities, Budapest, 14–16 June

O'Brien, A. 1988 *Poverty's Prison: The Poor in New South Wales 1880–1918* Melbourne University Press, Melbourne

Oakley, A. 1974a *Housewife* Penguin, Harmondsworth

——1974b *The Sociology of Housework* Martin Robertson, London

——1992 *Taking it Like a Woman* Flamingo, London

Office of the Status of Women 1991 *Selected Findings from Juggling Time: How Australian Families Use Their Time*, OSW, Canberra

Ogburn, W.F. 1950 *Social Change* Viking, New York

Okin, Susan Moller 1989 *Justice, Gender, and the Family* Basic Books Inc, New York

Orloff, Anne Shola 1996 'Gendering the Analysis of Welfare States' *Gender, Politics and Citizenship in the 1990s* eds Barbara Sullivan & Gillian Whitehouse, University of New South Wales Press, Sydney

Pahl, Jan 1989 *Money and Marriage* Macmillan, London

Pahl, R.E. 1988 'Historical Aspects' *On Work* ed R.E. Pahl, Blackwell, Oxford

Parsons, T. 1951 *The Social System* Free Press, Glencoe, Ill.

——1966 *Societies: Evolutionary and Comparative Perspectives* Prentice-Hall, Englewood Cliffs, NJ

Pateman, C. 1979 *The Problem of Political Obligation* John Wiley & Sons, Chichester

——1983 'Feminist Critiques of the Public/Private Dichotomy' *Public and Private in Social Life* eds S.I. Benn & G.F. Gaus, Croom Helm, London

——1988a 'The Patriarchal Welfare State: Women and Democracy' *Democracy and the Welfare State,* ed. A. Gutman, Princeton University Press, New Jersey

——1988b 'The Fraternal Social Contract' *Civil Society and the State* ed. J. Keane, Verso, London

——1989 *The Disorder of Women* Polity, Cambridge

Percucci, C., Potter, H.R. & Rhoads, D.L. 1978 'Determinants of Male Family-Role Performance' *Psychology of Women Quarterly* vol. 3, no. 1, pp. 53–66.

Pinkney, Sarah 1995 'Fights Over "Family": Competing Discourses in the Two Decades Before the International Year of the Family *Just Policy* no. 2, pp. 17–25

Pixley, Jocelyn 1991 'Wowser and Pro-Woman Politics: Temperance against Australian Patriarchy' *Australian and New Zealand Journal of Sociology* vol. 27, no. 3, pp. 293–314.

——1993a 'When Conservatism Meets Liberalism in the Family' *Australian Journal of Public Administration* vol. 52, no. 1, March, pp. 121–6

——1993b *Citizenship and Employment: Investigating Post-Industrial Options* Cambridge University Press, Melbourne

——1994 'After the White Paper—Where?' *Just Policy* no. 1, pp. 20–26

——1996 'Economic Democracy: Beyond Wage Earners' Welfare?' in *The Australian Welfare State* eds J. Wilson, J. Thomson & A. McMahon, Macmillan, Melbourne

Pleck, J.H. 1985 *Working Wives/Working Husbands* Sage, Beverly Hills

Pollock, Linda A. 1983 *Forgotten Children: Parent–Child Relations from 1500 to 1900* Cambridge University Press, Cambridge

Poster, M. 1978 *Critical Theory of the Family* Pluto, London

Queensland Domestic Violence Task Force (QDVTF) 1988 *The Report: Beyond These Walls* QDVTF, Brisbane

Radcliffe-Brown, A.R. 1952 *Structure and Function in Primitive Society* Cohen & West, London

Reiger, K. 1985 *The Disenchantment of the Home: Modernizing the Australian Family 1880–1940* Oxford University Press, Melbourne

Riley, D. 1983 *War in the Nursery* Virago, London

Robinson, J.P. 1980 'Household Technology and Household Work' *Women and Household Labor* ed. S.F. Berk, Sage, Beverly Hills, pp. 53–68.

Roe, J. 1983 'The End Is Where We Start From' *Women, Social Welfare and the State in Australia* eds C.V. Baldock & B. Cass, George Allen & Unwin, Sydney

——1987 'Chivalry and Social Policy in the Antipodes' *Historical Studies* vol. 22, no. 88, pp. 295–410

Rubery, J. 1988 'Women and Recession: A Comparative Perspective' *Women and Recession* ed J. Rubery, Routledge & Kegan Paul, London

Russell, G. 1983 *The Changing Role of Fathers?* University of Queensland Press, St Lucia

Ryan, E. & Conlan, A. 1975 *Gentle Invaders: Australian Women at Work 1788–1974* Nelson, Melbourne

Sainsbury, D. 1996 *Gender Equality and Welfare States* Cambridge University Press, Cambridge

Saunders, Peter 1993 'Married Women's Earnings and Family Income Inequality in the Eighties' *SPRC Discussion Papers* no. 40, Social Policy Research Centre, University of New South Wales

——1994 *Welfare and Inequality* Cambridge University Press, Melbourne

Saunders, P. & Matheson, G. 1991 'An Ever Rising Tide? Poverty in Australia in the Eighties' *SPRC Discussion Papers* no. 30, Social Policy Research Centre, University of New South Wales

Savage, Elizabeth 1994 'Unemployment and Social Security Reform: A Lost Opportunity?' Symposium of the Department of Economics, The Pursuit of Full Employment, University of Sydney, 8 April

Schor, Juliet B. 1991 *The Overworked American: The Unexpected Decline of Leisure* Basic Books, New York

Schultz, T.W. 1974 'Fertility and Economic Values' *Economics of the Family* ed. T.W. Schultz, University of Chicago Press, Chicago

Segal, L. 1990 *Slow Motion: Changing Masculinities, Changing Men* Virago, London

Seiter, Ellen 1987 'Semiotics and Television' *Channels of Discourse: Television and Contemporary Criticism* ed. R.C. Allen, University of North Carolina Press, Chapel Hill

Shaver, S. 1993 'Women and the Australian Social Security System: From Difference Towards Equality' *SPRC Discussion Papers* no. 41, Social Policy Research Centre, University of New South Wales

Shorter, E. 1977 *The Making of the Modern Family* Fontana, Glasgow

Siedlecky, S & Wyndham, D. 1990 *Populate and Perish: Australian Women's Fight for Birth Control* Allen & Unwin, Sydney

Singh, Supriya 1994 'The Money-Go-Round Banks Can't Grasp' *Business Review Weekly* 27 June, pp. 78–81

Singh, S. & Lindsay, J. 1996 'Money in Heterosexual Relationships' *Australian & New Zealand Journal of Sociology* vol. 32, no. 3, pp. 57–69

Sluckin, W., Herbert, M. & Sluckin, A. 1983 *Maternal Bonding* Basil Blackwell, Oxford

Snooks, G.D. 1994 *Portrait of the Family with the Total Economy: A Study in Longrun Dynamics, Australia 1788–1990* Cambridge University Press, Melbourne

Soriano, G. 1995 'Filipino Families in Australia' *Families and Cultural Diversity in Australia* ed. R. Hartley, Allen & Unwin/AIFS, Sydney

Spiegel, David 1982 'Mothering, Fathering and Mental Illness' *Rethinking the Family* eds B. Thorne & M. Yalom, Longman, New York

Stone, L. 1979 *The Family, Sex and Marriage in England 1500–1800* Penguin, Harmondsworth

Stretton, H & Orchard, L. 1994 *Public Goods, Public Enterprise, Public Choice* Macmillan, London

Stubbs, Julie & Wallace, Alison 1988 'Protecting Victims of Domestic Violence?' *Understanding Crime and Criminal Justice* eds M. Findlay and R. Hogg, The Law Book Company Ltd, Ontario

Summers, A. 1975 *Damned Whores and God's Police* Penguin, Ringwood

Szalai, A. et al. eds 1972 *The Use of Time: Daily Activities of Urban and Suburban Populations in Twelve Countries* Mouton, The Hague

Tancred-Sheriff, P. 1993 'Gender, Sexuality and the Labour Process' *The Sexuality of Organisation*, eds J. Hearn et al., Sage, London

Tannen, D. 1991 *You Just Don't Understand: Women and Men in Conversation* Random House, Sydney

——1992 *That's Not What I Meant!: How Conversational Style Makes or Breaks Your Relations With Others* Virago Press, London

Tapper, A. 1990 *The Family in the Welfare State* Allen & Unwin/Australian Institute for Public Policy, Sydney

Taylor, Ella 1989 *Prime-Time Families: Television Culture and Postwar America* University of California Press, Berkeley

Tennyson, Alfred Lord 1847 *The Princess*, iv, Introductory Song, line 477

Thompson, E.P. 1967 'Time, Work-Discipline and Industrial Capitalism' *Past and Present* 38, pp. 51–96

Thomson, M. 1995 *Blokes and Sheds* Angus & Robertson, Sydney

Tiger, L. 1969 *Men in Groups* Random House, New York

Tiger, L. & Fox, R. 1972 *The Imperial Animal* Secker and Warburg, London

Titmuss, R. 1963 *Essays on the Welfare State* Second Edition, Allen & Unwin, London

Vanek, J. 1974 'Time Spent in Housework' *Scientific American* 231, pp. 116–20

Vasta, Ellie 1995 'The Italian-Australian Family' *Families and Cultural Diversity in Australia* ed R. Hartley, Allen & Unwin, Sydney

Wajcman, J. 1991 *Feminism Confronts Technology* Allen & Unwin, Sydney

Wallace, A. 1990 'Homicide: The Social Reality' *Criminal Laws* eds D. Brown et al., The Federation Press, Sydney

Weber, M. 1968 [1922] *Economy and Society* University of California Press, Berkeley

Wheeler, L. 1989 'War, Women and Welfare' *Australian Welfare* ed R. Kennedy, Macmillan, Melbourne

Wheelock, J. 1990 *Husbands at Home: The Domestic Economy in a Post-Industrial Society* Routledge, London

Williams, F. 1989 *Social Policy: A Critical Introduction* Polity, Cambridge

Willis, R.J. 1974 'Economic Theory of Fertility Behaviour' *Economics of the Family* ed. T.W. Schultz, University of Chicago Press, Chicago

Women's Bureau 1996 *Women and Work* vol. 17, no. 1, March, Department of Employment, Education & Training, Canberra

Wynne, L.C., Ryckoff, I.M., Day, J. & Hirsch, S.I. 1967 'Pseudo-Mutuality in the Family Relations of Schizophrenics' *The Psychosocial Interior of the Family: A Sourcebook for the Study of Whole Families* ed. G. Handel, Aldine, Chicago, pp. 443–65

Young, C. 1990 *Balancing Families and Work: A Demographic Study of Women's Labour Force Participation* AGPS, Canberra

Young, M. & Wilmott, P. 1973 *The Symmetrical Family* Routledge & Kegan Paul, London

Zaretsky, Eli 1976 *Capitalism, the Family and Personal Life* Pluto, London

Zijderveld, A. 1983 'The Sociology of Humour and Laughter' Trend Report *Current Sociology* vol. 31, no. 3, Sage, London

Index

Vasta, Ellie, 115
violence 'domestic', 2, 54, 117, 222, 251
  descriptions of 44–6
  extent in Australia, 42–4, 46–7, 233
  extent in Queensland, 42
  extent by sex, 43–7
  hospital reports, 43
  laws, 213, 226, 234
  other violence, 43–4
  suppression of 41–2, 241–2
  under-reporting of, 45
voluntary work, 95
  definition of, 274n.3

wage labour, 59, 60–2, 71, 73–4, 122; see also human capital
  aggregate hours of, 94
  consequences for governments and families, 213, 214, 243
  cf. domestic service, 93
  cf. housework, 87, 89, 91, 122–3
wages, men, 92; see also family wage; social policy
  impact domestic division of labour, 174–5, 177, 188
  and marital power, 179–80, 183, 209, 220–2
  rates, 176–7
  why higher, 180–1, 183, 202–4, 217
wages, women, 92, 93, 119; see also choice; money in families; sex-segregation

effects lowers rates, 188, 219–24
motivation for, 220
rates, 176–7, 204, 218
recent improvements, see arbitration
why lower, 174–5, 183, 201–8; see also family wage
War Over the Family, The, 96
Watson, J.B., 56
Weber, Max, 49
wealth flows, 190
welfare, 59
welfare state, 216; see also governments and families
  Australian variant, 216, 247, 250
  comparative variation, 243, 250
  'feminist', 227
  impact on family type, 228–9
  'patriarchal', 227, 245, 247
  public and private care, 242
wives see spouses
women's refuge movement (Australia), 43
Women's Safety, Australia, 273n.8
Wynne, Lyman, 81

You Just Don't Understand, 83
Young, M. & Wilmott, P., 116–18
young people see adolescence; daughters; sons

Zaretsky, Eli, 63–4, 69